John O'Farrell is the author of two best-selling books, *The Best A Man Can Get*, a novel, and *Things Can Only Get Better*, a memoir. His name has flashed past at the end of such productions as *Spitting Image, Have I Got News For You* and *Chicken Run*. He writes a weekly column in the *Guardian* and a collection of his journalism was recently published as *Global Village Idiot*. He lives in London with his wife and two children.

this is your life

JOHN O'FARRELL

Doubleday

LONDON · NEW YORK · TORONTO · SYDNEY · AUCKLAND

TRANSWORLD PUBLISHERS
61–63 Uxbridge Road, London W5 5SA
a division of The Random House Group Ltd

RANDOM HOUSE AUSTRALIA (PTY) LTD
20 Alfred Street, Milsons Point, Sydney,
New South Wales 2061, Australia

RANDOM HOUSE NEW ZEALAND LTD
18 Poland Road, Glenfield, Auckland 10, New Zealand

RANDOM HOUSE SOUTH AFRICA (PTY) LTD
Endulini, 5a Jubilee Road, Parktown 2193, South Africa

Published 2002 by Doubleday
a division of Transworld Publishers

A catalogue record for this book is available from the British Library.
ISBN 0385 600984

Typeset in 12½/15½ Ehrhardt by
Falcon Oast Graphic Art Ltd.

Printed in Great Britain by
Clays Ltd, Bungay, Suffolk

1 3 5 7 9 10 8 6 4 2

For Pat O'Farrell

THIS IS YOUR LIFE

— I —

SCRIPT FOR THIS IS YOUR LIFE – JIMMY CONWAY

UNAWARE OF THE SURPRISE AWAITING HIM, JIMMY APPROACHES
THE ENTRANCE TO THE RESCUED OTTER SANCTUARY. ONLOOKERS
APPLAUD. BUT THEN A FAMOUS TELEVISION PRESENTER (STILL
EAMONN ANDREWS??) APPROACHES CLUTCHING A BIG RED BOOK.

FAMOUS PRESENTER: Jimmy Conway?

JIMMY CONWAY: Yes? (JIMMY SEES TV CAMERAS AND
                     PRESENTER'S FAMOUS RED BOOK) Oh I
                     don't believe it!

FAMOUS PRESENTER: Yes, you thought you were here to open
                     another otter sanctuary as part of your
                     tireless work for various animal
                     charities, but you're not because, Jimmy
                     Conway, THIS IS YOUR LIFE!

JIMMY LOOKS STUNNED, THEN LAUGHS AND LOOKS SKYWARDS IN

DISBELIEF. WE 'CUT' TO THE FAMOUS STUDIO WHICH IS IN LONDON AND IS VERY BIG.

FAMOUS PRESENTER: You were born 'James Elliot Conway', second child of John and Valerie Conway of 27 Elms Crescent, East Grinstead, Sussex, England, Great Britain, Europe. Your family didn't realize that you were destined for great things as your big brother Nicholas is now forced to admit . . .

VOICEOVER FROM NICHOLAS (NOW GROWN UP, FAT AND BALD):
Oh, our little Jimmy was always joking and laughing. I used to tease and bully him and say he'd never achieve anything, but he's proved us all wrong. We're all very proud of him. He's certainly turned out much better than me if the truth be known.

FAMOUS PRESENTER: After leaving a very respected university with a good degree in an intellectual yet commercially useful subject that you could always fall back on if needs be, you began a glittering career in show business. You started out as a humble stagehand which was very sensible because it's a good idea to get to know the ropes first rather than diving straight in at the deep end.

Anyway, a week later the star and his understudy were travelling in a car together when they were involved in a tragic collision with a lorry load of animals destined for laboratory experiments. Fortunately the actors were not seriously injured, and none of the animals were badly hurt either, but it took firemen twelve hours to cut the two actors out from all the mangled cages while all the animals, like rabbits and things, escaped to a nearby forest, which luckily didn't have any foxes. With no one to play the biggest part in that night's performance, the director got the cast together to tell them he was forced to cancel the show, which would also by the way bankrupt the whole theatre and put everyone on the dole including poor people like cleaners etc., etc. At this point a young unknown stagehand called Jimmy Conway (you) stepped forward and bravely announced that he knew the lead part off by heart. The director takes up the story . . .

FAMOUS DIRECTOR: Jimmy was really brilliant. He was a real revolution to us all, he was far better than the famous comic actor that we'd got but no one liked anyway. Soon afterwards, Jimmy got the star part for good, we moved to the West End theatre, he became a famous comedian and, as they say, 'the rest is in history'.

I folded the well-worn script and placed it carefully back in my breast pocket. It was over twenty years since I had painstakingly typed it out on the Silver Reed typewriter I had received for my thirteenth birthday.

I lay back on the tatty sofa and closed my eyes. I wanted to empty my head of all thoughts but somewhere an insect was buzzing loudly. At the window a wasp seemed to be struggling with the insect equivalent of Fermat's last theorem. Problem: you are confronted with a half-opened window. How do you get to the other side? Wasp answer: keep head-butting the glass over and over again. 'Aah,' says the wasp professor, 'you would think so, wouldn't you? But if you repeatedly fly into the glass of the *half-opened* window and you find for some reason that you cannot seem to go straight through the glass, then what do you do?' Hush falls over the wasp tutorial as their eager brains are taxed to the limit of wasp logic. Until one brilliant young wasp, the intellectual superstar of Wasp College, Cambridge, tentatively puts up his front leg, the answer slowly coming together in his insect head.

'If . . . one . . . cannot fly straight *through* the glass' – he cogitates as the lecture room falls silent, the other wasps sensing that they are in the presence of wasp genius – 'and we have established that the window is *half open* . . .' he continues, his brow furrowed in total concentration, 'then surely the logical thing to do . . . would be . . . to fly repeatedly at the glass, buzzing a lot?'

The other pupils glance eagerly across at the professor to see if this pupil has hit upon the solution, but their tutor smiles knowingly and shakes his head. 'No,' he says. 'The answer is that there is no solution to this conundrum. It is an impossible problem, like predicting prime numbers or putting a definitive value on pi. It is a philosophical trick question that cannot be answered.'

I stood up and rolled up a newspaper to strike the stupid wasp dead, but then thought better of it and used my improvised swatter to guide him gently over the top of the window and away into the outside world. A year earlier I don't think I would have spared him but now I felt in a position to act with generosity and benevolence.

I lay back on the sofa once more and closed my eyes. How nice it would be if I could just go to sleep now, if I could forget where I was and what I had to go and do. Then, as if somebody was aware of my escapist fantasy, there was a loud distorted crackle, and from the old speaker hanging off the wall came the startling message: 'Jimmy Conway, this is your five-minute call! Jimmy Conway to the stage please.'

In 300 seconds' time I was supposed to be walking out onto the stage of one of London's most famous theatres in front of two thousand specially invited guests. Here, I was to stand on my own under the glare of the lights and perform a brand new stand-up comedy routine, a performance which was, incidentally, being transmitted live on BBC1 to millions of homes across the country, who even now were glued to the spectacle of an all-night charity gala featuring dozens of their favourite stars.

The prospect made me wonder what it would be like to be a librarian. That must be a nice job, I thought. Surrounded by books all day; warm and quiet, occasionally stamping the return date on a Catherine Cookson novel, smiling at the old lady and handing the book back to her. 'Due back on the twenty-fourth, Edna.' Yes, I could live with that. There must be some stresses and personal pressures I suppose, having to stay late when there was 5 pence missing from the fines box or whatever, but I bet you don't often have to go out and perform a stand-up comedy routine live in front of millions of people.

I pulled myself upright and looked in the long mirror. I was wearing an immaculate light grey suit, my shoes were polished, my face was clean-shaven and I'd now removed the tiny bits of torn-off toilet paper that had been placed on all the cuts. There was a small speck of fluff on my jacket and I carefully picked it off. 'Time to go and knock 'em dead, Jimmy,' I said to myself, slightly unconvincingly. 'Jimmy Conway to the stage please!' replied the tannoy, slightly more insistently. There must be some other preparation required, I thought; some other avoidance task I could invent just to keep me in this private cocoon for another few seconds. I know, I should gargle. It's very good for your voice, gargling; everyone knows that actors gargle before they go on stage. I picked up a plastic cup on the side of the washbasin and turned on the tap. At which point a high-pressure jet of cold water shot out of the tap with such powerful fire-hose force that it ricocheted off the bottom of the sink and out all over me.

'Shit!' I said. I looked down to see that my groin was completely soaked: a large soggy dark grey patch spread outwards and downwards from the epicentre of my flies. 'Shit! Shit! Shit!' I repeated. I grabbed a towel and tried to dab my trousers dry.

Comedy is all about making your audience feel comfortable, about reassuring them that they are in safe hands; they need to believe that you are relaxed, not the slightest bit nervous or on edge. I knew my routine off by heart, I had a flashy suit; the only slight imperfection that might make an audience feel I was not completely comfortable about being up on stage was the fact that I'd obviously wet my pants. When you're looking for signs of nervousness in a comic, I'd say that a big damp patch around his groin was probably a bit of a giveaway.

I threw the towel to one side and ran out of my dressing room. Maybe there was an electric hand-dryer I could use in the gents' toilets. The stairs down from the dressing room were austere uncarpeted concrete and the bricks on the walls had long ago been painted with nicotine-yellow gloss paint. In theatreland every effort is made to present a glittering spectacle before the paying audience, while the parts of the building they don't see are inversely utilitarian and tatty. When I reached the floor below, I burst into the gents' to see a large electric hand-blower on the wall in front of me.

'Thank you, God!' I said to the ceiling and I pressed the big metal button. Nothing happened. I stabbed at it again several times but it was completely dead. There was a switch on the wall that I flicked on and off but it made no difference. I heard an electrical crackle which for a split second I hoped was some sign of life but then a voice bellowed through the speaker. 'Jimmy Conway to the stage now PLEASE. You are on in two minutes. Jimmy Conway to the stage immediately!'

There was no escape. I ran out into the corridor, now in a state of uncontrolled panic. Maybe they had hand-dryers in the big star dressing rooms down here on the first floor. I hammered on the door of Dressing Room One but there was no reply so I pushed open the door and there lying on the table before me I spotted the Holy Grail – an electric hairdryer. Salvation was at hand. It was already plugged in so I switched it to the maximum setting and directed it at the big wet patch between my legs. The dark grey of wet cloth quickly dried to light grey, but I could still feel the dampness in the lining of my pockets underneath, and since there was not a second to spare, I undid the buttons of the trousers and attempted to dry my crotch from the inside, wiggling the hair dryer, jumping slightly as the hot air scalded my skin. It was at this moment that the door to Dressing Room One opened.

I'd always wanted to meet Dame Judi Dench. I'd say she was one of my all-time favourite actors and I'd always hoped that one day our paths might cross.

'Hello,' said Judi Dench looking at me, apparently only slightly surprised to see a man in her dressing room with her hairdryer on full blast down inside his trousers.

'Um, hello,' I replied. 'Sorry, is this your dressing room?'

'Yes.'

'Look, I'm really sorry, but I splashed water all over myself and I'm on stage in two minutes and I was desperate.'

'Two minutes? Was that you the SM was just calling on the tannoy?'

'That's me, yes, Jimmy Conway,' I said, offering the wrong hand to shake because the other one was still fiddling around in front of my pants.

'Judi Dench.'

'Yes, I know. I thought you were brilliant in *Iris* by the way. And *Mrs Brown* for that matter.'

'Thank you.'

'What's Billy Connolly like?' I said, hoping that casual theatrical chit-chat might distract slightly from what I was doing with Dame Judi's personal hairdryer.

'Billy's lovely. Hadn't you better get a move on?'

'Well, yes, it's just I didn't want to go on stage with a big damp patch on my trousers . . .'

She laughed. I made Judi Dench laugh.

'Jimmy Conway? You're the comic that everyone is talking about, aren't you?'

'Oh. Well, not everyone – um – just some people,' I

stuttered, trying to sound modest but secretly delighted that the reigning queen of British theatre had heard of me.

'I've not seen your act, I'm afraid, but I've heard you're very good.'

'Well, fewer people have seen me than you'd think . . .' I said.

'Until tonight, that is.'

'Oh my God, they said two minutes about two minutes ago, didn't they?'

'Don't worry. I'm sure the stage manager's allowing a few minutes spare, especially with this going out on the telly as well.'

'Do you think so?' I said.

'Look, why don't I go and tell him you're just coming while you sort yourself out in here?'

'Oh, thank you so much, I really can't thank you enough. Tell him I'm in your dressing room, and I'll be there as soon as I've done my trousers up.'

'Well, I might not put it quite like that,' said Judi Dench with a smile, and then she was gone.

What a nice lady, I thought. She really was very nice indeed.

Judi (as I felt I could now rightfully call her) had been quite right, of course. The panicky cry of 'Jimmy Conway, you are on stage in two minutes!' had meant more like ten minutes, although the stage manager still mimed a mock heart attack when he saw me and called back the runner he had sent out to search the local pubs.

The trouser crisis had at least allowed me briefly to forget the next stage of the evening, but having got myself into a state of extreme anxiety about one problem, I was denied the opportunity to use that wave of adrenalin to surf right out onto the stage. I had to build myself up all over again.

Through a crack in the curtain at the side of the stage I could see the audience staring as one straight ahead of them. In a few minutes all those telescopic sights would be aimed at me. They seemed in quite a jolly mood until the dear compère started talking about the dreadful suffering their ticket money would go a tiny way towards alleviating. Did he not realize that a comedian was about to take the stage? What better way to warm up an audience than to talk about disabled children living in poverty in Britain's inner-cities? 'Honestly!' I said to the stage manager. 'Why doesn't he flash up some pictures of neglected kids to make them feel really miserable and guilty?'

'They are flashing up pictures of neglected kids,' he replied. 'You just can't see the monitors from back here.'

'Oh. Spiffing.'

I watched from the sides for a few more minutes, feeling numb and totally alone. At one point I got out my script and glanced over the opening paragraphs, but it was ridiculous; I knew it so well I was in danger of forgetting the meaning of the words.

'Haven't you learnt it yet?' teased the stage manager in a whisper loud enough to be pointless.

'Of course I have,' I said, a little too defensively. 'I couldn't be better prepared.' A boast that was rather undermined by my mobile phone suddenly ringing loudly in my breast pocket. I decided on balance not to take the call. I always think it's a bit rude to talk into mobiles when other people can over-hear you, like when you're on a train, in a café or walking out to perform in front of two thousand people at the London Palladium. 'Hiya, I'm on a stage!' It would be hard for the audience to pretend not to be listening.

'Sorry!' I whispered as I turned the phone off. The

compère was introducing me and I tightened my tie and checked that my hair wasn't all sticking up.

'Ladies and gentlemen, it's the moment you have all been waiting for . . .' roared the compère. 'You've heard so much about him, but now, making his BBC debut, put your hands together for a very, very funny man, the one and only . . . JIMMY CONWAY!'

The applause was louder than I had expected, and there was some whistling and a lone cheer. My senses were highly tuned, seeing, hearing, smelling everything; absorbing it all at once. The compère gave an exaggerated gesture to welcome me on stage and I stepped out from that shady sanctuary into the exposed bright open space of the vast arena, like a nervous rabbit thinking about crossing the motorway. The compère skipped offstage patting me matily on the back as if we knew each other well. For a moment I thought I must seem rude for not remembering ever having met him before.

The microphone stand lay ahead like a solitary blade of grass on a World War One battlefield. I walked towards it. What the fuck am I doing here? I thought to myself. The applause of two thousand people was dying down as they waited for my first words. I thought about all those millions of people watching me on their televisions at home, including just about everybody I knew. And as the applause finally gave way to an electrified tightrope of silence, I wondered if I should perhaps have shared my little secret with someone else by now.

That I'd never performed any stand-up comedy ever before.

— 2 —

27 Elms Crescent,
East Grinstead,
West Sussex,
England

Dear James,

Please find enclosed the script for your appearance on This Is
Your Life. Of course it may not be exactly like this when it
happens – it's just a rough plan.

I have decided to write it all down and put it in a safe place
for you to find when you are a grown-up just in case you have
forgotten to become successful and rich and famous. Because
most adults seem to just let it slip their mind. Then they
suddenly remember and laugh and say, oh yes, that's right,
when I was young I wanted to be a pop star or a football player
or whatever, but now they're all working in the bank or
something and, well, how can you forget to do something like
that? Obviously I know they can't all be famous – I'm not

stupid; I am nearly fourteen, which is virtually an adult anyway. For example, yesterday when Nicholas was dealing at cards I waited until he'd put down all seven before I picked them up to look at them. But by the time I am 100% grown-up with a car and proper facial hair and everything, I do not intend to settle for anything other than being a rich and famous comedian, actor and entertainer, so I have taken the trouble to plan it all in advance.

It's like everyone else in my class gets their homework and starts writing an essay straight away without doing a plan first, and surprise, surprise, they get a C+. But I do a plan beforehand on a separate piece of paper like Mr Stock says and I always get an A or A— (except one D— which doesn't count because I wasn't there when we did 'Lord of the Flies'). And then everyone leaves school and they don't do a plan of what they are going to do any more than they ever planned their essays and so it's no wonder they have lives that are only C+. So I am now going to write a plan of everything I am going to do on a separate piece of paper, and that is why in my life I think I am going to get an A or A— unless something really terrible that's not my fault happens, like I get bitten by a dog in France and catch rabies.

I should say that I only want to be really successful so that I can help those who through no fault of their own are less fortunate than myself. It's not for my sake that I want to be a celebrity or anything. I only want to be really famous for doing good for others, not for shooting John Lennon or something like that. And if I was really rich I'd be able to give some of my money away to charities and stop people pouring lots of oil into the sea near where there are lots of gannets. Instead they should be made to give that oil away to people in the third world who probably don't have any oil of their own.

The important thing, Jimmy, James (people call you James now like you always wanted them to), is how you use your good fortune, although it won't just be good fortune, you will have worked very hard for it as well. I mean, OK, so you're fabulously rich and everything but at least you earned every single penny through your own efforts. Just because you are really important now does not mean you have to be all pompous and stuffy. On the contrary, it means you can be the kind of adult who still wears jeans, for example. And when a group of sixth-formers come to hear you give a lecture about all your work for animal charities, you could turn the chair the wrong way round and sit on it back to front when you are talking to them.

But I've been going on too long again (just like my homework!!) and so I will stop now and write again in a few days' time. ~~When I've finished all these letters I'll put them in a shoebox in the attic, so if you've forgotten where you put this letter twenty years ago and you can't find it, that's where it will be.~~

Mine sincerely,
Jimmy

A year before I was to make my showbiz debut at the London Palladium, I was indeed performing for a living, albeit to a different sort of crowd. Many entertainers boast of playing difficult audiences. I'd never played the Glasgow Empire on a wet Tuesday in February, I'd never done an open spot at the Tunnel Club in Woolwich, but no performer could have had a tougher grounding than standing up and talking for a hour in front of the beginners' class of brain-dead teenagers at the Sussex Language Centre. To say they were slow to respond would suggest any response whatsoever. Teaching English as a foreign language to this particular group was like explaining quantum physics to a bowl full of goldfish, except at least goldfishes close their mouths occasionally.

The beginners' class at the Sussex Language Centre was where they sent people if they were unsure whether or not they'd come out of a coma. The students would sit at their desks, slumped forward and staring blankly at me, as I cheerily spouted an endless stream of meaningless syllables at them. 'Blah blah blah blah blah blah blah blah? Blah! Blah blah, blah blah blah, blah blah blah! Blah blah blah blah blah blah blah blah blah.' I did actually say that to them once just to see if it might provoke any sort of reaction, which I soon realized was wildly optimistic of me. Of course, it is possible to begin to teach English to students who only know the words 'OK', 'taxi' and 'Beatles'. You can teach any language to anyone who wants to learn, but this, I think, was the problem. These adolescents had been exiled to this dismal suburb-on-sea against their will, leaving behind their friends in Turkey or Algeria or Brazil. Denied the opportunity to smoulder at their parents, they sulked at the nearest available adult, who happened to be me.

'Ball!' I said brightly, holding up a ball. '*Ball!* Now you try.'

And I pointed to a young Russian sitting at the front. After about five seconds he blinked, which was progress of a sort; it was the most reaction I'd had all week. 'Ball!' I prompted him again, because after all it was a lot of lines to learn all at once. He looked at me. Not even a blink this time; we were going backwards now. There had been quite an exciting break-through earlier in the week when one of them had coughed. I had wanted to telephone his parents to share this exciting development. 'Wonderful news! Nadim lives! Young Nadim actually coughed!' and they would weep with joy at the first sign of life since their son was stunned into a silent stupor by finding himself imprisoned in a language school in some dreary English coastal town.

I had moved to the south coast at the age of twenty-one and got myself a temporary job at the local language school, where I was now their longest-serving teacher. I had only come to Seaford to be with my Truelove-for-Evermore but six months after we'd self-consciously set up home together and got proper jobs we had split up; the white-hot comet of our love had burnt up on entry into the atmosphere of the real world. We parted amicably; I got her Hermann Hesse novels and she got the interesting life away from Sussex.

Seaford is not the glamour capital of Western Europe. There are plenty of swinging songs about New York and LA, but I'm struggling to think of a single line that ol' blue eyes ever sang about the bleak weather-beaten collection of bungalows that I'd made my home. 'Seaford, Seaford, that's my kinda windswept English coastal resort.' Nope. 'I wanna wake up in a town that fell into a coma in 1957.' It wasn't ring-ing any bells. On the plus side, the town did have a wool shop, so if knitting was your passion then I suppose it might possibly have justified a brief diversion off the A259. I'd lived in Seaford for thirteen years now, which was quite a short amount of time compared to how long it takes most of the local inhabitants to find the right change when they get on the bus. The wind blowing off the sea is so strong on this part of the coast that the indigenous population grows up at an angle. Like those bent-over trees you see on clifftops, some of the old people have spent so long staggering along the seafront leaning inland at an angle of 75 degrees that their bones are permanently set in that position. It must be impossible organizing the over-60s music and movement classes. Every time they turned around they'd bump heads.

I didn't plan to be around here for quite as long as that. I managed to make my job tolerable by not turning up to it every other week – I had a loose arrangement with the school's owner to work alternate weeks or mornings only. This was when I would turn my attention to what I privately considered my real job: my comedy screenplay. The film idea was such a good one that I was sure someone would be desperate to make it. Ever since the concept had first popped into my head I'd had a positive spring in my step, sensing that my life was on the cusp of a great change. The thought of that brilliant opening scene up on the screen at the Odeon Leicester Square filled me with excitement. I had considered giving up teaching altogether so that I could concentrate on the screenplay full-time, but I had no idea how long it took to write a movie so I thought I'd better keep some money coming in until I sold the script. But the boredom of my everyday routine, the relentless aggravation of never having any money – none of the things that habitually got me down had bothered me much since I'd had this brilliant idea. It was my ticket to another life. I was tempted to tell every-one I met, but it was so precious that I had to keep it locked up inside in case someone stole it from me.

As I finished my last class of the week I was excitedly looking forward to the prospect of a whole clear week getting to
grips with the next scene. These were the times I lived for. I
had to admit there wasn't much job satisfaction spending
weeks teaching a class English only to drop them off at the
ferry terminal and have them turn and shout a final fond
'hello'. I dumped a few books in the office and gave a goodbye
wave to Nancy, a fellow teacher and friend, who seemed to be
involved in a serious phone call.

'How can you be so bloody stupid!' she shouted into the
phone.

Either she was talking to her daughter or the speaking clock
had forgotten to bring its watch that morning. Like me,
Nancy worked irregular hours at the Sussex Language
Centre, fitting in alternate weeks between her fourteen-year-
old's court appearances. How fate had conspired to give such
a kind-hearted, generous spirit as Nancy a daughter like
Tamsin was one of the great mysteries of life. She did once
bring her mother some flowers but even that ended up in an
argument. Tamsin said that whoever tied them to the lamp
post obviously didn't want them any more.

Nancy slammed down the phone and put her head in her
hands.

'Shit! Shit! Shit!'

'Everything all right?' I said, disguising nosiness as
concern.

'Guess who's been suspended from school again?'

'What's it for this time?'

'Setting off the fire alarm.'

'Setting off the fire alarm? Why on Earth would she do a
thing like that?'

'She says there was a fire.'

'Honestly! Is that the best excuse she can come up with?'

'The fire brigade put it out and everything, but she's still suspended for two weeks.'

'This fire? It wouldn't have been started by Tamsin by any chance, would it?'

'Well, obviously the head has jumped straight to that conclusion. But they're picking on her again. Just because she was seen near the rubbish dump with matches and a box of firelighters. Oh God, why does she do these things?'

The phone rang again and I stood there trying to do a bit of supportive hovering while Nancy and her daughter argued back and forth.

'Let me have a word with her,' I said.

'Hi, Tamsin. It's Jimmy here . . . Er, look, while you're suspended, do you think you could walk the dog for me? I'll pay you and everything.'

Tamsin was delighted at this prospect. In the background her mother was hissing: 'Don't pay her! She's supposed to be being punished!'

I continued chatting as Nancy listened to me with growing incredulity.

'So, was it a big fire? Right. What sort of firelighters did you use? Oh yeah, Zip, they're good, aren't they? That was very forward-thinking of you, firelighters and matches and everything. Oh, was it? Well, say hello to him for me. Yup, see you soon.'

'What was all that, "Oh yeah, Zip, they're good, aren't they"?' exclaimed Nancy. 'Why didn't you suggest she used petrol next time?'

'I thought you were supposed to show an interest in a kid's hobby?'

'Not when it's arson.'

'Well, it turns out that Kelvin brought in the firelighters and everything – he obviously put her up to it, and it was only a load of old leaves and stuff. She doesn't deserve to be suspended.'

'Oh God. What am I going to do with her?' Nancy sighed a world-weary sigh. 'I'm working all next week but I can't leave her in the house on her own all day. She's only fourteen and anyway I can't afford the bills from the Home Shopping Channel.'

'Take next week off,' I heard myself say. 'I'll cover for your lessons here.'

'But you were desperate not to work next week.'

She's right, I thought. What am I saying? Take this chance to back out while you can . . . 'Er, that's OK,' I said. 'I'll try and grab some time around the edges.'

'Oh God, Jimmy, you are such a star,' and she gave me a peck on the cheek and suddenly a precious five days on my script had evaporated.

Many moons ago I'd actually had a brief relationship with Nancy, but her having had a child by a former boyfriend made it all a little complicated. One can only put up with so many childish tantrums and eventually she got fed up with them and we split up. I think I probably hadn't felt ready to become a stepfather, especially before the real dad had finally disappeared from the scene completely. But when she'd said, 'I don't want to lose you as a friend,' for once it had been true. I still thought she was attractive with her big blue eyes and her infectious laugh, but we were living proof that it was possible to be just good friends with an ex; over the years we had disproved the theory that former partners only ever remained friends in the vague expectation of eventually getting back together.

In any case, I wasn't on my own any more. Now I lived with the beautiful Betty. Betty was young and happy and loved me with all her heart. If she hadn't been a Border collie she might have been the answer to all my problems. She was, however, a constant companion for me – wherever I was in the house, she wanted to be there too. I drew the line at allowing her into the toilet with me, so while I sat on the lavatory she lay on the floor outside with her nose pressed against the crack at the bottom of the door, snuffling and inhaling deeply for any clue as to what I might be doing in there. For the first couple of years I'd also had a rule that Betty was not allowed into my bedroom at night. My reasoning had been that no woman I brought home would feel particularly inclined to throw aside her inhibitions and embark upon a wild night of naked sexual passion while a Border collie sat there watching, wagging her tail and barking at sudden movements. At some point I must have realized that the absence of a voyeuristic panting sheep-dog in my boudoir was not making much difference either way, and so now Betty was permitted to sleep in the same room as me.

The next morning, I climbed out of bed at around half past nine and went downstairs to make myself a cup of tea. Not a particularly exciting or surpassing sequence of events for a Saturday, but my dog was never one to appear indifferent to anything going on around her. I imagined Betty's approximate thought process for what followed *la grande levée*:

'Oh wow – he is getting out of bed! I don't believe it, how exciting, he is putting on his dressing gown and he is going downstairs; ladies and gentlemen, he is going downstairs!!! Quick! Quick! Follow him down, hurry, I'm not missing this, excuse me, excuse me – I've got to get down before him to be there first. Whoops, nearly tripped

him up on the stairs there, oooh he didn't like that, but it was worth being shouted at, I wouldn't have missed this for all the world, and now what's he going to do? Oh incredible, he is flicking on the kettle! Can you believe this? This is extraordinary – spin around in excited circles – he just flicked it on, without so much as a by-your-leave! Clear my diary, cancel licking my bottom and chewing my basket, because right now I have simply got to sit here and watch what happens next. Oh God, I'm shaking with excitement . . . Here we go, here we go, he's going to the cupboard and, yes, yes, he's opening the cupboard door and, this is amazing, he is getting a tea bag from the tea bag box and, oh wow, he is putting the tea bag in the mug, ladies and gentlemen, HE IS PUTTING THE TEA BAG IN THE MUG!! Oh dear, I barked, I couldn't help it, he didn't like that, I'm sorry but it was pretty phenomenal you must admit, and oh God I'm sorry I barked but sometimes the excitement is all too much and oh dear, oh no – he's opening the back door and telling me to go out for a wee. Oh God, oh God, oh God, he's so right, he is so right, I do need a wee, he's so clever like that; that's why I love him so much but I couldn't bear not to be here to see what he does next, and now I'm really torn because I don't want to miss any of this but I really do need a wee, and if he wants me to go out then it must be the right thing to do, because he just knows, he really does . . .

The kettle clicked itself off and luckily Betty managed to rush back inside in time to witness the event. I proceeded to make myself a brew, only tripping over the dog three or four times before I sat down on the sofa to drink from a Princess Diana commemorative mug, which I hid from those visitors I feared would not appreciate the irony. I noticed that my answerphone was flashing. The strange electric lady informed me that I had: 'THREE, new, *messages . . .*' and her voice went up at the end as if she was about to add something more important but she never did. The first caller was my mother. 'Happy birthday, Jimmy darling!' 'Many happy returns, son!' chipped in Dad, adding the cheery afterthought, 'Oh, and Brian Meredith's got Parkinson's.' Message two was my nephews who sang 'Happy birthday' in such perfect close harmony that it would have relegated the Von Trapp family into second place at the Salzburg folk festival. This was followed by another birthday greeting from my brother's wife, Carol, who generally did all that remembering-the-family-stuff for him, adding cheerily, 'See you later for the gathering of the clan!'

Today was my thirty-fifth birthday. Halfway through my three score years and ten, and the first birthday greeting of the day was still from my mum and dad. I treated myself to a cooked breakfast, and since it was a special occasion I dished my egg and bacon onto a plate instead of eating it out of the pan while standing up. It's surprising how table manners deteriorate when you are on your own. When the Queen has a slice of toast in bed on her own does she stuff it in all in one mouthful, chewing with her mouth open and then forcing out a satisfying baritone burp? For me, eating seemed to have become a simple bodily function: feel-need-for-food, ergo put-food-in-mouth. Now when I dined out I had to try to remember to remain sitting down and not to eat with my bare hands, wandering aimlessly across the restaurant to stare out of the window.

For my birthday last year, Mum and Dad had given me a special cookery book to communicate that they had finally come to terms with my long-term single status. Entitled *One Can Be Fun*, it was based upon the Goebbels-esque mendacity that cooking and eating alone can be every bit as joyful as a dinner party with your oldest and dearest friends. I checked the back page of *One Can Be Fun* but they had failed to come clean and print the telephone number of the Samaritans. If it had been a little more honest, *One Can Be Fun* would have had just one solitary recipe along the following lines: 1) Take one can of baked bins. 2) Open and put into saucepan. 3) Heat on stove. 4) Eat straight from saucepan in front of telly. 5) Drink several strong cans of lager after abject failure to find whole bottle of sleeping pills for dessert.

Despite it being my birthday, I had now resolved to spend as much of the day as possible on my screenplay. Indeed, the night before I had read a whole chapter of *How to Write a Screenplay* and had even turned on my computer to retype the title page. 'Avoidance is the writer's greatest enemy,' said the book. I decided to re-read the entire chapter on avoidance, lest I should succumb to this insidious trap. Then it was down to work. The manual was quite specific on how a screenplay should be set out, and so by pasting everything I'd written to date into another template, I managed to make Scene One look much more professional. But then I'd type another line into the computer and the text would suddenly revert to the earlier format, so I had to try to edit the document template all over again. I printed out a page of various fonts: first Times New Roman, and then another in Bookman Old Style, until I decided that Courier New had the most pleasing old-fashioned-manual-typewriter look about it.

I printed out the whole of the first scene, punched a couple of holes in the margin and threaded little green string paperbinders through it. It looked fantastic. I read my name on the title page: modest and understated, just the right distance under the title of the film. The only thing that diminished my pride in my *magnum opus* was the slimness of the work. It was clearly only a few sheets of paper. It didn't look anything like a completed script. I propped it lovingly on the side of my desk and set about rectifying this situation by tackling Scene Two. 'Scene Two', I typed at the top of the page. All right so far. I underlined those two words and then stared out of the window. After a few minutes I turned my keyboard upside down to shake out all the fluff and dead bits of skin that had collected in there. I glanced again at my printed script. And then I took a half-inch of plain paper from my printer, about a hundred and twenty sheets in all, and punched holes in every one before attaching the blank pages under the title page and the opening scene. There. At last it looked like a proper screenplay. I felt its weight and dimensions; I imagined it landing on the desk of a Hollywood executive. It looked perfect. All it needed now were the words.

I had intended to progress to that next stage, but by now it was a quarter past five and suddenly Betty became excited about somebody bustling around my front gate, which I knew meant my mother and father had arrived. I put the screenplay out of sight and braced myself for the onslaught as I opened the front door.

'Hello darling we had a terrible journey that's a nice jumper is it new we missed the turning for Newhaven and ended up going into the middle of Brighton is it cashmere so we came along the coast road but it's quite pretty or is it angora well they're both goats anyway we went past that famous girls' boarding school where Persephone James was sent when her father was gored to death by that bull in Pamplona. You won't remember the Jameses, dear, very sad it was in all the papers and Persephone's mother moved to London after he was killed. I expect she was upset by the sight of cows poor dear and Persephone went to board at Roedean that's what it's called which was a shame because she used to babysit for your brother before you were born.'

'Gored to death by a bull?' I said, suspiciously.

'Well it wasn't quite like that,' said Dad. 'He was struck by the bull and fell back and hit his head and died two days later.'

'He was *Gored To Death*, darling, I've still got the news-paper clippings in the escritoire, there's a big headline, "Gored To Death!", anyway it's much prettier than the other way.'

'What is?'

'The coast road though it adds on twenty minutes make sure you handwash that or you'll ruin it . . .' and while I was still trying to work out what it was we were talking about she had marched straight past me and begun tidying up.

'Ooh you've lit a real log fire, I do love a real log fire, they used to have one at the Rose and Crown but they've replaced it with one of those lookalike gas things with the special rocks that glow when they're hot, volcanic lava the landlord said it was, that must be a dangerous job getting them out of the volcano, he's gone and got himself one of those Thai wives, doesn't speak a word of English but I suppose they must have a lot of sexual intercourse, the trouble is of course they do spit so terribly don't they?'

'What, Thai wives?'

'No dear, real log fires. I'll put the fireguard up then the house won't burn down while we're out. I checked for your sister-in-law they do a vegetarian option and a fish dish we had some lovely fish with the new couple who've moved in down the road, they're Korean but very friendly, they're away a lot so they've left me a key, lovely new fitted wardrobes with lights inside, I said I'd introduce them to the new Thai wife at the Rose and Crown because that's quite near Korea isn't it of course your father didn't touch the fish because it wasn't deep fried in batter where does this go?'

Trying to talk to Mum was like playing tennis with someone who sent back seven different balls over the net at any one time. In the end you just took cover until the barrage was over. The subject of my job was briefly touched upon out of a sense of dutiful good manners. 'And how is your *part-time* teaching job?' she enquired as if she was asking the question, 'And how is your homosexual Iraqi boyfriend?' or 'How are things in the world of pre-school heroin dealing?'

'Fine . . .' I began, but this was a sufficiently comprehensive summary for her to feel that she could now move on to more pleasing subjects, such as my elder brother.

'We had Nicholas and Carol over last weekend, the children are so clever, apparently little Jasper is "almost gifted", but it's hard to know before they start nursery, your reports were always very good until you fell in with those working-class boys, the Strongs, dreadful family I found a box of them in the attic the other day all you and your brother's old papers and postcard albums and everything. I gave them to Nicholas to sort out I'll just wash up these few things yes Betty hello good dog.'

'Old Gareth Strong died of natural causes,' added Dad. 'It was in the local paper. I went through it twice but that's all they said. "Natural causes".'

My heart sank at the prospect of my big brother Nicholas being in possession of my old school reports. I knew he'd read them and then be deliberately complimentary about how good they were. 'You were quite a high-flyer at school.' (Subtext: So what happened?) But I resolved not to feel oppressed by my family's pervading sense of disappointment in me. I pictured the freshly printed screenplay, hiding like a winning lottery ticket in the top drawer of my desk, and wondered how they'd react this time next year when my birthday meal was quickly grabbed between takes on the set of my first movie.

The fact that my family was treating me meant that this was the one day of the year when I could choose somewhere special for us to go. So I had opted for the place I went all year round, namely the Red Lion, a pub in the town centre. It served reasonable food and we could have a beer beforehand and I could meet up with my friends later, so it was as good a place as any if you had to eat out in the sort of restaurants that were to be found in a dump like Seaford.

'Seaford is not a dump,' I said defensively an hour later as my brother described his failed search for a semi-tasteful birthday card. We were sitting in the saloon bar of the pub, studying laminated menus with helpful photos of every dish described.

'It *is* a dump – most of the cards in the shop said "In Deepest Sympathy". I mean how can you live in a town where people are more likely to die than have a birthday?'

'Maybe they mean "In deepest sympathy that you live in Seaford",' chirped his wife Carol unhelpfully.

'Dennis Johnson died on his birthday,' said Dad. 'Double pneumonia.'

I knew everything my brother said was true, but I couldn't help feeling that only I had the right to say it. British commuters endlessly whinge about their public transport system, but that doesn't mean they want foreign visitors agreeing with them.

'So what are we doing later on this evening, Jimmy? Carpet bowls or over-60s water confidence classes?'

'There's quite a lot for young people to do round here, as well you know.'

'Great. So it's hanging around the bus shelter giving each other love bites.'

'And there are some lovely walks as you head out of the town.'

'Walks? Surely if you were heading out of town you would run?'

The onslaught was relentless.

'Well, I like it here,' I said sulkily. My brother lived in London, and Mum and Dad had followed him there some years back to be near their *only* grandchildren. The reason I felt personally offended by their constant digs about Seaford was that I couldn't help interpreting them as coded attacks upon me. Substitute 'where I lived' for 'the way I lived' and the criticism wasn't so thinly veiled.

'It's not all pensioners and bored teenagers you know,' I continued before casually playing my only trump card. 'Billy Scrivens lives in Seaford . . .'

This news prompted more surprise and excitement than I could have hoped for.

'Really?' said Nicholas.

'Billy Scrivens? Lives here?!' said my sister-in-law.

'Oh now, he's very funny,' said Dad. 'What's his pro-gramme called? *Gotcha!*'

'Does he live here all year round?'

'Well, no, I'm sure he has somewhere in London, but he has a cottage between Seaford and Cuckmere Haven. You often see him in the town or jogging up on the Downs.'

'Have you ever actually met him then?'

'Er, yeah, I bumped into him this morning, as a matter of fact.'

This was true, if a little misleading. I had indeed exchanged a few words with Britain's highest-paid TV star at around half past eleven that morning. I'd taken a break from my computer and was walking Betty up on the cliffs when I suddenly saw Billy Scrivens coming towards me. He must have been jogging because he was red-faced and dripping with sweat and was now reduced to a sort of lumbering half-run, which petered out completely as he approached. He was clearly on some sort of health kick and stopping jogging certainly seemed the healthiest thing he could have done. He looked scruffier than usual. When he skipped down the steps at the beginning of his TV show he always wore a spangly jacket and his trademark bow tie, but that morning I was disappointed to see that he was allowing his impeccable standards to drop for a jog on the South Downs with his Labrador. But it was still unmistakably Billy Scrivens. His famous face seemed to announce to me 'Hi there, Jimmy, it's me!' and for a split second I had the sensation of bumping into an old friend. I checked myself; I should treat him as I would anyone else, even though I was not just another ordinary member of the public. In fact, I had a direct connection with him that I wanted to share. As an undergraduate, Billy Scrivens had been in the Cambridge Footlights and my old English teacher at school had *also* been in the Footlights about ten years before him. I paused for a moment, wondering how to broach this, but Betty was not so reserved and ran right up and sniffed his dog's bottom.

'Bit windy today,' said Billy Scrivens. I laughed heartily because I presumed the word 'windy' was a fart joke referring to his dog's posterior and my dog's interest in it. He seemed thrown by my laughter, which made me realize that all he'd meant was that it was a bit windy today. I searched for some witty rejoinder to demonstrate that I was totally unfazed at having bumped into a TV superstar.

'Yes,' I said. And then he walked on.

*

'So did you chat for long?' said my brother-in-law as my family focused on me with a level of concentration that felt as pleasing as it felt unfamiliar.

'Not that long, I had to get back . . .' In fact, I had turned and watched Billy as he ran off and was then stopped by an attractive girl asking for his autograph. Funny how she'd recognized him when she hadn't even looked up from the ground when she'd passed me.

'What did you talk about?' said Mum.

'Er, well, you know, the usual stuff . . .'

'No we don't know! Tell us!' demanded Carol.

'Um, well, look, I don't want to sound pompous or anything but with someone as famous as Billy I think one should treat private conversations as exactly that. But Billy's just an ordinary person like anyone else . . .' Nothing I had said so far was actually a lie.

'So you often stop and chat with him, do you?'

'Yeah, quite often.'

Oh. That was.

'*Billy*, he calls him,' said Mum. '*Billy*, not Billy Scrivens. So is *Billy* coming to your birthday drinks later this evening?'

'Er, no – I decided not to invite him in the end. It's hard enough for him in a little town like this without all my mates from the language school asking him to repeat his catchphrase all night.'

It felt good being the friend of a superstar. I'm sure he would have appreciated me protecting him like this.

'Well I never! My son, a pal of Billy Scrivens's, just wait until I tell the girls.'

'No – don't go round broadcasting it, Mum.'

'Would he like to have dinner with us now, then, if he's not coming for drinks later? Give him a ring, ask him if he wants to come and have some chicken in a basket. It looks nice in the photo.'

'No, Mum, really, I don't want to disturb him now.'

Even though 'Billy' would not be joining us for dinner, there was a noticeable shift. For the rest of the mealtime I was more interesting. Mum and Dad were visibly more proud; I had gone up several notches in status. All because I had exaggerated a chance encounter with a celebrity. Now they were basking in the warmth of the stardust that had rubbed off on me.

'Maybe Billy Scrivens could help you get a job in television, darling,' said my mother. Though I had promised myself I wouldn't tell my family about my secret project, the moment suddenly seemed ripe. They were temporarily impressed with me, and since Mum had alluded to a change of career I proudly told them my big news.

'Screenwriter?' said my dad, sounding momentarily optimistic about this turn of events. 'What's that, like a computer thing, is it?'

'No – writing films. A writer who writes scripts for the big screen.'

'Oh lord,' he said with a world-weary sigh.

I didn't expect them to understand. At least my brother was interested, as I might have expected since he was a bit of a movie buff himself.

'What's it about?'

'Well, it's very early days; it's hard to explain.'

'What is it, action adventure? Romantic comedy? Hardcore snuff movie?'

'No, none of those. I don't really want to say yet. I might let you read it when it's finished.'

'Wow! What a pitch! If I'd been a Hollywood producer,

I'd have signed you up there and then, no question!'

After dinner and kisses and family thank-yous, Mum and Dad finally headed home, while Nicholas and Carol came through to the bar to join me and the usual suspects for a birthday booze-up. The friends I'd accumulated during a dozen years in Seaford were drawn from the small pool of like-minded people who also wouldn't be seen dead in the town where they lived. We had eventually found an ingenious solution to the problem that there was nothing to do in Seaford by going to the pub and moaning about the fact that there was nothing to do in Seaford. My family had got to know most of my friends over the years, but when they were all together like this I still felt embarrassed that my brother and his wife were so cosmopolitan and smart and that my friends were so scruffy and provincial. Although I could hardly blame my expensively dressed sister-in-law for recoiling slightly as smelly Norman, our resident biker, plonked himself down beside her.

There are people who don't believe in eating meat; there are religions where you are prevented from cutting your hair. Norman's particular credo apparently prevented him from washing. For a while he had had the nickname 'Dogbreath', but personally I thought this a little harsh – my dog's breath didn't smell anywhere near as bad as he did. He believed it was unnatural to wash your hair. 'If you leave it for a while, it might smell a bit,' he conceded, 'but eventually the hair will start to cleanse itself using the scalp's own natural oils.' I'd known Norman for ten years and there was still no sign of those natural oils kicking in. Maybe they were still recovering from that last splash of shampoo they'd experienced in the early 1990s. Norman was one of the last surviving males of a once populous species referred to by anxious 1960s newscasters as 'rockers'. Every summer huge flocks had migrated to this coastline, but their numbers had plummeted because of the problem of oil on the beaches. There wasn't enough of it. And now his grubby leather jacket was rubbing up against my sister-in-law's expensive suit and she leapt up and generously offered to buy a round of drinks.

As the person who made the least effort with his appearance, it was only fair that Norman was the only one of our crowd of social misfits who was in a long-term relationship. Sitting on his other side was Norman's girlfriend, Panda. She was also clad in denim and leather, although she had omitted to have an old beer towel sewn into her jeans. The name 'Panda' was a bizarre corruption of 'Miranda' and I had known her for a couple of years before I realized that she'd been educated at Cheltenham Ladies' College and the whole biker's moll image was a reaction against Alice bands and pearls. She dyed her hair black, but sometimes you could see her blonde roots coming through. It was an effort for her to remember to hold her cutlery incorrectly. Carol passed her the last of the drinks from the tray.

'And yours was the glass of port. It's Cockburns, is that all right?' said my expensively dressed sister-in-law.

'It's pronounced Co'burns, actually,' said the grubby rock chick.

Confusing class friction aside, the alcohol was soon working its magic and everyone was chatting and laughing. Norman was moaning to me that Panda's parents didn't like him.

'Just because I've got a skull and crossbones on my helmet.'

'Well, you must admit it's an unusual place for a tattoo.'

My brother was deep in some political conversation with another of my friends. Dave was a gruff and cynical Yorkshireman who had stopped voting Labour long before anyone else, not because of any yuppy hijack or abandonment of socialist policies, but because the Labour Party had adopted the red rose as its symbol. 'The red rose of bloody Lancashire!' he snorted in disgust every time politics was discussed. 'What's wrong with the white rose of Yorkshire?' It was not that Dave was someone who bore grudges; he just needed a little bit longer before he could forgive Lancaster for winning the Wars of the Roses in 1485.

Despite living about as far from Yorkshire as it was possible to get, he continually tutted at Southern prices and the lack of foam on his beer while castigating us soft Southerners for needing namby-pamby luxuries like coats. An almost obsessive fear of being taken for a ride or being ripped off made him so cynical that he believed old ladies in the High Street collecting for guide dogs were only pretending to be blind. You'd show him a report from some third world charity saying, 'Hey, Dave, did you hear, they've stamped out smallpox world-wide.' And he'd tut and say, 'Typical drug company scam.' His outrageous statements compelled you to challenge him and then you'd find yourself stuck in a pointless argument, which was Dave's favourite means of communication.

'How can you possibly say there is no such animal as a badger?' shrieked my astonished brother.

'It's true. They're made up. An invented species,' asserted Dave.

'That's ridiculous. Of course there's such a thing as a badger.'

'Have you ever seen one?'

'Well, no, but . . . there are lots of people who have . . .'

'Lots of people say they've seen flying saucers and all. Doesn't mean they exist. Norman, have you ever seen a badger?'

'Well, yeah, on nature documentaries and stuff.'

'Doesn't count. I saw a flying saucer on the telly.'

'I saw a badger in a flying saucer once,' I added, a bit unhelpfully.

'Actually, I *have* seen a badger,' announced Nancy. 'Well, a dead one, squashed on a road.'

'Any hoaxer can forge a dead badger. It's like corn circles. That would have been put there for the very purpose of making you think there was such a thing as a badger.'

Eventually my brother was forced to concede that it was possible there may not be such a species as a badger and he attempted to change the subject. Five minutes later I heard him exclaim, 'How can you possibly say nothing happened in the 1940s!'

I was sitting next to Nancy who announced that the photos of our holiday were finally back from the developers. Every August a crowd of us went camping in Normandy, and thanks to Nancy's camera we had a great record of what her thumb looked like extremely close up. The more blurred efforts had oval stickers on them indicating what the problem might be: *Problem: Lens obstructed. Solution: Do not let Nancy take the photos. Keep Nancy as far away as possible from anything vaguely technical.*

'This could be the next big idea in photography,' I suggested. 'First they develop the disposable camera. Now Nancy's gone one better and taken disposable photos.'

The evening wore on and everyone was laughing and joking as novelty cards and little joke presents were unwrapped and I realized I was really enjoying myself.

'What did your brother get you, Jimmy?' said Nancy.

'Oh, well, we don't get each other presents any more . . . I just get them for the kids,' I said diplomatically.

'Except this year,' cut in my brother, looking mischievous and producing an old shoebox from under his chair.

'Although this isn't actually from me,' he continued. 'It's from *you* . . .'

A present from myself? What on earth was he talking about? And then from the box he carefully withdrew a large bundle of old letters wrapped in a faded ribbon and passed them over. Silence fell around the table as I stared, puzzled, at the pile of letters in my lap. The envelopes were all addressed to me, *but in my own handwriting*. At least, it was an early incarnation of my own handwriting, self-consciously adult and overelaborate in its loops and fountain-pen swirls. The pages inside were typed on an old-fashioned manual type-writer. And suddenly I remembered. These were letters from me, to me, written more than twenty years before.

As I scanned the first epistle a vague memory stirred, that in my early teens, during a particularly boring summer holiday, I had not only planned my future life but had written letters to my adult self, setting out every step of the way. Lots of teenagers keep secret diaries recording all the things they have done. I had written down all the things that I was yet to do. It wasn't that I had been a precocious teenager, I'd just written my autobiography in advance. Mixed in with this epic teenage fantasy were warnings against some of the unbearable habits that grown-ups develop. Some of the pitfalls I had managed to avoid: I hadn't spent thousands of pounds building a conservatory, for example. But that might be because I didn't have a garden on which to build one. I didn't make my kids look around the inside of churches on holiday, but that was because I didn't have any children.

'What are they, what do they say?' said Dave.

'Oh, it's just some old letters . . .' I said dismissively,

realizing that everyone had been sitting there in silence watching me read and waiting for an explanation.

'I found them in the box of our stuff that Mum got out of the attic,' explained my brother. 'It appears that in the absence of a proper childhood pen friend, Jimmy wrote a whole series of letters to himself as an adult, to be hidden away and read once he was a grown-up.'

There was a buzz of interest around the table.

'Well, lucky you didn't post them,' said Dave, 'or they wouldn't have got here yet.'

'No doubt you've read some of them?' I said anxiously.

'How dare you!' said Nicholas. 'I've read *all* of them.'

'Oh, read a bit out! Read a bit out!' demanded Nancy.

'Yes, well, now they are back in the hands of their rightful owner,' I said, putting them back in the old shoebox and pointedly replacing the lid, 'so if you think I'm about to expose myself to your ridicule you can just forget it.'

There were groans and pleading but I was unmoved.

'I knew you'd say that,' said Nicholas, pulling some pieces of paper from the pocket of his blazer and announcing, 'which is why I have some edited highlights for this evening's entertainment!' and a huge cheer went up as he put on his glasses and unfolded a few sheets.

'Read it out! Read it out!' chanted the dangerous drunken mob and he regally gestured for them to be silent.

'"Dear James",' he began with a grin.

'James?' heckled Dave. 'Oooh, very posh!'

'"As a multimillionaire, it is very important that you should not forget those less fortunate than yourself . . ."'

This ignited a roar of derision from around the table. He read the opening sentence again while I attempted, and no doubt failed, to adopt the expression of a good sport who was happy to take this sort of thing on the chin.

'"Despite being so wealthy, you should not be tempted to waste your money buying yourself a Rolls Royce or a Ferrari."'

'Well done, Jimmy, you've stuck to your principles there!' shouted Dave. 'Does it predict the Nissan Sunny with the coathanger for an aerial?'

'No, no – it's all here,' Nicholas continued, suppressing his own mirth. '"Instead, you should get a smart but un-pretentious car like Uncle Kenneth's Austin Princess, perhaps, and then just give your money away – not all of it, obviously, just a bit, like a thousand pounds or something, to carefully chosen charities that don't spend too much of their money on administration."'

For some reason this last detail triggered another huge explosion of laughter. Norman convulsed so much that he fell off his stool, while I merely smiled and nodded and attempted a long-suffering tut at my own adolescent foolishness. For a second I had hoped that Norman's drunken backwards lunge might deflect the attention away from myself, but this pack of hyenas had already selected their victim and were shrieking and howling for more blood.

'"However, it might be advisable to have tinted windows fitted to the Austin Princess in order that you are not repeatedly recognized off the television as you try to go about your everyday business without being constantly mobbed by your fans."'

The laughter was out of control now; it had tipped over into frenzied hysteria.

'"The important thing is not to look down upon ordinary unfamous people just because they seem to have such dull and uninteresting lives. Many of them, especially vets and people like that, do good and important work, and though it may not seem very glamorous to you, if it wasn't for all of them being so ordinary, it would be impossible for you to be so special." '

'Don't look so miserable, Jimmy,' said Nancy. 'You're not a bit like that now.'

'What, millionaire superstar?' said Nicholas. 'You can say that again!'

It was then that a terrible thought struck me. It wasn't what I'd written that embarrassed me, it was the obvious and enormous gulf between what I'd hoped to become and who I now was that made me feel so humiliated. The letters included the imagined script for my appearance on *This Is Your Life*. But with all the details of a showbiz success story that was not to be, these predictions were more like my own personal 'This Isn't Your Life'.

Further lines were read, but I was no longer listening; instead I was staring at the scene of myself surrounded by friends and family all shrieking and banging the table and drunkenly braying for more. Pretending that it was still all in good fun, I eventually managed to snatch the remaining letter off Nicholas and quickly placed it inside the box. I answered a few serious questions about whether I remembered writing them and what I was going to do with them now. Perhaps Carol could see from the expression on my face that her husband had gone too far in front of all my cackling friends and so she rather belatedly attempted to come to the rescue.

'Well, you never know, this time next year he might be famous. He is writing a screenplay, aren't you, Jimmy?'

'Are you really?' said Nancy. 'What about?'

'Oh, it's early days at the moment. I'd rather not say.'

'Come on, Jimmy, you can tell us,' pleaded Norman.

'You'll only take the piss.'

'No we won't, go on, what's it about?'

'Umm, no, really, I don't want to risk somebody else stealing my idea.'

'We won't tell anyone, honestly,' whispered Nancy.

'You've got to practise telling the story, Jimmy – pitching your idea is one of the basic skills of the screenwriter,' said my brother.

Nicholas was right, and having been made to feel such a failure, now I was desperate to do anything to restore my pride. The glass slipper had been produced – once they all saw how well it fitted I'd be the one who was laughing.

'OK. It's just that the whole thing is reliant on the idea, really. It's a comedy but it's a sort of thriller as well.'

'OK, buster, you've got two minutes!' said Nicholas, miming a cigar in an unconvincing impression of a Hollywood movie mogul.

'Right, imagine this: a millionaire tycoon decides he is going to murder his wife. But when he goes home to kill her, he discovers his wife has been kidnapped!' There was a buzz of impressed interest around the table and I continued. 'Everyone is saying, "Pay the ransom!" but this guy refuses. He says, "No, we've got to stand up to these bullies!" Only we, the audience, know that really he's hoping that the kidnappers will do the evil deed for him!'

I held my hands out ready to accept a little round of applause but my brother just unleashed the four devastating words: 'What, like *Ruthless People*?'

'Er – I never saw that. What happens in that?'

'A rich man comes home early to murder his wife and discovers she's been kidnapped.'

'Stop it, that's not funny.'

'And everyone says, "Pay the ransom," but he says, "No, we've got to stand up to these people."'

'Oh yes, I remember that,' chipped in Nancy. 'Danny de Vito, Bette Midler. It was quite good.'

I tried to salvage my precious project from this devastating revelation. 'Yeah, but in my story the joke is that the kidnappers are the ones who are desperate, because they're stuck with this really unbearable hostage, so they keep lowering their ransom demand to try and get rid of her, but the husband won't pay a penny.'

'Yes, that's it, that's what happens, it's all coming back now,' said Carol.

'Oh yes, I think I rented that once,' Dave added, unhelpfully.

I'm not sure if I said anything else for the rest of the evening. Oh no, that's right, about an hour later I distinctly remember mumbling 'Sure' when Nancy whispered, 'Are you all right, Jimmy?' I sipped my pint from time to time, feeling the laughter and chatter becoming separate and distant, like the echoey shouts inside a municipal swimming pool. I didn't want to be there any more. Just before closing time a big cake was produced and everyone sang 'Happy birthday' and I blew out the solitary candle. Yet another year effortlessly extinguished. Yeah, happy bloody birthday, Jimmy. Bloody Danny de Vito. He bloody nicked my idea, the bastard. When I eventually staggered home I read a few more of my teenage letters, describing a wonderful life of fame and success and money and adoration. And then I went to the bookshelf and looked up the offending film in my movie guide. There was an exact summary of the plot on which I had been pinning all my hopes. *Ruthless People*. Four stars. See, I knew it was a good idea.

And then I tossed my screenplay into the dustbin.

— 3 —

27 Elms Crescent,
East Grinstead,
West Sussex,
England

Dear James,

I know it is only two days since I last wrote but I was just
sitting down to start my project on the Tudors and I thought
I'd quickly write another letter to you before I start. No
doubt most of my class will leave their projects right until
the beginning of September but I think it is far better to get
it out of the way early on rather than have it hanging over
you all summer and then rushing it all at the end.

I don't know where you will be going on your summer
holidays but I imagine it is somewhere really hot with a
fantastic apartment that leads straight out onto the palm-
fringed beach, but there is also a lot of very interesting
culture and history there as well in case it rains. I'm sure

you are certainly not the sort of person who'd make your kids spend two weeks at their grandparents' and call that a summer holiday. Also, because you are not a male chauvinist pig, you sometimes let your wife choose what she would like to do on some days, so the two of you do not spend the entire holiday arguing. You treat her very much as an equal but fortunately she likes to do exactly the same things that you do anyway. Your wife is like a feminist, but beautiful as well. But not beautiful in a tarty way. In fact, she is actually very intelligent and it would even be all right if she wore glasses like Felicity Kendall did occasionally in The Good Life.

Your children are much more like you were. They are not all bossy like your brother Nicholas. You are a good parent who realizes that your children are more mature than you give them credit for and they are allowed to watch programmes that may offend some viewers, especially those watching in family groups. Your wife would never take your son to get his hair cut at a woman's hairdressers where his French teacher was having her hair done at the next mirror.

I suppose the trouble with your level of fame is that it seems like there is nowhere you can go where people don't recognize you! Some people will probably envy your wealth and fame but it's hard for them to understand that the grass always seems greener on the other side. From where they are it might seem much nicer being really rich and having a huge house and being able to buy whatever you want and having everyone love you and giving you whatever you want all the time. From where they are that must seem like a really attractive lifestyle. But they're only looking at the positive side of all that, they don't think about the downside, like having to give autographs sometimes.

There are pros and cons to every lifestyle. I'll write again soon.

Mine sincerely,
Jimmy

The depression I felt on the night after my birthday was no doubt deepened by the realization that the teenage Jimmy had had such high hopes for me. The more I read of these hubristic letters, the more I sensed that I must be a terrible disappointment to myself. I suppose if you are going to attempt to predict the future, there's no point in prophesying the mundane. Nobody would have been very interested in Nostradamus if he'd written: 'And in the land of the Angles, there will be much drizzle, And a great nuisance shall be felt, when no buses come for ages and then three come along at once.' When we watch toddlers playing with Lego we say: 'Oh look, he's going to be a great architect when he grows up.' Not: 'He's going to work for a building company, but be mainly based in the office, sorting out everyday software problems on their integrated network system.' So I understood why I had foreseen such an exciting life ahead of me – it must have been more fun to write about. And now I was supposed to smile at my naïve fantasies and think, Well, thank goodness none of that came true, thank goodness I'm where I am now. Except I didn't feel like that at all. I still would have loved to appear on *This Is Your Life* and listen to a catalogue of my successes and pretend to blush as it was revealed how much tireless charity work I had put in to help the otter sanctuary. I still desperately yearned to be someone. Here was Jimmy Conway's success story, and that was all it was: a story.

I wonder if in the old days ploughmen ever felt they were stuck in a bit of a rut? It was now 3 a.m. on the third Sunday in September in the wet and windy seaside town of Seaford. All night the wind had whistled like a *Scooby Doo* soundtrack, banging wooden gates and spinning polythene bags along the seafront. Betty was sitting beside the bed staring at me expectantly, shaking with excitement as to what I might do next.

'Go to bed, Betty,' I mumbled, and she reluctantly slunk off to her beanbag. Before she finally lay down she liked to walk around in little circles a few hundred times, endlessly scrunching the squeaky polystyrene gravel inside like some ancient Chinese torture for irritable insomniacs.

Just as football matches generally start at 3 p.m. and school always began at 9 a.m., three o'clock in the morning is the long-established kick-off time for the traditional 'where did my life go wrong?' meditation. There is no better moment than the low-energy loneliness of the small hours to enter that innermost cavern of self-pity and regret. They ought to market special negative-thinking tapes that you could play to yourself when you wake up in the middle of the night, just in case you weren't convinced of your own worthlessness. To the echoey background music of distant panpipes and mysterious tubular chiming, a Californian with a gentle but authoritative voice could assert, 'You are a worthless piece of shit. You have achieved nothing. Your life is a mess and it's all *your* fault.' Apparently over 50 per cent of suicides happen in the small hours of the night. I'm sure with my negative-thinking-tape idea they could get that figure up another 10 per cent or so.

As you grow older, you gradually realize that the gulf between where you are now and where you had hoped to be is never going to be bridged. In your daily life you pretend that you will catch up, make up all that lost ground and suddenly be catapulted to that elusive magical place called 'Success'. But slowly it starts to seep through from your subconscious to the conscious: this is your fate, this is who you are, *this* is your life. I seemed to live permanently with that feeling you have when you're lost on a car journey and you just keep on driving further and further in the wrong direction hoping there'll be a turning or signpost somewhere up ahead.

Maybe everyone experiences this sense of creeping disappointment. When Alexander the Great was still in his twenties he had conquered most of the known world. Did he lie awake at three in the morning thinking, 'I dunno. I just always imagined I'd have done so much more by now . . .' Did Michelangelo feel the Renaissance had sort of passed him by? This theory failed to cheer me up since there was no escaping the fact that, unlike these rather poorly chosen examples, I had neither conquered Persia nor painted the Sistine Chapel; most days the sum total of my achievements was walking the dog and maybe hoovering the stairs. Youth is like the mornings: if you don't make a good start before lunch, you're in danger of wasting the whole day. Well, I must have spent my entire twenties clearing up the breakfast things and reading the paper and then having another cup of tea and suddenly it was the lunchtime of my life and I really should have made a start on something by now.

How did those famous people originally know in which area they should apply themselves? Does having a gift for something automatically impel you towards that outlet for your talent? Or was it just good luck that matched great people with the means to achieve their greatness? If Beethoven's dad had sent him to martial arts classes instead of piano lessons, would young Ludwig have developed into a rather disappointing sumo wrestler? If Kasparov had been given some other game instead of a chess set, would he have eventually found his true gift or struggled to become a grand master at Buckaroo? Perhaps the thing that I was great at hadn't been discovered yet. What did great goal-scorers do before the invention of football? It seems a bit unfair that Mary, Queen of Scots got her head chopped off for being a failed monarch; for all we know, her real talent might have been as the greatest female goalkeeper of her generation. If the rules of Association Football had been drawn up four hundred years earlier, she could have represented her country at the Women's Soccer World Cup finals and become the heroine of all Scotland after stopping the ball three times in the penalty shootout that settled the 1566 final against the Holy Roman Empire.

Unlike me, my brother had always achieved to order. A good degree followed by a good job, a nice flat; married a nice wife, two lovely children now living happily in a lovely house. It wasn't fair. Why wasn't Mum shouting through from the kitchen, 'Nicholas! Let Jimmy have a turn with the nice life now!' As children we had niggled and bickered and fought like any two inmates sharing a small cell, and I lost every encounter. He was stronger, smarter, more experienced, more confident and just plain older than me. There had been a period when his ascendancy had been very directly expressed. For about a year and a half, I do not think Nicholas ever once broke wind unless he had first tracked me down, forcibly pinned me to the ground and sat upon my head, where his fart would finally be detonated with a triumphant 'Yes!' For eighteen grim months it was only in these precise circumstances that he deemed it right and proper to break wind: when his bum was pressed as close to the head of his little brother as possible. He would save them up, search the house and garden for me, then suddenly wrestle me to the ground, place his posterior on my head and release a methane blast while I struggled and protested underneath him. Sometimes my day would begin with this animal brutality. I would be awoken, not with a gentle kiss from mother, not with the melodic birdsong drifting in from an English country garden, but with a loud bottom burp blasted right into my eardrum at point-blank range, followed by the delighted cackling of my older brother.

For an outsider to our society looking for clues as to the pecking order in this particular social grouping, I'd say that my big brother's version of wind power might well indicate his supremacy over me. If you were observing a meeting of the council of European ministers and trying to discern who had status over whom, this sort of tell-tale body language would definitely point you in the right direction.

'Hmmm, they're both speaking French, but which countries do they represent?'

'Ah look, that minister has just leapt up, grappled the other delegate to the ground and farted on his head. So the bloke on top must be France and the one underneath must be Luxembourg.'

My brother was indisputably the boss, the master, the führer. Mao said that power comes out of the end of a gun. In our family power came out of my brother's bottom.

Of course, this ritual humiliation only took place due to the breakdown of the *pax parentis* – the real power brokers in our family did nothing to safeguard the human rights of the weaker sibling under their supposed safekeeping. I might try to protest and wail, 'Mum! Nicholas farted on my head again!' but somehow this made me party to a disgusting act for which it seemed I shared responsibility.

'Stop fighting, both of you! It's disgusting. You're both as bad as each other!'

I felt then and I would still humbly maintain today that we were not 'as bad as each other'. He was the farter and I was the fartee. And to have your head used as a fart cushion for a year and a half does something to your self-respect. Eleanor Roosevelt said, 'No one can make you feel inferior without your consent.' I'd like to have seen her say that with my brother sitting on top of her, farting into her right ear. It is very hard to maintain an air of composed dignity, I can tell you.

The digital clock blinked and now it was four o'clock in the morning. I thought about Billy Scrivens: rich, successful and popular. He must have achieved everything he ever hoped for. He had his own TV show, he'd written books, he'd launched his own charity, he had a number-one novelty record and he even went bloody jogging in the mornings. How do other people find the time to achieve so much? I have this theory that nobody else in the world sleeps. They're all conspiring to tell me that I have to get some rest but as soon as I nod off everyone else gets up again and busies themselves practising the piano or learning clever Latin phrases or reading novels. And then I go to some party and they're all talking about the latest Martin Amis or chatting in Russian to the guest from Moscow and I'm left thinking, Er if anyone wants to know the precise wording of any Monty Python sketches, I'm right here.

Now that I considered the matter, it seemed strange that someone as busy and famous as Billy Scrivens found the time to go jogging. I thought the super-rich paid other people to do all that boring stuff for them. Shopping, cooking, cleaning, answering letters ... If I was a millionaire, going jogging would the first thing I'd delegate. Maybe it isn't the half-hour spent exercising that's the point. Maybe it's what it does to the rest of your time. Perhaps the reason I never seemed to achieve very much on any given day was because I failed to attack the early morning with sufficient vigour. Was this why you always saw pictures of have-it-all high-achievers like Billy Scrivens and the American president going jogging? If I too started the morning with some strenuous exercise, perhaps the rest of my day would continue on the same high-octane go-getting level. I'd return home supercharged and ready to whizz through all my tasks for the day, ticking off each duty on my to-do list with a bold sweep of my pen before sitting down to read a little poetry before my fencing lesson.

My mind was made up. Instead of my usual morning work-out (gently turning the pages of a newspaper and sipping a mug of tea), from now on I was going to leap out of bed at 6 a.m. and go for a vigorous run along the beach and up onto the clifftops, whatever the weather. Starting in two hours' time. This was it: the start of a dynamic new regime, and I set the alarm accordingly. With the riddle of how to sort out my life finally solved I felt at peace with the world again . . .

I was on a steam train with my old maths teacher when the station tannoy suddenly emitted a similar buzz to the noise of my alarm clock. And then I woke up and it was all a dream. I looked at the clock, which said 6:00, and then I felt depressed that my alarm had gone off accidentally early, and then even more dejected when I realized it hadn't. Right, come on, Jimmy, get up! You're going jogging! Today is the first day of the rest of your life, go for it, just do it, feel the force or whatever.

I closed my eyes for a split second and then I fear I must have been kidnapped by aliens or sucked into a time warp or something, because even though I opened them again immediately the clock tried to claim it was three hours later. It glowed '9:15' at me mockingly, in that annoying digital clock font that looked slightly futuristic for about five minutes in 1973. Ten minutes later I was dashing along the pavement towards the beach, being dragged by a Border collie unable to believe her luck. Betty would pull me along faster than I could possibly run until she smelt a bit of abandoned food, when she would suddenly slam on the brakes, nearly yanking my arm out of its socket, and then refuse to budge.

Betty was quite picky about what she ate in the sense that it had to have been a foodstuff at some point in its history. To dine on driftwood or an old flip-flop that had been washed onto the beach would have been an offence to her polished canine etiquette. But if it were food, or rather had possibly been a human dinner in any former incarnation, then she was very open-minded about its preparation. Here's a favourite recipe from the *Larousse Gastronomique de Betty*: take one KFC chicken leg, strip most of the flesh and dump in a grass verge for several weeks until well rotted. The decayed bone should be sprinkled lightly with dirt and ants before serving and then it is customary to attempt to swallow the bone whole before gagging violently.

By the time we reached the path up to the cliffs I could run no more. I let Betty off the lead and staggered, exhausted, up the path in my now sweaty T-shirt and shorts, my plimsolls slipping on the sodden rabbit-mown grass. This is where I had pictured myself racing across the skyline, occasionally overtaking less energetic athletes. Instead I was bent double, panting with nauseous exhaustion. I felt stupid for having gone out of my way to contrive another failure as I staggered wheezily up the path.

Coming up the hill was a herd of determined walkers. They overtook me on the path as if I was standing on the wrong side of an escalator, their determined pace and self-consciously swinging arms showing the world that they were 'Walking' while I was just shuffling aimlessly along. How is it that people can make you feel as if you're doing something as basic as walking incorrectly? I had always presumed that walking at least was a skill I had mastered some time ago, but apparently not. At the head of the pack was a confident guide who had an Ordnance Survey map in a plastic cover swinging like a giant pendant around his neck. Why can't we have these route-finders to tell us where we should go in our everyday lives, I wondered. I could have used this bloke's directions a few years back.

'No, come back, Jimmy, you've taken a wrong turning there. You want to head towards that town there, then apply for this job here. On the desk on your left you'll see a girl called Linda. Ask her out for a drink and then a year later propose marriage and have three children called Polly, Sean and Samantha. All clear?'

As I clambered breathlessly to the first summit I turned and looked back at how far I had climbed. On the hills up towards the cliffs was a small golf course and a couple of golfers were now looking around seemingly confused as Betty tore over the brow of the hill with a small white object in her mouth. In the car park at the bottom of the hill was a van with a large satellite dish on top, an unusual sight in a cultural backwater like Seaford. Perhaps they were filming *The Antiques Roadshow* from the prosthetic limb shop. I tried to start running again. I thought I'd veer to the left today, which happened to be the path where I had passed Billy Scrivens the day before. But as I came over the brow of the hill I could see an unfamiliar cluster of people who looked strangely out of place. A smart-looking woman in a coat more suited to the fashionable streets of London or Brighton than the howling winds of the South Downs was standing in front of a TV camera looking sombre and significant, while a couple of other slightly less important people clutched clipboards and talked into mobiles.

Being unimpressed by such things I carried along my

intended path. About 1.5 seconds later I turned sharply towards them in the hope of gleaning some indication of what could possibly have attracted what looked like a documentary film crew to a muddy hilltop in East Sussex.

'What's all this in aid of?' I asked a girl in a puffy anorak holding a clipboard.

* * *

Premature deaths of famous people are always a shock. Their celebrity makes you feel intimately connected to them, making it impossible not to feel some personal loss. But this was different. I really wasn't just another of Billy Scrivens's viewers; I had exchanged a word or two with him up on this hill the day before. And today I had come out jogging here, yes, I admit it now, hoping to bump into him again, not quite sure what I would say if I did. But instead I discovered that a couple of hours earlier he had been out jogging on this very hillside, had felt unwell and returned home, where he'd had a massive heart attack and died.

'God. I was talking to him up here only yesterday . . .'

'Really?' said the girl with the clipboard excitedly, before calling to the presenter. 'Maggie! This guy knew Billy Scrivens.'

Her boss strode over and shook my hand.

'Maggie Belfitt. BBC News South. How do you do? Very sad news.'

'Yeah. I can't believe it. I was talking to him up here only yesterday.'

'He was only forty-four . . .' she mused ruefully.

'God. I was talking to him up here only yesterday.'

She nodded sympathetically although in her eyes I detected the slightly forced attention of someone being compelled to listen to an elderly relative with Alzheimer's.

'Was Billy a keen jogger like yourself?'

I was so impressed by this presumption about my own dedication that my brain-to-mouth transmission was jolted out of sequence.

'Er – well, he jogged yesterday and again today so I suppose he must be pretty fit. I mean apart from having the heart attack, obviously. Er – and, you know, dying.'

The cameraman shook his head in contemptuous disbelief.

'Sorry,' I said to the producer. 'That wasn't meant to be a joke.'

'That's OK. Billy would have seen the funny side.'

'Yeah, he would have done, wouldn't he?' I said, already using his death to justify my actions, and I realized all over again what she was saying, that this national treasure had died at the peak of his fame, had died so unexpectedly.

'Look, would you mind saying a few words on camera?'

'Me?' I said in astonishment. 'But, what do you want me to say?'

'Just what you told me – that he was jogging here only yesterday and what a shock it is for everyone. And you know, just something about Billy Scrivens in your own words.'

Subtly the shocking reality of this celebrity death seemed to be mutating into some shamefully thrilling drama for which I seemed to have passed an audition for one of the minor roles. Of course I was upset by the news, but there was a perverse excitement to it as well. A national tragedy that involved *me*. When the whole country briefly comes together to feel a unifying sadness, we all want to place ourselves as close to the event as possible: 'Of course, it was especially poignant for me. I'd been up the Twin Towers only three years earlier.' Here I was being asked to be that special person; my proximity to this drama made me feel like some peculiar sort of hero.

Betty had her nose in a rabbit burrow and I knew that unless I called her off, she would dig and sniff for hours.

'Er, yeah, of course . . .' I said, failing to sound laidback about this suggestion.

'Great, thanks.' And then she called out. 'Mike! This guy's just going to do a piece to camera. He used to jog up here with Billy Scrivens.'

I wasn't quite sure what she'd meant by that. Did she think that I used to sometimes happen to be running on the Downs at the same time that he was up here, or had she imagined that the two of us jogged side by side, chatting about life and then shouting US Marines-type encouragement to each other as we pushed ourselves through the pain barrier.

'Melissa, can you just put a bit of powder on him. Mike, what do you think, with the sea behind or the Downs . . .' All of a sudden, I felt important and interesting. A beautiful blonde was leaning right over me, wiping the sweat from my brow and putting a little powder there. It was surprisingly intimate.

'Single?' she asked.

'Yeah, well, I just never found the right girl, you know . . .'

'Sorry, I was talking to Maggie. Is this a single or a two-shot?'

The cameraman shook his head with rancorous pity and swore about me under his breath. They debated whether or not to clip a little microphone onto my T-shirt. The camera-man merely glanced at the perspiration soaking through the cotton to indicate there was no way he was risking ruining his equipment by exposing it to my disgusting sweat. So he fitted a long microphone onto the end of his camera, efficiently locking it on like a foam bayonet, and then it seemed we were ready to begin.

'OK, Jimmy. Just tell me what you had for breakfast,' said the cameraman.

I was unsure how a national news report on this shocking death was going to strike a sufficiently sombre tone by cutting to some anonymous local resident saying, 'Now, let me think, I had a bowl of multi-cheerios 'cos I'd just run out of sugar puffs, oh, and half a pop-tart I found at the back of the bread bin.'

Maggie saw the surprise on my face and elucidated.

'It's just for sound level.'

'Oh I see.' My chance to be witty, I thought – to show them I could think on my feet. 'Er – I had a bowl of cereal,' I said. Well, you had to be there.

'OK, Jimmy – I'm going to ask you a question, but I'll be cut out in the edit so make your answers completely self-contained, OK?'

I didn't really follow, but nodded anyway.

'Jimmy, when did you last see Billy Scrivens?'

'Yesterday!' I said, but their faces suggested that I had earned no points for getting this particular quiz question correct.

'Erm, sorry, Jimmy, just to explain again: my question won't feature when this goes out, so someone just saying "yesterday" won't mean anything. Can you give us a bit more? Did he seem his normal self? Did you chat about the usual things?'

She really did think I'd known him. The time had surely come to step back for a second and explain the truth here. Maggie was waiting for me to respond; I looked at the pretty assistant who regarded me with sympathetic sadness as a man who had just lost an old friend; I saw all the equipment; the monitor, the cables, and the camera pointing right at me.

'I was chatting to Billy only yesterday,' I said sombrely. 'He was on such good form, it's such a shock to us all . . .'

'Was he as funny off the screen as he was on it?' said Maggie eagerly.

It was too late to come clean now. This was probably costing thousands of pounds; I had to play along, give them what they wanted. And so what if I exaggerated our brief exchange on the Downs yesterday? I was only going to say nice things about Billy; I wasn't planning to hurt anyone or make money out of this tiny deception. So I resolved to go for it, to do my very best for them, and so I really concentrated, slowed right down and said as mournfully as possible: 'Billy was a great guy. A true professional, but that rare thing, a comedian who was as funny off the screen as he was on it . . .' This was amazing stuff. These lines were coming into my head like some standard tribute speech I'd subconsciously learnt from watching too much television. 'A great guy' – I never used the word 'guy'; where did that come from? Paul McCartney describing an ex-Beatle? Tony Blair mourning a former cabinet colleague? 'And though he will always be remembered for the joy and laughter he brought to millions, we should not forget the tireless work Billy did for charity. We'll all really miss him.' And then I did a little sad shake of my head, staring at the ground with my mouth hanging slightly open as if I still couldn't believe it.

I was brilliant, I was sure of it. As I finished, astonished at my own perfect performance, I realized that my speech had in fact expressed little of the genuine sadness and shock I felt at the news. After all, Billy Scrivens had been talking to me from that box in my living room every Saturday evening for so many years it really did feel as if I had lost someone I knew.

'That was excellent, Jimmy, thank you very much,' said the

producer, touching my arm in sympathy. 'You must be very upset.'

'Er, yeah, well, you know, I was only talking to him yesterday.'

'Mmm,' she said, with a slight suggestion that I might already have mentioned this. And then, as if she had just thought of the most poignant tribute possible, as if it would be what Billy really would have wanted, she added: 'Jimmy, can we get a shot of you jogging down the hill?'

'I'm sorry?'

'It's a linking shot, to talk over while we're saying who you are. If you could just jog towards us from that bench over there.'

'Oh, I see. Um – OK. Do I know that Billy has died at this point?'

'Er – Mike – what do you think? Should he look sad or just normal?'

'Erm – well, neutral I think, I mean obviously not happy, but not running along blubbing either.'

After my word-perfect speech, 'Jimmy one-take Conway' felt pretty confident about an easy task like running down the hill. So I flattened down my hair and pulled my socks up and tried to jog as athletically and gracefully as possible. I imagined the *Chariots of Fire* theme as a soundtrack to my running across the horizon.

'Er, that was OK, Jimmy, except for some reason you were running in slow motion. Could you just do it once more for us, and this time try jogging a teensy little bit more naturally? Just try and forget the cameras are here, OK?'

I felt my face go red, and hoped they'd put it down to the exercise, except that my slow-motion interpretation had not involved any actual exertion. OK, cut the *Chariots of Fire* theme, I said to myself as I skipped back up to the bench, and when they were ready, I ran towards them much more quickly, determined not to repeat this mistake. I tore past the camera like Jesse Owens on whizz and Maggie shouted, 'Whoa! Whoa! You're just out jogging; it's not the hundred-metre dash at the Olympics!'

'Sorry, sorry, too much the other way!'

'That's fine, don't worry. Just relax and, when you're ready, give us a normal jog down from the bench.'

'Sorry. Bit nervous . . .'

'Don't worry,' she said, and I noticed her glance at her watch while the cameraman's loathing reached new heights. He spat at the ground as if no words could ever express his contempt.

'A normal jog' she had said. You wouldn't imagine that the simple act of running could be difficult, but I seemed to have lost the knack. Each step became self-conscious and contrived. Suddenly I couldn't remember how far I should stride with each step, how high to bring up my knees, how much I should swing my arms; I was paralysed by the embarrassing image of myself bobbing across the television screen like the wooden marionette of some 1950s children's TV show. It was difficult enough concentrating on which limb to move next without simultaneously having to focus upon what sort of facial expression I should present. I settled on the gritty 'loneliness of the long-distance runner' look, and lumbered towards the camera with the forlorn look of a recently bereaved jogger. Perfect! I thought. The cameraman turned to the producer and without lowering his voice said:

'Nah, the fucking idiot looked into the camera.'

'Sorry, Jimmy, we should have said. Don't look at the camera lens, look straight ahead to the side of it, and keep running straight past.'

'Oh, OK, so I'll keep my eyes on an imaginary object to the left of camera.'

'Great idea!'

Notice how I said to the left 'of camera' not 'of the camera' – I couldn't help picking up the jargon after only minutes in the biz. I did my little dash once more and kept running straight past as instructed. But then I was unsure whether or not the cameraman had swivelled round to film me running off into the distance, so I thought unless instructed otherwise I should probably just keep going.

Unbeknown to me the crew had stopped filming and gathered round a little monitor to check back the footage. Which is why they didn't notice me dashing off up the hill, not daring to slow up in case I ruined another take or was shown on national television to be a rather weedy jogger. It must have been a minute or more later that the producer looked up from her screen to turn to me and ask what I thought, when she realized I was not in fact by her side but was still running with all my might up to the clifftop, desperately listening out for someone to shout 'Cut!' They got me back before I ran all seven miles to Beachy Head.

'Are there any other joggers who might have seen Billy up here yesterday?'

As she said this I could see running down the hill the young woman who had stopped Billy Scrivens the day before and asked for his autograph. He had taken her pen and made her giggle by signing his name right across her naked upper arm.

'What about her?' they asked me. As she came closer I could still make out the smudge; she'd obviously not washed it off. What a great piece of TV news footage that would make.

'No. She wasn't here yesterday,' I said. 'Never seen her before.'

I felt myself shiver slightly. It must have been colder than I thought.

This is how famous Billy Scrivens was. The flyer outside the newsagent's said, 'BILLY IS DEAD'. Not 'TV COMEDIAN DIES', and you buy the paper and discover that it was some-one who used to be in some long-forgotten American sit-com. Not 'TOP COMIC DIES' and you buy the paper to find out which one. Not even 'TV'S BILLY SCRIVENS DIES', but just his name, that was enough; they knew you'd be interested. 'Billy is dead.' That's the true definition of fame, when they only have to say your first name when you die. What a proud moment for him.

Naturally it was the first item on the lunchtime news. Just the way the newsreader said 'Billy Scrivens', his voice dropping a couple of notes for the last syllable – that was all you needed to hear to know instantly that this superstar's life was over. It was all very sad, very shocking and I checked that my video recorder was taping the right channel. There was a photo of him behind the newsreader with the dates of his life underneath and then they cut to the scene of his heart attack: 'his holiday cottage just outside the Sussex coastal town of Seaford'. Seaford was pronounced slightly incorrectly, like it was a forerunner of the Model T Ford, but there was no time to be annoyed about this because there was Maggie Belfitt talking to camera, describing how Billy Scrivens had suffered a fatal heart attack after going jogging. And then suddenly there was me – jogging down the hill, looking pretty cool if I say so myself, as she was saying that these cliffs were a popular spot for local joggers, which they weren't, adding that Billy often jogged here, which he hadn't. Then the whole picture was filled with my talking head. 'Billy was a great guy. A true professional, but that rare thing, a comedian who was as funny off the screen as he was on it . . .' I sounded so convincing. Then a caption popped onto the screen. 'Jimmy Conway. Billy Scrivens's jogging partner.'

'And though he will always be remembered for the joy and laughter he brought to millions,' I continued, 'we should not forget the tireless work Billy did for charity. We'll all really miss him.' But they cut my little sad shake of the head. I couldn't believe they cut my little sad shake of the head. That was the best bit! Did these people have no idea?

The phone went immediately. Even though they were still talking about Billy's sudden death and tracing the early years of his career, an even bigger news story had just broken for anybody who knew me: namely that I had just been on the television. And now they were phoning me for comment and reaction to the story of the day: Jimmy Conway was on the lunchtime news.

'Jimmy, I can't believe it – I just saw you on the telly.'

'Oh hello, Dave. Yeah, they filmed it this morning. Terrible, eh?'

'No, you were really good, mate. Like a real pro.'

'No, I mean the news. About Billy Scrivens.'

'Oh yeah, what was all that bollocks about you being his jogging partner? They do talk some rubbish, don't they? You never knew Billy Scrivens, did you?'

I couldn't help feeling slightly insulted by this, as if he was undermining my one moment of glory.

'Well, actually we were chatting on the Downs only yesterday . . .'

'You mean you really knew him then?'

'Well, I didn't want to sound like I was bragging about it or anything . . .'

'Oh, sorry, mate, I didn't realize.' And then his voice turned from embarrassed sympathy to boyish excitement. 'So will you be going to the funeral then? 'Cos there'll be loads of celebs there!'

'Come on, Dave, that's not really the point, is it?' I said.

'Er, well, no, I suppose not, but I was just saying, you know . . .' and he apologized and I told him not to worry about it, and explained that I was still a bit in shock from what had happened.

But Dave was right, there would be loads of celebrities there: soap stars, footballers, rock legends, quiz show hosts and maybe a couple of politicians hanging self-consciously around the edges. Just imagine being invited to that, being in the same room as all those people at once. But of course it was part of another world, a world in which I didn't have any place. There was no question of me being invited, even though the BBC had called me Billy Scrivens's jogging partner. Whoever got the job of drawing up the list of people to invite was never going to say, 'Oh, and we must ask that bloke who was on the news, you know, the one down in Sussex who used to jog with Billy.' It's not as if any of them had ever met me or knew anything about me; just seeing the lunchtime news would never prompt them to invite me. They didn't even know where I lived.

It was about this time that I wondered if it might be a thoughtful gesture to send a letter of condolence to Billy Scrivens's wife. Just a few words to say that my thoughts were with her at this difficult time and perhaps mentioning how Billy had seemed in such good form when we'd chatted the day before he died. I thought in order to explain who I was I should say that although she and I had never met, I was the one on the lunchtime news given the dubious title of 'Billy's jogging partner'! And then I thought twice about the poor taste of this and removed the exclamation mark. Before I could change my mind, I dropped the letter in by hand to the big empty cottage in Cuckmere Haven that had been their holiday home and then went back to listen to all the excited messages on my answerphone.

Four days later I received a black-edged card inviting me to Billy Scrivens's funeral. 'Yes! I'm going to the funeral!' I exclaimed to my excited dog. 'What a result, way to go, Jimmy! Oh joy! Oh happy day!' I couldn't remember ever being so delighted.

— 4 —

27 Elms Crescent,
East Grinstead,
West Sussex,
England

Dear James,

Fame is a two-edged sword. But they're not both good edges, one
of them is a bad edge. And the trouble with being the major
celebrity that you are is that there are some pretty weird
people out there who will probably stop at nothing to get
close to you. Most will probably just want a brief taste of
your exciting world, but others may have more sinister
intentions. I don't want to spoil all the fun of being rich and
famous or anything but I feel I should warn you that there is
a chance that you'll be gunned down in the street by a crazed
psychopath.

It is now eight months since John Lennon came to the end of

his 'Long and Winding Road', except it wasn't as long as it should have been, it was more of a short and winding road, well he was forty, so it was medium length, I suppose, but anyway certainly not as long a winding road as it should have been after his life was tragically ended by a crazed fan. Actually, I don't call people like that fans, they're not real fans, they're murderers. That's the only word for them. The point is that if John Lennon had never been famous he would probably still be alive. His music gave pleasure to millions, including pensioners. But then one so-called 'fan' went and killed him. As usual, it's always a small minority who have to go and spoil things for everyone else.

So, James, I am writing to advise you that perhaps you too should take a few precautions. Don't give autographs to people pointing guns at you. No, on second thoughts, do give them autographs. It's probably advisable to do whatever they want. But if, say, a scary-looking man with lots of handguns and grenades and a dagger in his mouth climbs up the side of your house and wants to come in the bedroom window, then don't let him in. He could be dangerous.

Of course, when you become famous, a certain amount of constructive criticism is to be expected. You've put yourself in the public eye and you have to be prepared to accept the odd dig or two. But if people try to shoot you then frankly I think that is going too far. Ronald Reagan, the Pope, JR — they're all getting shot at the moment. And I blame the gunmen.

So, Jimmy, keep an eye out for a crazed assassin, and if you see one, stand behind a stone pillar or a bus until he's gone. Because there are some pretty weird people out there.

Mine sincerely,
Jimmy

It's true, there really are some pretty weird people out there, I thought as I prepared to gatecrash the showbiz funeral of a celebrity I was pretending I'd known. But I wasn't obsessed, I wasn't a stalker; I was just a fame tourist. Some people liked to wander around Rome taking snapshots of the deities of a bygone age. I merely wanted to see the icons of today, to see all the new gods lined up on display.

Back in Seaford, of course, I was already a little bit holy myself. Following my distinguished appearance on the BBC news, a tribute which, I am proud to report, was also included in that night's specially extended evening bulletin, every single person I knew or had ever known had heard the good news: that Jimmy had been modestly keeping mum about a friendship with Britain's biggest TV star. Everyone wanted to talk to me to console me, to buy a few shares in the death of Billy Scrivens, to make this shared national experience have something to do with them. 'Yes, a friend of mine is going to the funeral . . .' they'd say to their workmates when the subject came up. 'I've been trying to help him come through it but it's very hard for him, you know, with the telly and newspapers reminding him of what's happened every five minutes.'

They had suddenly discovered that they had a place in this solar system. At the centre was the supernova Billy Scrivens. Around that star had revolved various planets, including, as it turned out, their friend Jimmy Conway, around whom they orbited themselves. And suddenly I noticed that the various satellites that looped around me were all at their closest proximity all at once, all in full view, lined up and shining brightly into my life. After the lunchtime news the phone rang continuously for the whole of the day of Billy's death and for every day in the build-up to the funeral.

The second friend to call had been Chris. Chris was a very

nice person, but he'd never been the same since he nodded off on the beach at Rio de Janeiro. He'd been victim to a gang of criminal surgeons selling human organs on the black market. They must have whipped his brain out while he was asleep; there was no other explanation. He was the only person I knew to get a negative score in an IQ test.

'Hey, Jimmy. You were just on the television!'

'Yeah.'

'Amazing!'

'Yeah, it's weird.'

'You must have run home really quickly.'

'What?'

'I was expecting to get your answerphone but you're back already. That's amazing!'

'No, it wasn't live . . .'

There was a pause while Chris thought about this.

'Right. So they know the news in advance, do they?'

'What?'

'I thought the news was live.'

'Well, most of it is, Chris. But it's amazing what they can do with modern technology these days.'

'Yup. I'm with you. You've got your home phone diverted to your mobile, haven't you . . .'

The next caller took me slightly longer to place.

'Is that Jimmy?' said the voice of an elderly lady.

'Yes.'

'Hello, dear, it's Audrey Lacy.'

'Sorry?'

'Audrey Lacy. Brian and Audrey – your Mum and Dad's friends. You sound different, your voice has broken.'

'Oh blimey. Hello, Audrey.'

'Brian and I just wanted to say how sorry we were

about your friend Billy Scrivens dying like that.'

'Oh. Right. Yeah.'

'Your mother had only just let on that you were friends with Billy Scrivens when she rang at eleven o'clock last night. So then when we heard the sad news on the wireless this morning, well, we just had to ring and say how sorry we were . . .'

'Oh well, um, thanks, Audrey. Nice of you to ring. Yeah, it still hasn't really sunk in yet.'

'Oh dear.'

There was a momentary silence during which I suppose I had expected her to say goodbye.

'So, was he like that in real life as well?'

'Hmm?'

'Always joking and playing practical jokes on you and such like?'

'Er, yeah – he was just the same,' I confirmed, and she seemed to have found the solace she'd been seeking.

This was a reassurance everybody demanded of me. That the friend who beamed out of their television set had not been deceiving them, that they'd been right to take him into their hearts. In the course of various conversations about 'me and Billy' I had found myself being forced to embellish my fantasy with little details about things we had chatted about or done together. 'No, we never talked about ideas for the show; when he was down here he wanted to get away from all that.'

More than one person volunteered to accompany me to the funeral. 'You know, just in case you need a bit of support or whatever.' Honestly, these morbid groupies, they're so voyeuristic; it's sick, it really is. I'd got myself a ticket, I mean an invitation, and they hadn't, and that was all there was to it.

Although I began the morning with plenty of time to spare,

the hours were rapidly slipping away from me. I popped into Mr One Pound because I seemed to remember they had some cheap plastic belts but I quickly found myself being press-ganged into assisting Edna Moore who lived next door to the language school and for whom every aspect of the modern world always seemed completely baffling.

'Oh hello there, Jimmy, could you give me a hand, dear, I've forgotten my glasses again – I can't read any of the prices.'

Obviously I was perfectly happy to find the time to assist a widowed pensioner like Edna, I didn't mind at all, nothing could give me greater pleasure than explaining the complex pricing system in the Mr One Pound shop.

'Jimmy – how much is this?'

'That's a pound, Edna. Everything in here is a pound. That's why the shop is called Mr One Pound, because everything you see costs exactly one pound.'

'Oh I see. What about this?'

'That's a pound as well. Everything here costs a pound.' In the background a tape loop was endlessly booming out the message: 'It's all a pound at Mr One Pound, everything costs a pound at Mr One Pound.'

'What about two of these?'

'That would be, um, two pounds for those two items, yes, I think that's right. Two pounds.'

'I only want one of them.'

'That's one pound then.'

'A pound for one of these? Haven't they got anything cheaper?'

I ended up carrying Edna's bags up the hill to her house, which left me less time than I had planned to walk the dog and somehow I managed to turn a leisurely drive up to London into a frantic race against time. There are some social occasions at which you are not expected to arrive at the time stated on the invitation; indeed, it's actually quite cool to walk in a little bit late. Funerals, however, are not one of them. In *Debrett's Guide to Bereavement Etiquette* it is most definitely not the height of good manners to burst in through the doors towards the end of the ceremony, elbowing past the pall bearers going in the opposite direction down the aisle with the weight of the deceased on their shoulders.

Fortunately I just made it, but I had cut it so fine that I found myself trying to do the slow dignified walk into the church at the briskest pace possible. Behind temporary crash barriers, dozens of photographers and TV cameramen leered out at the invited guests. A soap actress was ahead of me and they called out her names, both real and fictional, and flash-bulbs exploded like party poppers but she didn't stop for them. This was not the BAFTAs or the Oscars; it was a colleague's funeral. Though she did glance both left and right, towards both sets of photographers, as she walked slowly in. I suppose if you are going to spend that much on a fancy black hat you are going to want people to see it. It occurred to me that she probably didn't shop at Mr One Pound very often. I was next up. They raised their cameras once more, looked at me through their lenses and then put their cameras down again. 'Is this a celebrity?' said the first action. 'Nope, it's not . . .' said the second.

Just inside the church a couple of girls were collecting invites and cross-checking them against the lists on their clip-boards. I was momentarily nervous that there might be some sort of test to check that everyone really did know Billy Scrivens, such as, 'What was his favourite drink?' or, 'What was his first job in television?' As it happened I knew the answers to both these questions; like thousands of other people this week I had bought and devoured his biography, which was now racing back up the bestseller lists. I noticed that on these girls' name badges was the logo of *Hello!* magazine, which struck me as peculiar. Then I saw that at various strategic points around the church were photographers' lights set up on stands, with stepladders and tripods and cables and all the paraphernalia of a major fashion shoot. The men behind the crash barriers had been the unofficial photographers. You couldn't possibly have flashbulbs going off inside the church during a religious service. That would be inappropriate. So dazzlingly bright arc lights were set up for the official photographers all the way through.

It was a large, impressive church, a fine example of the unmistakable architecture of the period known as 'the olden days'. Every pew was packed. The trouble was that from the few remaining seats at the back, the view was terrible. You could see the vicar and the organist and everything, but you couldn't see the congregation. The back of one celebrity's head looks pretty much like another, with the exception perhaps of Mr Blobby and Tinky Winky, neither of whom seemed to have been invited from where I was sitting. It was only once I was in place that I noticed an usher starting to fill up the two rows of pews along the side of the church. You must be able to see everyone from there, I thought. So after a moment's hesitation I squeezed past the mourners beside me and fought my way for the best view in the church, or second best after the photographer who was clambering to the top of his squeaky metal stepladder. Some of my fellow mourners looked a little perplexed by my suddenly clambering across them, but I shook my head sorrowfully, bravely biting my bottom lip, and so my reasons were not questioned. In fact, everyone seemed to be wearing the same courageous expression: a clenched, sad smile that greeted fellow mourners with the message, 'I know, yes, I understand, it's nice to see you too, but how dreadful it had to be in these circumstances.' There was real grief on famous faces. The photographers from *Hello!* were having a field day.

Once I had a clear view of the whole church I was amazed and thrilled by the number of celebrities who were gathered in this one building. Would it seem a little improper to ask that weeping Spice Girl for her autograph right now? Maybe I should wait till the hymns to ask that bloke from *Coronation Street* if he gets found guilty in that court case. There was what's-his-face from Manchester United, behind him was a newsreader who was posing a question (a cooking query maybe?) to the presenter of *Mastercook*, and just behind them looking slightly different in her glasses was Norma Major, wife of the former prime minister. Even the people who weren't famous looked as if they ought to be. Their suits were smart and fashionable and they had an air of importance about them that made me conclude that the people I didn't recognize probably wrote out the cheques for the people I did. As well as most of today's top twenty there was a sprinkling of golden oldies, people who had been at the peak of their careers ten or twenty years ago, some of whom I'd completely forgotten about. There was that actor who was in *Upstairs Downstairs*, for instance, although he was obviously trying to play this down because now he was wearing modern clothes. And then my eye would wander again and I'd be brought bang up to date once more: coming in last of all were the really big stars, Kylie Minogue, Prince Edward, two out of six 'Friends' and the Dalai Lama. The young girl with the clipboard looked at his invite, ticked off his name and said, 'Take a seat on the left, please, Mr Lama.'

It was almost as if the more famous you were, the less time you could be seen to be kept waiting in the aisles. But I suppose that's just the way it happened to work out. I can't believe they were sitting in their cars around the corner till the last moment. Each face prompted a different Pavlovian emotion from thousands of hours spent watching television. Seeing England football stars made me instantly think, 'Goal! England are safe!' Seeing the bad guy from *EastEnders* made me want to shout, 'You bastard, you broke your poor mum's heart!' Spotting a TV quizmaster recreated the sensation of, 'Ooh, I know this one, don't tell me!' One or two of the stars seemed to have a slightly resentful air about them, as if deep down they rather objected to being cast with a mere walk-on role in this particular drama. 'Why should Billy Scrivens be the centre of attention?' they seemed to be thinking as flowers were placed around his coffin. 'It should be me up there.'

Edging his way past the official photographer and stepping over the cables, the world's most nervous vicar tentatively shuffled up before his celebrity congregation like some rep actor suddenly finding himself auditioning in Hollywood. For most of his sermons he must have felt confident that he was the best public speaker in the room, that he could project his voice and bring out the meaning of the text better than any of the dozen or so pensioners dotted about the otherwise empty pews. But just glancing around today's packed congregation I could spot the winners of three Oscars, four BAFTAs, and the TV Quick Award for Best Daytime Weather Forecaster. The vicar was trembling so much he could barely get his words out. He rushed through his first reading, desperate to make it to the first hymn, at which point he looked even more thrown because this new congregation sang up with such projection, clarity and feeling that he must have thought he had been transported to the front row of *Phantom of the Opera*.

It seemed strange to be worshipping some unimaginable made-up God in a room full of living, breathing deities. How bizarre that we had gathered together in a church, the religion of celebrity hijacking the temple of the previous established faith. Billy Scrivens had toured the sick and incurable in hospital and had touched them; was it not him we had come to worship today? In this century it was not the illuminated saints in the stained-glass windows we venerated, but the figures shining brightly through our television screens. Did not more believers worship at the altar of television on Saturday night than ever entered a church the following morning? In every home in every street we gathered around the god-box to hear the gospel according to St Oprah, for yea, daytime television is the truth, the light and the way.

The organist missed a few notes, the sermon was irrelevant and overlong, and frankly the whole show was a rather amateurish production. It was only at the end of the service when the speakers relayed Billy Scrivens's TV theme tune that the atmosphere picked up and the audience started to respond. When the jaunty tune finished everyone spontan-eously applauded. It was quite moving. We were at a funeral in a church but this was show business and it was Billy's lifetime curtain call. Take a bow, Billy Scrivens, you put on a great show, you gave us some great laughs, thank you.

As the applause died down six people took their places on either side of the coffin. But not six ordinary people, not undertakers or Billy's relations. No. Standing by ready to lift and carry out the coffin were six of the most famous celebrities in the country, each one from a different sphere of entertainment. There was the premiership's most expensive footballer, the lead singer from Britain's biggest boy band, a team captain from a top comedy panel show, the hottest British actor in Hollywood, a leading member of the cabinet, and just in front of him the winner of *Big Brother*.

If you'd wanted to arrange the perfect celebrity photograph, the vision of these six stars solemnly and humbly carrying Billy's coffin out of the church would have been it, I thought, as the official photographers eagerly clicked away. Once the coffin was taken outside, it was placed in a hearse and whisked off to a private cremation that would be taking place away from the public gaze. No details of this part of the proceedings were provided on the service sheet, but I knew that if it was for Billy Scrivens, it wouldn't be just any old conveyor-belt ashes-to-ashes job; he'd have the luxury cremation, a sort of executive super-cremation plus, with every frill and comfort laid on for the customer's convenience and peace of mind. It was hard not to be jealous of him, but I just had to accept it: this was how the other half died.

While all this was taking place everyone filed slowly out of the church, showing their sorrow and their best sides to the waiting paparazzi. They inched their way down the road to a nearby hotel that had been requisitioned for the purposes of the wake. It was a disappointing, unglamorous location, a modern post-war hotel that would normally cater for sales and marketing conferences for middle managers. But today the delegates didn't need name badges; their faces did the same job.

My excitement at being alone in this strange company was beginning to wane and with no one to talk to at the party I started to feel awkward and self-conscious.

I hovered on my own for a while next to a plant, which proved disappointingly inadequate camouflage and so I attempted a faint half-smile to various people walking past.

Their internal computers quickly scanned my face, instantly calculated my importance to their careers, registered the score 'zero' and swiftly redirected their eyeline to the next person along.

Hanging around beside the various groups of industry movers and shakers, I could overhear various snippets of what I presumed must be typical TV conversations: 'Yah, I'm doing a new Channel Four series called *Icons Uncovered* – you know, a sort of dish-the-dirt-on-the-modern-saints thing. We're exposing the real Anne Frank – there's some evidence that the blank diary wasn't given to *her* after all, she borrowed it off her sister and then failed to replace it. It's dynamite . . .'

Another pitch was going on behind me. 'We're trying to salvage the ratings for current affairs. I've got in the producers of *Pop Idol* and *Soap Stars* and we're holding auditions for people who want to become real-life politicians. The winner stands as an independent at the next by-election and with all the TV publicity we reckon they ought to walk it.'

I noticed an abandoned glass of champagne on a nearby table, which sat there fizzing away for ten minutes. I was dying for a drink and finally I strode past it, deftly picked it up and continued on my way as if I'd just spotted someone I needed to talk to. I glugged it back and my nerves began to ease. I found the purposeful searching-for-a-work-colleague technique quite an effective means of feeling less self-conscious. I walked from one end of the room to the other, exaggeratedly craning my neck, looking for this elusive imaginary friend, and then when I got there, I walked all the way back doing the same thing over again.

Although I was sure that thousands of pounds must have been spent on food and drink, there was no actual meal laid on as such. Instead elfin waitresses flitted around the groups of guests offering them a selection of expensive looking meal-substitutes. I found it hard to get too excited about this feast. '*Another* sliver of carrot! I shouldn't really, I've already had one, I might explode if I eat any more! No, no, just *half* a quail's egg for me please – I'm on a diet.'

These beautifully presented little nibbles, artistically arranged on silver platters, had clearly required a great deal of care and money to prepare but they failed to leave you feeling as if you'd eaten anything. In fact, the dainty morsels of spiced prawn or sculpted radishes dipped tantalizingly in exotic sauces only served to remind you how bloody starving you now were, how much you really fancied a couple of big cartons of Chinese takeaway. Even on the culinary front, image had triumphed over substance. It must take real expertise to create dishes that leave you hungrier than eating nothing, I thought; to pull off the gastronomic conjuring trick of combining garlicky breath with a rumbling empty stomach in order that guests leave the party belching spicy reminders that they're completely famished. Of course, any true gourmet will know that this burp food is only intended as a starter. If you wish to avoid a fierce headache when you wake up next morning, you're strongly advised to follow such dainty entrées with a large bowl of Weetabix for your main course when you get home. Only then can you lean back with the satisfaction of the replete diner, taking care not to stab yourself in the leg with the grubby cocktail sticks you secreted in your pocket earlier in the evening because there was nowhere else to put them.

The waitresses dispensing these morsels were petite and skinny as if they had been raised on a meagre diet consisting only of this negative-calorie food they were now bearing before them. They appeared like holograms around the edges of the circles and the guests acknowledged the platters but never the bearers, as if the selections were somehow hovering in front of them by magic. It puzzled me that no one was talking about Billy or even bothering to appear particularly bereaved – even drinking champagne seemed a little odd. I thought you were only supposed to have that when you were celebrating something. Then an approaching waiter offered me a glass.

'How much is it?' I enquired.

This prompted a big laugh from some nearby guests.

'Yeah, I wouldn't put it past him, the old bugger. That's just the sort of thing Billy would do, isn't it, charge for the champagne at his own funeral!'

'Er, yes, ha!' I said, taking a glass from the tray. *It was free.* Obviously it was free. I can't believe I could have been so stupid.

'So where do you fit into all this?' I was asked.

I had prepared for such a question on the drive up from the coast. Someone was sure to ask me, 'How did you know Billy?' and I would reply, 'Well, we were sort of neighbours . . .' and then if necessary I could talk a little more about us occasionally jogging together . . .

Unfortunately the question was asked by a very striking young woman, who added the irresistible bonus query, 'Are you in the biz as well?'

'Yes,' I tutted long-sufferingly, immediately realizing that more information was expected. And then I thought about my teenage letters and how they'd reminded me what I had always wanted to be; what people had always said I was good at.

'I'm a comedian.'

'Really,' she said, sounding impressed. 'I always think that must be the hardest job in the world.'

'Er, sometimes . . .' I quipped effortlessly.

'Are you doing the circuit at the moment?'

'Oh yeah, The Circuit,' I said casually, 'and, you know, a few other clubs beside that one,' and then they all laughed some more and I wondered if I really was just naturally very funny.

'What's your name?'

'Jimmy Conway?' I replied, tentatively phrasing my name as a question that could only prompt the answer, 'Never heard of you!'

'Oh yes . . .' she said hesitantly. 'Yes, I've definitely heard the name . . .'

'Can't say I've ever seen you on the telly,' said a posh man dismissively. He emptied his glass and clicked his fingers to summon more champagne. I wanted to assert myself, to stand up to this showbiz snob.

'No, I won't do television,' I said defiantly. 'It's killing real stand-up.' I had read this line in a magazine in an interview with some comic who had clearly repeatedly failed to get his own television series. 'Pure stand-up comedy is just the comic, the microphone and the audience, nothing else, live, right there in that room,' I declared, emboldened by the free champagne. 'Sure, telly might pay more. But which is better – to make a million people mildly entertained for five minutes, or to have a hundred people in the palm of your hand, weeping with laughter for a whole hour or more. Telly's a sell-out.'

It was my best performance since my tribute to Billy on the news and they all looked a little dumbfounded.

'That is so refreshing,' she said. The woman introduced herself as 'Arabella from the *Sunday Times*' and we chatted a little more about my experiences playing the various comedy clubs.

'You must know Mike Mellor then,' she said and before I could stop her she waved across a short stocky bloke with a shaven head.

'Mike, do you know Jimmy Conway? Jimmy's a stand-up comic like you.'

'Er, no, can't say the face rings a bell.' He shrugged. Mike Mellor was drinking champagne like the rest of us. But he was drinking it straight from the bottle. 'Just starting out, are you?'

'No. Jimmy's on the circuit, a proper comedian.'

I attempted a smile but it wasn't returned.

'So where might I have seen you recently?' he said, taking another swig.

I said the name of the only comedy club I'd even been to, hoping that he was unlikely to have ventured that far out of London. 'The Chuckle Cabin at Brighton?'

'Oh yeah, you must know Chris.'

'Chris, yeah. He's a good bloke, Chris.'

'She.'

'Oh, *that* Chris! Sorry. I was getting it mixed up with another club run by a bloke called Chris.'

'Which one?'

'Sorry?'

'Which other comedy club run by a bloke called Chris?'

'Oh it's a little one down there, tiny really, above a pub in Seaford, the, um, the Funny . . . the Funny Place.'

'Never heard of it.'

'No, Chris needs to do a bit of work on his publicity I think . . . but that's Chris all over,' I said, shaking my head in despair.

'Jimmy doesn't do television like you, Mike,' said Arabella.

'I do telly,' he insisted. 'I've got my own show!' and then he felt forced to add, '. . . being piloted on BBC Four.'

'Well, Jimmy won't do it on principle,' continued Arabella. 'He only performs live.'

'I've played most comedy clubs and I can't say I've ever seen you,' said Mike Mellor. He took another big swig from the champagne bottle and wiped his mouth like the hard man in a cowboy film.

'No, I haven't done much in this country for a year or two,' I replied, the drink making me even more reckless. 'I've been, um, gigging in the States for a couple of years, actually. They seemed to really go for me but, you know, it's a great scene they've got over there now.'

'Wow, the British comic who broke the States *before* he made it big in England!' said Arabella.

'Well, I wouldn't say I was that big in the States, you know . . . I get by.'

'You must be good if you're here. Billy wouldn't be seen dead with an unfunny comic.'

'Poor choice of phrase,' said Mike Mellor.

Soon after this Arabella spotted someone she urgently wanted to speak to and I was left on my own with this scowling skinhead of a comic. We stood together in awkward silence for a while.

'So how did you know Billy?' I asked him.

'I didn't. I'm here with my girlfriend. She knew him through work.'

'Oh well, he was a great guy,' I reflected. 'A great guy . . . I'm really going to miss him.'

I chatted with one or two other people over the next hour or so and maintained the same persona, becoming increasingly confident in the role of stand-up comic returning home after storming every comedy club from New York to LA. I was a little shocked at myself, weaving such elaborate webs of deceit, and eventually I felt overwhelmed by the need for somewhere to hide for a while. I slipped out into the lobby and wandered along a corridor. On a trolley outside the door was an abandoned platter of food and, after a furtive glance in each direction, I picked up a paper serviette and packed it with half a dozen chicken sticks, garlic prawns and asparagus spears, and looked for somewhere to stuff my face in private.

I found a little ante-room, walked in and closed the door behind me. The room was small and private but it was only after twenty seconds or so that I realized with a start that I was not alone. I'd been so preoccupied with my own hunger that I'd failed to notice a woman sitting silently in a chair in the corner. I could tell that she was a guest rather than a waitress, but I couldn't see her face, nor did she choose to look at me, even though she must have been aware of my presence all this time. She just sat immobile, her face in her hands, not so much in despair but in world-weary exhaustion. Like me, she had evidently come in here to escape.

'Oh, I'm terribly sorry!' I blurted out through a mouthful of battered prawn Szechwan. 'I didn't see you there . . . I'll leave you in peace.'

'No, you're all right, don't worry,' said the voice from behind the hands.

Her defeated posture reminded me that I was at a funeral. This was someone who had needed to get away from the gossipy cacophony in the main hall.

'I just needed a moment away from the crowd,' I volunteered, deciding to put the smuggled supplies to one side for later consumption.

'I know just how you feel,' she said, and then she lowered her hands and I recognized her immediately. Back from the cremation and now hiding from the hordes of drunken celebs next door was Stella Scrivens. I had gatecrashed a celebrity funeral and now I found myself confined in a tiny room with the widow and forced to make small talk.

'You're Stella Scrivens, aren't you?'

'That's right, yes. I'm sorry, I don't recognize you . . .'

This was not said in a suspicious or accusing way, but still I could feel the warm rush of blood to my face.

'Sorry, no, we've never met. Jimmy Conway – are you sure you don't want to be on your own?'

'No, you're fine, it's actually quite nice not to recognize someone. I don't know half the people here. I just keeping thinking I do because I've seen them on the television.'

'Oh, that's not just me then?' I said, and we shared a smile of recognition.

'No, everyone does it. Even Billy does it,' and she sighed and corrected herself. 'Did it.'

'I'm very sorry,' I said helplessly.

'Thanks,' she said.

Apart from the embarrassment of talking to the widow at a funeral I had no right to attend, I was doubly discomfited by her almost oppressive loveliness. She was so strikingly beautiful I felt I had to look away, that it would seem like I was staring at a disabled person. She couldn't help it; it wasn't her fault she was born that exquisite. I had not been so attracted to anyone for a very long time but something told me I should banish any thoughts of finding out if she was available at the moment. *So, tell me, are you seeing anyone right now?* It might not go down very well. *No need to blub, darling. There's nothing wrong with being on your own.* No, it definitely felt wrong, I've always been a good judge of these things.

Trying not to be too obvious about my fascination with all

the people who had turned up, I quizzed her a little further about the celebrity guest list.

'Some of the stars out there didn't even know Billy,' she revealed. 'They'd never even met him, not once.'

I winced inside, while shaking my head in disbelief at the cynicism of some people. 'Really?' I tutted. 'That's awful. But then again, you know, the whole country *felt* like they knew him. When you're as famous as Billy was, it's like you're an old friend for people who you didn't even know existed.'

'No, it's not that.' She smiled. 'They're here to get on the front page of the newspapers. To be seen as one of the in-crowd. They're not here for Billy's sake or my sake. They are here because it's today's place to be famous.'

I searched for something pertinent yet philosophical to say. 'Blimey,' I finally mumbled.

'Their grieving comes later,' she added, 'when they buy *Hello!* magazine and discover that the photographer failed to snap them here.'

'Er, yes, I noticed that *Hello!* were helping organize things in the church. Are they here as well then?'

'They offered a fortune for the exclusive rights to photograph all the mourners at the church and reception. Said I could give it to charity if I wanted. But I said no.'

'Quite right. What a vulgar thought! I mean, it's a private wake, isn't it?'

'No, I said I wasn't giving it to charity. Why should I give all that money away when there's this whole funeral to pay for?'

'Er, yeah, right – I see what you mean. Good for you!'

So *Hello!* were paying for the entire funeral! I'd heard of magazines paying for celebrity weddings, but surely this was a new development. 'Still, they must be pleased with the turnout,' I said. 'All those stars carrying the coffin will be one of their most famous front covers ever, won't it?'

'Well, that was a bloody nightmare to organize I can tell you!' Stella laughed, and rolled her eyes heavenward. 'First of all *Hello!* said the chief mourners weren't famous enough and so we had to change them for bigger stars, even if Billy hadn't known them.'

'My God! Didn't you object?'

'If they pay for the show, they get to choose the cast.' She shrugged. 'But then it got worse. Can you imagine six different agents and publicists arguing over who should be at the front of the coffin?'

'How charming. So, how did you resolve that one?'

'In the end it came down to whose publicist had the most power. That's why the deputy prime minister was at the back,' she chuckled, almost revelling in the cynicism of it all.

I wanted to offer some sort of consolation, to try to reclaim the funeral for her. 'Well, anyway, it was a great send-off.'

'Thanks.'

'And it was a lovely service.'

'Hmm.'

And then six words slipped out.

'It's what he would have wanted.'

She looked up and did her best impression of a widow thankful for those few crumbs of comfort. Beyond all the grief and anger that death brings to the nearest and dearest, there is another, unexpected form of suffering the chief mourners must endure. The torture of being subjected to an endless barrage of platitudes. 'It's what he would have wanted,' I had said, and she smiled and thanked me for my kind words. *No, it's not what he would have wanted*, is what she should have said. *A big showy funeral paid for by* Hello! *magazine is not what he would have wanted at all; staying alive for another forty years and dying peacefully in his sleep surrounded by lots of grandchildren – that's what he would have wanted.* Of course, no grieving wife is permitted to say this. Manners demand that she graciously react as if this latest cliché was the most appropriate, touching and thoughtful comment that any guest at a funeral could possibly come up with.

I thought perhaps the time had come to leave her in peace, so I said it was nice to meet her and reluctantly returned to the coalface of chit-chat. I stood around a little longer, but realized I wasn't enjoying this at all and since I'd only come along for the experience, for the fun of it, I told myself I might as well head home.

'Ah, Jimmy! I've been looking for you everywhere,' said Arabella from the *Sunday Times*.

'Oh, hello again.'

'Look, do you have a card or anything?'

'A card? What do you mean, like a postcard or something?'

'No – a card, you know, with your number on.'

'Oh I see. Erm, no, no – didn't bring any with me today.'

'It was just that I've been thinking of doing a feature on the state of British comedy and I was wondering whether I ought to include you, "the stand-up comic who won't do television". I've been chatting to Mike Mellor but I think I'd rather interview you, if that's possible?'

I know I should have thought long and hard about agreeing to do this but I didn't think long and hard at all, I thought short and easy.

'Er, yeah, that would be OK, I suppose.' I shrugged, my heart suddenly racing inside. 'I'll have to try and fit it around my gigs, of course,' I said coolly, but then I worried that she might decide it was all too much trouble. 'Although I could always cancel if you were stuck for dates,' I gabbled. We exchanged mobile phone numbers and then one of the people from *Hello!* magazine asked us to move to the side slightly, as we were standing behind a couple of stars who were obligingly posing for the camera and our anonymous faces obviously weren't adding anything to the shot. Everywhere there were shallow celebrities who only turned up to this wake to further their own career prospects. Could their egos really be so enormous as to lose any sense of what was decent and appropriate?

'Great, Annabel, I'll look forward to hearing from you!' I said as I headed off. A feature on stand-up comedy including me, I thought. My name in the *Sunday Times*. What a result! This is the best funeral I've ever been to!

— 5 —

27 Elms Crescent,
East Grinstead,
West Sussex,
England

Dear James,

Lady Diana Spencer got married to Prince Charles today, which beneath all the pomp and circumstances was just a normal family wedding and it's good for tourism as well. A while after the engagement was announced she actually broke down in tears because she was so fed up with being photographed wherever she went, but I suppose you get used to that after a while. They say that all publicity is good publicity, but there must be exceptions, like the Yorkshire Ripper, for example, he can't have got many more driving jobs after his name was in all the papers. But now that you are a celebrity, James, you just have to accept that the press are always going to be prying into your affairs. It's a bore, I know, but I'm afraid that's the price you have to pay; everyone is endlessly fascinated with every aspect of your life all of the time. That's why I don't mind that at the moment no one is the slightest bit interested in me. That's actually a _good_ thing, because one day I'll look back and envy the privacy I have now. The total absolute privacy I am lucky enough to have at the moment, never being hassled by people ringing up for me, no one writing letters to me or expecting to see me all the time, or any of the time really. These are precious times for me, and I keep reminding myself of how fortunate I am.

The important thing when dealing with the press is to keep your eyes open when they take the pictures. Obviously the East Grinstead Observer is only a local paper and a Fleet Street _professional_ would never have used that particular shot of the school's summer fete. But even if you do appear in the newspaper in a group shot with your eyes closed, remember no one pays it as much attention as you do yourself. Although in this particular case, everyone at school seemed compelled to point it out several times a day for far longer than would have been amusing if it had ever been funny in the first place, which it wasn't, as a matter of a fact. It was very immature.

Basically you have to remember that the newspapers need the celebrities, but the celebrities also need the newspapers. It is a special sort of relationship, what they call 'a two-way relationship' in which they both need each other as much as the other one needs them.

Anyway, I have to dash now as I have so much that I have to be getting on with. I was going to start my project on the Tudors today but I decided that watching the royal wedding would be good background research. I'll write again soon.

Mine sincerely,
Jimmy

'Interview with Jimmy Conway for *Sunday Times* review section, tape one.' My interviewer announced these words into her gleaming dictaphone and then placed the little gadget upright on the table between us. A little light flashed on and off continuously throughout our talk. I presumed this indicated that the machine was recording, although part of me worried that it had a built-in lie detector that caused the red light to come on every time I made something up.

'So, Jimmy, question number one: how long have you been a professional stand-up comic?'

'Er, well, I'm not a professional stand-up comic. I was making all that up because I've always wanted to be somebody. Unfortunately I've grown up to be not the slightest bit interesting or significant, so I thought I'd try lying and pretending that I was and see where that got me.'

This answer flashed through my head but I decided not to give it because I feared it might possibly set the entire interview off on the wrong foot and spoil the atmosphere.

'Well, I've always seemed to be able to make people laugh,' I mused. 'But I suppose my first professional engagement was when I was eight years old. My older brother told me an obscene joke that I didn't understand and then promised me 50 pence if I recited it in front of all my relations at Christmas. I had two of my presents taken away and he still owes me the money.'

This much at least was true. It was the only time I felt she didn't believe me.

'Did you find it was a good way to deal with the bullies at school? That instead of fighting them you could deflect their aggression by making them laugh and so comedy became a matter of survival in, like, the playground jungle?'

'Er, not really.'

'Interesting, that's fascinating,' and she made a note of this as if it was a critical piece of information in the analysis of a psychiatric patient. I felt very important to be under such scrutiny. When I ordered a pint of Guinness she said, 'Are you Irish at all, Jimmy?'

'No – it's just they don't sell draught bitter so I thought I'd have a Guinness.'

'I see, I see,' and she nodded significantly as if I'd just described my childhood experience of seeing my mother having sex with my scoutmaster.

We were sitting in a London club with huge armchairs and more tiny waitresses where Arabella was a 'founding member', whatever that was, and I was the wide-eyed newcomer who had to stop himself going from table to table collecting up all the designer matchboxes that were given away free in every ashtray. She had rung me up a couple of days after the funeral saying she would like to do a whole piece on just me, prompted by my 'return from the States'. She made it sound like the Beatles getting back together. 'When are you free?' she asked. 'Ooooh, let me see . . .' and I stared at the Arctic tundra of endless blank spaces in my diary.

'I can only do Thursday next week,' she interjected. 'How's Thursday for you?' As it happened there was something in my diary for the following Thursday. It was Waitangi Day in New Zealand. It was a clash, but one I was sure we could work around.

'Thursday's fine,' I said.

'Is Soho House all right with you? I usually find people prefer to meet somewhere in the centre of town.'

The centre of town? I thought. Which town's that then? I'd never heard of a club called Soho House in the centre of Seaford, that was for sure. The Royal British Legion, maybe, but I'd stopped hanging out there recently, you know; it was so full of cokeheads and media poseurs. I guessed Arabella must mean that town called 'London' that people were always on about; we arranged a time and so on the Thursday I travelled to the capital and decided to head towards Soho and then look for a House.

'Are comedians really very sad people inside?' she asked me next, biting the end of her pencil meaningfully. 'It's just a little theory of mine,' she added.

'Hmmm – interesting,' I said. 'You mean like that song "The Tears of a Clown"?'

'Yes. Exactly. "The Tears of a Clown", possible headline maybe,' she said, leaning towards the dictaphone. 'I think those lines are so true, don't you? About making a joke or two, but deep inside being blue.'

'That's "The Tracks of my Tears".'

'Tell me, talking of music, do you think it's almost as if comedy has now become the new rock and roll?'

I was sure I had read this line somewhere before but I was making such an effort to be polite and positive that I may have overenthused at the brilliance and originality of this observation. I think she was quite flattered. She said she'd never met such a modest performer before.

'OK, now the sixty-four-million-dollar question.' I braced myself a little as she gave a grin in anticipation of playing her ace of trumps. 'Where do you get your ideas from?' I wondered if this wasn't really a sixty-four-million-dollar question. I think it may not have even been a £6.40 question.

She declared it was time for a coffee and I gratefully agreed to join her.

'Excuse me!' she called to the waitress. 'Could we have two cappuccini please?' *Two cappuccini*, she said. Not two *cappucinos*, but two *cappuccini*. That would be the correct Italian plural, I supposed. To think I'd been saying it wrong all this time.

Agreeing to do this interview had been the moment I had crossed the rubicon of premeditated deception. Before this point any dishonesty on my part had been spontaneous and unrehearsed, often just obligingly confirming what other people had wanted to believe. But when Arabella had called me and said that she wanted to do a whole feature just about me, I'd been so completely flattered and delighted that I'd agreed to bring along some of my reviews from America. And then as I reflected on my predicament, I felt dangerously out of my depth. I was just a nobody who would have liked to be famous in another life; I had to leave it at that. But the following evening I was sitting alone in my house in Seaford watching an old black and white film called *All About Eve* and it was a revelation. We trace the rise of a famous star and discover she got her big break by cheating. A film about fame, made in Hollywood, saying how it was done. You cheat. It was suddenly so obvious.

How naïve I had been all these years to think that a commodity as precious as fame would be doled out on the basis of merit. Of course not. It is ruthlessly embezzled, stolen, hijacked – and, in my case, why not forged? 'Phoney fame' – was such a thing possible? Maybe they were all pretending; maybe they had all cheated and lied their way into the celebrity party before quickly blending in with the other guests. For once you were in, you'd made it; you became the genuine article by default. Like millionaires who had stolen their first ten thousand, you just needed a head start on everyone else.

So a few days later I proceeded to print out some of the

reviews I had received from various newspapers in America; reviews that it had taken me all weekend to write. I didn't manage to think up any jokes that I could share with the readers, but my famous 'fish' routine was mentioned in every notice. In fact, in terms of the pure creativity I'd always sought, I seemed to have finally found my métier. Inventing an elaborate account of how successful I was saw me at my most creative ever. Pasting my words into a page copied off the New York Times website was a simple enough operation, but the photographs that Arabella later requested took all night. There was Billy Crystal with his arm around me, while Steve Martin looked on and laughed as I pulled that funny face that always cracked them up. It had required all my skill and patience to digitally decapitate the anonymous American producer who'd originally held centre stage of this picture I'd found on the internet. Using Windows Naughty Fotoforger XP, I imported my own goofy head from my personal photo collection and after much touching up and resizing it looked perfect. Billy Crystal and me, we go way back – the camera never lies, does it? By the time I met up with Arabella, I had constructed myself an entire career in the United States (I latter added 'and Canada' – the pointless detail seemed to add a ring of truth). People moaned that these days public figures were more interested in spin than substance. Well, I was going for no content whatsoever – I was going to be 100 per cent spin and zero substance.

Arabella was impressed by the material I gave her. She accused me of hiding my light under a bushel. I restrained myself from saying, 'No, I am not hiding my light, there is no light, there's just a bushel and that's it.' I elaborated upon my reasons for not doing television, which I could already sense would be the hook for the whole piece. As part of my anti-commercial, 'back to the roots of stand-up' philosophy, I explained that I'd gained my reputation in the States by turning up and doing impromptu sets at various venues, never publicizing an appearance beforehand or indulging in the vanity of a one-man show at some prestigious theatre. My appearance was always a surprise, a bonus. That way, I explained, I could never be cynically marketed or end up being hijacked by agents or the industry money-men. I was delighted to see how impressed Arabella was with all of this as I explained I was already doing the same thing over here. I was not on the bill of any comedy club, you wouldn't find my name in the listings of any magazine, and yet, I modestly conceded, my reputation seemed to be growing at the grassroots level where it counted most– among the fans. And I handed her another picture of me, this time on stage at the Comedy Store in London, and through the smoky haze you could make out the sheer delight in the faces of the audience doubled up in laughter as I stood impassively at the microphone.

I could feel the size of the feature growing as she gazed over the material. In this cynical world of desperate media wannabes, here was someone who seemed to be consciously rejecting celebrity. Privately I thought I could probably get quite famous doing that. I was particularly pleased with the way I had accounted for there being no records of my gigs. You never knew when I might turn up at Jongleurs or the Comedy Store or the Buzz in Manchester – it made the currency all the more precious for those that had seen me. I reckoned it was completely foolproof.

'So when can I come and see you?' said Arabella. Well, almost completely foolproof. 'Are you all right?' she added. 'You look a little pale.'

'No, no,' I stammered. 'As I say, I don't tell people in

advance. It's a question of whether I happen to turn up on the night that you've gone to a comedy club.'

'Yes, but my deadline is two weeks' time. I can't write this piece without seeing your act. So if you tell me where you're planning to make a surprise appearance, I'll make sure I'm in the audience.'

'Er, no, that's not how it works.'

'You don't honestly expect me to do a whole feature on you without ever having seen you perform, do you?'

'Um, no, of course not,' I mumbled. 'Er, I'll give you a ring when I know where I'm on next week.'

As I stared out of the train window on my way out of the metropolis, I wondered what on earth I could have been thinking. Dusk was falling as I was whisked past hundreds of ordinary homes; through the windows you could make out the electric glow of the television sets, every family gathered around the hazy blue hearth, all focused on the same formats and celebrities. Would my place always be on this side of the screen? I was back at the language school tomorrow with a new batch of the French teenagers who regularly came over on shoplifting exchanges. It was my job to teach them useful English phrases such as, 'I must have put it into my pocket by mistake,' and, 'Oh dear, did I forget to pay?' I felt depressed at the prospect of starting with another new class as I sped away from the bright lights of London. And then I realized that one radical option remained open to me. Not cheating. It was crazy, I know, but the more I thought about it, the more merit there seemed to be in this unconventional plan. I would do it the fair way. A journalist from a national newspaper wanted to do a big feature on me. Even better, she was very keen to see my act. How many struggling comics get such an opportunity?

OK, I didn't have an act to see, but this was quibbling over mere details. Her deadline was two weeks away. What was to stop me writing a twenty-minute stand-up set and performing it at a comedy club? People had always said I was funny. If I was good, then I'd get a glowing write-up in a national newspaper. If I was rubbish, well, at least I would have given it a go. I could retire gracefully and come up with another harmless way of drawing attention to myself, like claiming I was the killer in a high-profile mass-murder investigation, perhaps.

I had been to a comedy club in Brighton and so I knew the form for all the wouldn't-be comics who'd attempted to start their careers there. Amateur hopefuls were given the opportunity to get up and do an open spot immediately after the interval. The audience usually granted them a short period of time to demonstrate whether they were funny or not. This varied from anything between two and twenty seconds, and then they were booed, heckled, insulted or pelted with half-full plastic beer glasses. What on earth was I waiting for? It was time to make my famous 'fish' routine a reality.

First of all I would have to book the gig. Rather than risk being seen by Nancy or Dave or any of my friends in Seaford, I enquired about open spots at some of the smaller London comedy clubs. I finally booked myself in for Wednesday week at a club in north London – which gave me ten days to write and rehearse the act, and Arabella a couple of days to write it up afterwards.

'No,' she said when I rang to give her the secret details of my next appearance. 'No, no, no, no, no. Wednesday's not good for me. It's Samantha's birthday,' she said in a tone of voice that suggested I too should have this notable date in my diary between Martin Luther King's and St Patrick's. 'There's a crowd of us going to her house for dinner.'

'But it's quite late in the evening,' I reasoned. 'Come along afterwards. Bring them too, if you want.'

'Can't you make it Tuesday? Hang on – nope, book launch Tuesday, Thursday out again, Friday too late,' and it quickly transpired that she couldn't make any other dates either and so she reluctantly agreed to cut short her dinner party.

'You will come, won't you?' I said, feeling significantly less important than I had when we'd last spoken.

'Of course I'll come. The review editor is taking a keen interest in this piece. "Comedy is the new rock and roll. But here comes comedy's punk," she said.'

I wasn't quite sure what she meant by that – though it left me feeling that the stakes were raised even higher. So the next morning I finally sat down to start writing my act. I didn't have to be in at the language school until the afternoon so I got some blank pieces of paper and tried to think of something funny. Observational comedy, that was the thing. 'Have you ever noticed how hard milk cartons are to open?' Hmmm. I had a feeling that this observation might have even pre-dated the advent of milk cartons. Something more up to date. Text messaging, maybe. Or digital television. 'They've got a channel for everything now, haven't they? Next they'll have a special channel for ... a special channel for ...' but I couldn't think of anything for which they didn't already have a special channel. Political comedy, maybe. 'New Labour, eh? They're not as left-wing as old Labour, are they!' It didn't feel very satirical and I screwed up the sheet only to find a used piece of paper underneath, completely blank except for the words 'Scene Two' written at the top.

Half an hour later an idea was just starting to hatch when the doorbell rang and I could make out the unmistakable silhouette of Doreen Cutbush blocking out any light that might think of coming through the glass in my front door. There was only one thing you could think on meeting Doreen: This is a woman who loves miniature schnauzers. This was partly due to the fact that she sported a bright yellow badge the size of a teaplate bearing the unequivocal declaration, 'I love miniature schnauzers'. But there was another clue that was hard to overlook: under her arms she was also holding a couple of panting miniature schnauzers – their moustachioed doggy heads were almost permanent features either side of her colossal waist-high breasts. Doreen was a figure from Greek mythology with a human head and body but with two doggy heads coming out from under her arms. In case you were in any doubt as to her feelings about miniature schnauzers, the big badge was backed up with an extensive collection of further schnauzer insignia: another thirty or forty little metal badges in the shape of her favourite dog breed or boasting membership of the Miniature Schnauzer Club of Great Britain pinned all over the front of her green gilet.

I opened the door and she sighed in her rushed-off-her-feet way.

'Jimmy dear, are you taking Betty out for a walk today?' This was the opening salvo of a two-part trick question that ensnared me every time. On answering, 'Er, yes,' I'd create the opening for her to ask if I could possibly take her dogs while I was at it. Bishop to King's Knight 4: checkmate. In fact, I had been planning to dash quickly up to the cliffs with Betty, but taking these dogs for a walk was a more complex operation, as you might expect with dogs that are not really used to walking anywhere. You didn't take them for a walk, you took them for a 'carry'.

Doreen ran the language school where I worked. She had even found me this house to rent a few doors down from her own when I first started. I'd been repaying the favours ever since. Because I worked part-time, people quite often asked me to help them out or just called round when they fancied a chat, and, well, you have to give people the time of day. I suppose celebrities employ other people to give people the time of day. 'Her Majesty has asked me to thank you for your letter,' somebody would always reply from Buckingham Palace when I used to write to the Queen about smoking beagles. Famous people don't give individuals the time of day, they give everyone the time of day, all at once. They don't chat with one neighbour, they chat with the whole country, the whole planet even – that's what being a star means. You don't do your neighbour a favour, you do millions of people a favour. So while I might do my bit for humankind by feeding Edna Moore's cat when she was in hospital, Bob Geldof might do a little good deed of his own like organizing a major concert for famine relief. They all have their place in the scheme of things. I mean, who's to say one is more significant than the other?

I'd read all about the determination and single-mindedness of stars on the way up. They never mentioned that they had to give up having time for people, but that must be the price of fame – that you have to keep putting yourself first over and over again. That point had now come for me. I did not enough have the spare time to walk Doreen's miniature schnauzers. I had more important things to do – I had a hit comedy routine to write. I'd just have to be firm and say no. In fact, I would look her in the eye and explain that I was so busy that actually I needed her to walk Betty for me. I gathered up my courage and began.

'The thing is, Doreen—'

'Because I've got to go and see my brother,' she continued, 'in hospital in Brighton. You know, the one with cancer I told you about . . .'

As I helped one of the miniature schnauzers over a particularly large clump of grass, I wondered if I'd ever achieve the destiny I had set for myself. On Odysseus's epic journey he had to defeat a one-eyed giant, or sail between the twin perils of Scylla and Charybdis, or resist the seductive song of the sirens. But you don't get so much credit for overcoming the mundane obstacles that stop you getting anywhere in the journey of everyday life.

'Lo, see how the hero resists checking his emails, for he is strong of will!'

'Yea, and marvel at his immense courage as he dares battle with the council over the parking ticket that was unjustly slapped on his Nissan Sunny!'

'But look, forsooth, now he faces the ultimate foe – the giant lady with the two dog-heads under her arms! Is our hero strong enough to say no to her request to walk her miniature schnauzers?'

'No, it would seem, he is not.'

It took Odysseus twenty years to sail home, which seemed approximately the time it was going to take me to write my stand-up set. But by the weekend I had the beginnings of a routine and I performed it pacing maniacally up and down my front room. It went like this:

'The dodo. What a crap bird that was!' I put an anxious note to myself in the margin – 'topical enough??' – and carried on. 'So the dodo is extinct. Well, I'm sorry but, like, whose fault is that? I mean, like, dodos – right? I'm sorry but you had it coming.' Maybe laugh here slightly. 'There must have been a point, right, where, like, there was one last breeding pair of dodos left in the whole world and the sailors thought, Well, what's it to be? Lose this species for ever more to Planet Earth or not have roast dodo à l'orange for dinner? Well, I'm sorry, but it's no fucking contest!' (I had tried that bit without the swear word but it didn't feel so funny.) 'Listen, dodos, you can't fly and you're delicious. I'd say that was pretty crap planning on your part, so tough shit! You're extinct. Get over it! Move on!' And then I would give a little shake of the head as if I still couldn't believe how ridiculous they were, and maybe repeat, 'Dodos. Crap birds!' just to myself, perhaps pretending to suppress another little laugh at this point. I practised these lines out loud and for some reason found my voice mutating into some weird outraged cockney, somewhere between Bob Hoskins and Dick van Dyke in *Mary Poppins*. I also found that by regularly inserting the words 'like' and 'right', I gave the piece an authentic, just-made-up feel.

Although I was encouraged that at least I'd now written something, I still had a problem with the length. I timed what I had so far and it fell short of the twenty minutes I'd been aiming for by nineteen minutes and twelve seconds. Maybe if they laughed a lot that would pad it out a bit. To be honest, I didn't have the faintest idea how the audience would react. Wasn't it all a bit dodo-ist?

On Monday I was at work all day, and during the morning coffee break Nancy told me that her daughter was now back at school.

'That's good to hear,' I said, adding, 'I'll tell you something, dodos were crap birds, weren't they?'

'What?'

'You know, dodos. OK, so they're extinct, well, I'm sorry but, like, whose fault is that? I mean dodos – right? I'm sorry but you had it coming to you. You can't fly and you're delicious. I'd say that was pretty crap planning on your part, so tough shit! You're extinct. Get over it! Move on!' I chuckled.

She stared at me for a second, not even cracking a smile. 'Sorry, what are you talking about?'

'Well, it just struck me as a funny thought.'

'Except that the dodo was the first significant animal to be hunted to extinction and now we are losing hundreds of species every year.'

'Mmm, good point,' I nodded.

I had tried the same routine out on Chris. He'd just looked concerned and said, 'Dodos? Extinct? When did that happen then?' I hadn't told Nancy or any of my friends about my situation. Perhaps I was embarrassed to reveal the depths of deception I'd got myself into, or maybe it felt unlucky to talk about my performance beforehand, but for the time being I had to keep it locked up inside. Not that I would have had any trouble making Nancy believe me; her generous spirit meant that she always gave people the benefit of the doubt. The downside of this admirable trait was that it made her chronically gullible. She could be convinced that Narnia was a former Soviet republic or that Princess Michael of Kent was so called because she hadn't been allowed to change her Christian name after her sex change. I think she quite liked me teasing her, but everyone did it. I once caught her putting a tea bag in a casserole 'to add flavour'. Several hours later I finally convinced her that this was not normal culinary practice, and that what she had seen her mother place in a stew all those years ago was in fact a *bouquet garni*. Her mum had obviously only been joking when she said it was a tea bag, but Nancy had been cooking Coq au PG Tips ever since.

I put the dodo routine to one side for a while and that night spent a couple of hours trying to come up with some more stuff. What about my famous 'fish' routine that New York's *Village Voice* had called the 'Hey Jude of British stand-up comedy'. Fish, they're funny, what could I say about fish? 'Have you ever noticed, right, how fish, like, have all these different fins? There's the dorsal fin, the pectoral fin, the pelvic fin and the tail or caudal fin.' No, too dry. Most fish have an anal fin; that might get a cheap laugh, I suppose. OK, I'll come back to the fish. I tried to remember funny things that I had said in the pub but it wasn't the same out of context. 'Anyway, there's this big German girl at the language school where I teach and there was a crowd of us in the pub one evening and she knocked back this pint of bitter in one go and then let out this huge burp and I said, "That finishing school was a waste of money!" ' Well, you had to be there, really.

And then I tore up the top sheet of paper and screwed it up and stared and stared at the blank nothingness in front of me. Several times I was close to ringing Arabella and telling her not to come and to scrap the feature and forget all about it. But then I thought about the possibility of really being someone, about what it must feel like to be a person of real significance, about how illogically proud I'd been when I'd read back those fictitious American reviews. I was closer than I had ever been in my life to really achieving something. Which was why I was so terrified. Because now I was faced with the imminent possibility that I might fail.

There was of course another reason why I wanted to be famous. From where I was standing, it seemed to unlock everything. I'd not been in a proper relationship for years. Why should anyone be interested in a part-time English-as-a-foreign-language teacher in his mid-thirties with nothing to his name except a neurotic dog and an assorted collection of Allen keys left over from self-assembly furniture kits? Everyone knows that fame makes a man attractive. You only had to look at the contrast between the plug-ugly Billy

Scrivens and his stunning wife to see just how famous he must have been. Fame was the ultimate in ostentatious peacock-feather mating displays. Fame wouldn't just bring status and respect and money and purpose. It would mean an end to being so bloody lonely all the time.

The next day I resolved to be strict with myself and work really hard on writing this stand-up set. I paid Nancy's daughter Tamsin to walk Betty for me. Tamsin was only four-teen but her face lacked the fresh innocence of most girls that age. Well, those parts of her face you could still see behind all the bits of metal sticking out of it. It had started with match-ing studs through her nose and navel; maybe Tamsin had been given a pair of earrings and had carelessly stuck them on her body without reading the instructions properly. But after that her mother had been unable to dissuade Tamsin from having her lip, septum, tongue and eyebrows seemingly attacked with a nail gun. In fact, what with the tattoos, pierc-ings and love bites, there was very little of her visible skin that was not mutilated in one way or another. Thanks to Tamsin's face, the jobs of British steel workers were safe for another few years.

My dog was one of the few creatures in Seaford that did not recoil on seeing her, and soon they were out on the beach and I had gained an hour's time in which to try to write. I stared interminably at the page, scribbling down half thoughts and then crossing them out again. But then, finally, a bite! To my astonishment, I actually thought of a fish joke! Quick! It's hooked, reel the joke in, careful now, draw it into the keep-net . . . Then the doorbell went and the thought escaped.

Tamsin was back and she wanted to talk. I don't know why but she always chose to talk about her problems when she was round at my house. Nancy had suggested that I was something of a father substitute, but from what I knew about fourteen-year-old girls they didn't really talk to their dads and I'm not sure I particularly wanted Tamsin shouting 'I hate you!' and running up the stairs and slamming my bathroom door. In any case, she didn't talk directly to me. She got round her embarrassment by pretending she was confiding in Betty while I happened to be in the room.

'Oh, Betty, what am I going to do?' she said as she tickled the dog's tummy. 'I think Kelvin's going to chuck me.'

'Look, Tamsin, thanks for walking the dog and everything, but I've got some work to get on with so I can't chat, I'm afraid.'

'That's OK. I won't disturb you, will I, Betty? Good dog!'

I had to be strong. This time I couldn't cave in.

'I'm sorry, but I really need the house to myself.'

Tamsin started crying. 'Betty! Kelvin is going to chuck me,' she sobbed. The tears ran down her face and over the metal studs and lip rings and I couldn't just leave her there to rust.

'Oh dear,' I lied.

Kelvin had not been good news for Tamsin. Although he was supposed to be her boyfriend, Nancy said the only time they'd spent an entire evening in each other's company was when their facial piercings got snagged together.

'So has Kelvin said as much then?'

She told the dog that he hadn't but she could just tell he was planning it. Betty wagged her tail at this development.

'Maybe he's just not very good about expressing his emotions . . .' I suggested to the girl who was communicating her own feelings via a border collie. I made more sympathetic noises and a cup of tea but eventually I told her I had to get on with some work now. She seemed embarrassed, as if she was holding something back and asked if she could just stay and play with Betty.

'I'm really sorry, Tamsin, but I can't work with you here talking to the dog.'

'But she's the only one who understands, and it's important . . .'

'Tamsin, I'm afraid nothing you could possibly say could be so urgent as to prevent me from working right now.'

There was a long silence.

'Betty, do you think it would stop him from leaving me if I got pregnant?'

About an hour later I finished listing the reasons why I thought this was not a very good plan. I found it faulty on many different fronts. Indeed, though I pride myself on usually seeing both sides of any issue, I struggled to spot a single merit to young Tamsin's idea.

'Where did you get such a stupid idea from?'

'It's not stupid. It was on *ER*.'

I must admit I was naïve enough to be shocked that sex should even be on the agenda for a fourteen-year-old girl. It was too young, it was wrong, it was immoral. And more to the point, if I'd had to wait till I was nineteen, why shouldn't the teenagers of today? Finally I was confident that she was dissuaded from this course of action, for the time being at least.

'Tamsin, you don't need Kelvin to tell you you're special, you are special,' I said. 'People notice you already.'

This was actually true. There was so much metal on her face that passing ships lost track of true magnetic north.

'A baby won't make you someone special. In fact, in this town it might make you pretty average. You're somebody special already, Tamsin. If Kelvin doesn't understand that, well, then he doesn't deserve you,' I concluded, feeling like the agony aunt in *Jackie* magazine.

Tamsin felt better after that and thanked the dog for

listening to her. It was all sorted. Then I realized I would have to tell her mother about the conversation and when I mentioned this, Tamsin got upset again and begged me not to and we talked for another half an hour. She said if I told her mum she would run away with Kelvin and have his babies and they'd make a living in London busking and juggling and stuff. The addition of the words 'and stuff' made me suspicious that this might be another plan that had not been fully thought through.

'Your mum is one of my best friends. I have to be completely honest with her.'

'Are you going to go back out with her?' she asked me directly.

'Don't change the subject.'

'I'm not, but if I wasn't around, she might find a boyfriend. So I thought if I ran away with Kelvin. . .'

'Tamsin, can you stop coming up with so many completely stupid ideas!'

Against my better judgement I promised not to tell her mum, and finally she was gone and I was free to do some work. At which point I opened a beer and collapsed exhausted on the sofa.

The idea of getting up on a stage had seemed like a logical solution when it had been an unimaginable ten days away. But now that D-Day was imminent it struck me as an absolutely insane concept. The early Christians didn't turn up at the Colosseum hoping they might be able to get an open spot with the lions.

'So you say you've never seen the lions and Christians show?'

'No, but I've heard it's very popular and I'm sure I'll pick it up as I go along.'

'Oh yeah, don't worry – the lions tend to lead and you'll find your role then comes to you quite naturally.'

And yet here I was, willingly volunteering myself to be sacrificed for the entertainment of the modern-day mob. I wanted to put it out of my head, but found myself thinking about it every moment of the day.

I wanted experience, but I wanted it now. I wanted instant experience: just-add-water-microwaved-experience-to-go. Already I was discovering the downside of celebrity. I had liked the idea of everybody admiring me, of people giving me free tickets and inviting me to exciting parties and paying me lots of money and making me feel really special wherever I was. I just didn't like the 'working-very-hard-at-something-it's-very-difficult-to-be-good-at' side of the deal.

Arabella rang my mobile the day before to check a couple of 'facts' for her piece and added, 'See you tomorrow' just when I was hoping she'd say she didn't think she'd be able to slip away from her friend's dinner party. With so many distractions I'd barely written ten minutes of material – not really enough for a proper set, but possibly enough for someone pretending to do an open spot. But it was great stuff, I kept telling myself. I was going to be fantastic. I was going to blow everyone off the stage. I was so funny, I was so hilarious that nothing could possibly go wrong. It was a deliberate self-conscious survival tactic; Mike Tyson didn't go into the ring thinking, 'Actually I'm a big sissy, me. I'll probably lose, but it's the taking part that counts.'

The comedy club was above a pub in Camden and the open spots were after the interval at around 10 p.m. I looked at my watch at quarter to ten and began my second pint. Three young lager-drinkers were huddled around a quiz machine, endlessly feeding it pound coins for the shallow gratification of being able to answer pitifully easy general-knowledge questions. 'How smart are you?' flashed the message across the top of the machine. 'Not very' must surely be the answer for anyone who fell for that one. The pub in which I was sitting managed to be noisy and smoky without having very many people in it. Oh, and it was also about eighty miles from Camden.

It is hard to pinpoint the exact moment that the decision not to go through with my plan passed from my subconscious to the conscious. That very morning I had even checked the times of trains from Brighton to London, still blithely pretending to myself that I was going to proceed with this foolhardy personal dare. Despite all the hours spent writing jokes and practising my delivery and working myself up into a state of phoney self-confidence, I wonder if deep down I ever truly believed I was going to go through with it. But by now it was a physical impossibility. I was sitting in the Red Lion in Seaford, having an ordinary night's drinking with the usual crowd. I tried to picture Arabella miles away in a London comedy club, settling down in a seat with a clear view, her notebook on her lap, smug in the knowledge that she alone was privy to the wonderful secret that there would be an extra performer on stage that night. And not just some scrofulous hopeful, but a real master of his craft, one of the greats, but as yet undiscovered by British audiences. Had she brought any friends along with her, promising them that they wouldn't regret it? Was she glancing around the room right now, hoping to give me a conspiratorial wink before I went on stage?

'Of course a football is round! Dave, how can you possibly say a football isn't round?' exclaimed an outraged Norman. I was unfortunate enough to be sitting downwind of Norman. Panda wasn't with him this evening; they'd had a row. She'd said you should always mount a motorbike from the left and he'd said, 'Why don't you have the bike today? You can take it bloody foxhunting!'

Now Dave was engaging him in an even more pointless argument.

'Sure, to us a football might be round. That's just the way we perceive it. It doesn't make footballs round from an objective point of view. To a Martian it might be square.'

'No, footballs are definitely round . . .' pondered Chris, perhaps a bit out of his depth discussing abstract philosophy. 'You can see them roll.' Chris was not the intellectual of the group. He was once asked to name his favourite opera. He thought about this for a while and then said, 'Winfrey.'

'Yes, to us they're round,' repeated Dave. 'But to a Martian they might be round.'

'There, you said round. There that proves it. You said to a Martian they might be round,' said Chris.

'I said square.'

'No, not second time. You said round, you said, "To a Martian they might be round." Here, Jimmy, didn't he say that footballs are round?'

'Footballs?' I said, my mind elsewhere. 'Oh yeah. They're definitely round all right.'

And Chris put his fingers in his ears to stop Dave even replying and eventually Dave got up to buy another square of drinks.

'You're quiet tonight, Jimmy,' said Nancy, bringing me back to reality.

'Hmmm? Oh yeah, bit tired. Couldn't get to sleep last night.'

'Are you worried about something?'

'Me worried? Nah! Well, you know, only the usual trivial things: whether the AIDS virus will mutate and become airborne . . .'

'Really?' she said anxiously.

'No, sorry, I just made that up.'

'Just for a change. I've found out something else you made up.'

'What?' I said anxiously.

'What you were saying the other day. Well, I took the trouble to check, Jimmy Conway. And they haven't taken the word "gullible" out of the dictionary. You were having me on, weren't you?'

'No no, it's still in Collins and everything. But it's been taken out of the new OED they've just published.'

'Really!' she said, amazed once more.

I had been chided by my friends for repeatedly looking at my watch as if I wanted to be somewhere else and so now I threw a furtive glance at the clock behind the bar. It was half past ten and now Arabella would surely be confused that I'd not appeared. Perhaps she might attempt to rationalize my non-appearance, explaining to her friends that the club's manager had been so delighted to have me there that he'd moved me to the top of the bill and I would probably be closing the show if they sat tight and waited.

It was not until I was finally inside my front door that I turned on my mobile to see if there were any messages. There were none. And no missed calls either. She had been too disgusted to want even to speak to me. Not only had I blown out her feature, probably forcing her to work on Saturday to cobble together something else, I had made her leave her friend's birthday dinner early and probably humiliated her in front of those friends as well. I considered ringing her office number and leaving some elaborate excuse on her voicemail but decided that it would be far better to do the decent thing and hide. Having never given her any contact details other

than my mobile phone number, I made myself in-
communicado for a few days by courageously switching off
the phone until after the paper was published.

And on Saturday night at around midnight I drove into
Brighton where you could get first editions of the Sunday
papers the night before. I bought a copy of the *Sunday Times*
and slipped into a café to see what Arabella had filled the space
with. The review section fell out and there was my face on the
front cover. I could feel myself starting to shake. There I was
with Billy Crystal and Steve Martin under the headline, 'He's
having a laugh'.

It's obviously a hatchet job, I realized – an exposé on my
whole scam, now laid bare for the entire country by an
investigative reporter I'd foolishly underestimated. 'He's
having a laugh' – suddenly it didn't feel very funny at all. I
flicked over the page and started to speed-read the feature,
which occupied a double spread:

I am in a slightly tatty comedy club in North London, where
the best joke of the evening so far is the amount they charge
for a warm glass of white wine. I have watched a succession of
comics attempting to extract comedy from the usual subjects
and now as I look around the strained expressions of the
audience, I can see their facial muscles are aching from endless
half-hearted attempts to laugh at these mediocre efforts. But
tonight the audience is about to be very surprised indeed.
Because the funniest comic is the one who was not on the bill.
Onto the stage walks Jimmy Conway, who proceeds to deliver
one of the most inspired sets to hit the London comedy scene
in years!

Confused, I read the sentence again. 'Onto the stage walks

Jimmy Conway.' What was she talking about? Had she gone mad? It was inexplicable. I read on and discovered that my act had in fact been far funnier than I ever dared hope it could be. My now famous 'fish' routine was fast becoming the stuff of comedy legend, apparently. For no obvious benefit to herself, Arabella was prepared to lie to millions of people that I had gone ahead with it and got up there and performed. And I was fantastic! I was a triumph! She must have liked me so much that she'd given me the benefit of the doubt when I failed to turn up, presuming that I really was every bit as funny as my American reviews asserted. In which case, why didn't she call to ask why I had let her down? Why wasn't she angry that I had made her leave her dinner party early to rush across London on a rainy Wednesday night to see a stand-up comedy show? And then it dawned on me. Because Arabella hadn't turned up either! That's why there had been no message left after the supposed gig. She had arrived at her friend's house on Wednesday night for a meal, kicked off her shoes and had a few glasses of wine on the sofa. No doubt the meal had been served up slightly later than she'd anticipated and eventually she looked at her watch in the middle of her dinner and just thought, What's it to be – lie to millions of readers or leave now and miss out on a portion of that chocolate tartine with the crème anglaise? Yeah, sod it – I'll just say he was good. 'More wine over here please, Samantha, and I think I might try a slice of the pavlova as well.'

I looked around the café to see if anyone else was reading the *Sunday Times* and if so to see if they recognized me. I gave a half smile to a cleaner, but she didn't seem to instantly place my face. I read on, almost aghast at the improbability of my success.

Having just returned from a couple of years spent building a cult following in the United States and Canada, Jimmy Conway is once more delighting British audiences with surprise appearances at ordinary comedy clubs across the country. With Conway there is no hype, there are no agents, no PR campaigns, no lager adverts or dodgy series on Sky One. Yet he is rapidly gaining a reputation via the best publicity machine in the business – word of mouth.

'It's just the way I like to do things,' he says when I meet him for drinks in one of London's trendy media clubs. Most celebrities are shorter than you imagine, but Conway is tall and good looking, with striking blue eyes and that hangdog scruffiness which is so often the sign of a great artist.

I was good looking! It said so in the paper! As for the scruffiness of the great artist, I privately had to concede it was more likely the sign of a person who was just scruffy.

'The ordinary venues are the lifeblood of Britain's comedy industry,' he explains, 'but they are being bypassed by television and big theatres who are grabbing the few big names and leaving the grassroots to wither away.' Except that now audiences know that if they go to enough clubs then eventually they will be treated to a surprise guest appearance by one of the funniest men in the country. Imagine going along to see Doncaster Rovers and discovering that David Beckham has decided to turn up and play for them this week. And Conway doesn't even expect a higher fee than the other performers. For the first time the comedy club promoters are laughing as much as their audiences.

While reeling in shocked delight at this unwarranted praise, I still found room to be puzzled by some of the comments in this almost perfect profile. Apparently I had admitted that underneath all the jokes I was probably a very sad person, and that I drank Guinness as a way of connecting with my Irish roots. But these were mere quibbles. The piece was prominent, with big pictures, great captions and the profile was so much better than it could have possibly been if we had both turned up to the gig. Now I was somebody. I had arrived. I read the entire piece again, more slowly this time, savouring its idolatrous climax:

> The *Los Angeles Times* described Jimmy Conway's most famous routine as a comic 'tour de fish'. But even this does not do justice to the highlight of his finely polished set. They said that comedy was the new rock and roll. Well, here comes comedy's punk. I have seen the future – and it's funny.

'You bloody liar,' I giggled delightedly, astonished that a journalist on a national newspaper could be so casually and brazenly dishonest. Now I noticed that the entire article never mentioned which comedy club Arabella was at, or who the other comics were – she covered herself by being deliberately vague. It was difficult to categorize all the different emotions I felt reading this profile of myself. Like any great trauma there were several stages. Shock was followed by incredulity, then excitement, then enormous gratitude, which finally gave way to the final stage: pride. Yes, I was very proud of how funny I was. It was all there in black and white. 'Well, you know, you've deserved it, Jimmy,' I joked to myself. 'Let's face it, you've put the work in, you've played all the clubs, you've served your time – no one deserves this more than you.'

Arabella sent me a short scribbled note a few days later returning my original photos.

Hope you liked the piece. Sorry I didn't stop and chat the other night; had to dash back to friend's birthday meal. But thought you were great, etc., etc. Photos enclosed. Comedy Store rang and asked if they could have copy of that picture of you performing there for their Wall of Fame. Keep in touch. Yrs, Arabella

PS Several people in the office say they think they remember seeing you before you went to America. They said you were great back then as well!

Shucks, yeah, I suppose I was.

— 6 —

27 Elms Crescent,
East Grinstead,
West Sussex,
England

Dear James,

In his song about fame, called 'Fame', David Bowie asked
fame what its name was. I thought about that long and hard
today. Then I decided that I didn't have the faintest idea what
he was talking about. But the kids from <u>Fame</u> said, 'Fame – I
wanna learn how to fly', and that's definitely true. It would
be much easier to do that sort of thing if you were famous.

But becoming a celebrity isn't just about being able to get
flying lessons or whatever. It also gives you the chance to do
some real good in the world. For example, if a worthwhile
cause was having problems raising money, you could come along
and go, 'Hello – let me help! I'm famous, you can use me to

publicize your charity.' And all the girls who work at the charity would be really grateful and feel so lucky that you'd come on board and then the newspapers would take a picture of you shaking a can for the disabled people or whatever, and you might even, sort of stand next to a disabled person to show that you don't mind doing that either. Then you'd be in the paper raising money for charity and everyone would think, 'Oh, that's good!' I mean, 'that's good, that charity', not 'oh that's good, good old James Conway is doing work for charity'. Although there's no point in doing it anonymously, because otherwise you might as well just be an ordinary person shaking a tin in the High Street and that takes ages just to get a couple of quid.

I always think that the more you put into something the more you get out of it. Except those fraudulent pyramid-selling schemes, of course. You're better off putting less into them, or nothing at all in fact if you know they're a swindle, which many of them are, sometimes deliberately. But the point is that far too many people these days take out more than they put in. They take out all their money, and things . . . no, not money, because they have to earn that. They take out all the nice things they buy, except then I suppose they are not really taking them, they are purchasing them legally. Well, whatever it is they are taking out, they are not putting as much of it back and it's not on. As a famous person it will be up to you to set an example to show everyone how good you are. Because when that Fame finally comes knocking on your door the temptation will be to drive around in your flashy car and buy yourself expensive things and go to parties where everyone thinks you are great, but you shouldn't just do all that, you should also put a couple of hours a week aside for thinking about people less

fortunate than yourself. Which with a bit of luck should be
just about everyone by now.

Mine sincerely,
Jimmy

'I didn't know you were bullied at school, dear,' said my mother on the phone that incredible Sunday morning.

'I wasn't.'

'It says here in the *Sunday Times*: "Jimmy Conway sipped his beer, almost as if the memory was too painful. 'I first learnt the craft of comedy as a teenager. I discovered that I could deflect the aggression of the school bully with a well-timed joke, and so for me comedy became a matter of survival in the playground jungle.'" Mind you, you're right about the jungle, darling,' she continued without drawing breath, 'the time I spent picking burrs out of your school jumper and they never pulled up the bindweed it always looked such a mess round the gates, but that's state education for you I suppose, encourage the weeds as well as the roses, I wanted to send you private they had much nicer grounds at Charterhouse but your father wouldn't hear of it after the money we'd spent on Nicholas who rang this morning they're back from the Dordogne they're having trouble with planning permission for the farm-house but that's the French for you, obstructive by nature like de Gaulle with the Common Market . . .'

The habits of a lifetime are not easily surrendered and despite my sudden increase in status she still found herself moving straight onto the subject of my elder brother. I had got used to this over the years. If my mother's butterfly brain should find itself settling for a second on the comprehensive bindweed of her youngest son it would then immediately flit off and settle on the richer nectar of the privately educated prize bloom that was Nicholas. But on this day an incredible thing happened. She fluttered back again and settled on me!

'Nicholas saw the piece in the newspaper as well, everyone's very excited about this secret career you've developed, darling,

I'm so glad you had a word with Billy Scrivens like I said. One of Nicholas's friends rang him and asked if he was any relation of Jimmy Conway, how about that? We're all very proud of you, dear!'

How about that, indeed! All the years that I had been Nicholas Conway's younger brother: 'Any relation of Nicholas?' people would always ask me, 'Oh yes, you're Nick Conway's little brother aren't you?' and now Nicholas had been asked if he was any relation of mine. Yes! Yes! Yes! Finally I had sat on his head and let rip a stinker! Dad had a brief word; the success of his younger son seemed briefly to have cheered him up but he quickly returned to his usual subject of conversation: 'Did Mum tell you George Howe's had another stroke? He can't have much longer I should think.'

'OK, Dad, lovely to talk to you . . .'

'And Arthur Lloyd has got to have a triple heart by-pass. Not many people survive those . . .'

I felt a slight pang of guilt at allowing this deception to extend to my own family, but it was not enough to make me feel I had to put them straight. Obviously there were some people I was more comfortable about deceiving than others, and when I thought about this I realized that ultimately it came down to levels of resentment. The more I resented someone, the easier I found it to lie to them, but a certain measure of resentment was required in all cases.

One of the first people I had lied to on this journey was my older brother. Obviously I resented him, but I imagine this is perfectly normal behaviour: isn't it exactly what successful siblings are for? My parents' adoration of him brought resentment by proxy which allowed me to mislead them as well. *Sophie's Choice* would have been a very short film if it had been our family captured by the Nazis. 'Mrs Conway, only one of your children may live and you must make that choice.'

'OK; Nicholas please.' The End.

Nicholas had towered over my childhood and twenty-five years later continued to metaphorically fart on my head by outperforming me in every single department. His life story was one of uninterrupted success, wealth and happiness; unless of course you happened to read his entry on *Friends Reunited*, which recorded a catalogue of abject failure, bankruptcy and prison. He still hadn't discovered what I'd written on his behalf. Actually *Friends Reunited* had provided me with a whole new supply of people to resent. I'd forgotten about many of my classmates but this website meant I could look them all up and resent them all over again. 'Jamie Kerslake – Database manager for software company in Reading. Married to Denise; two girls aged 2 and 4.' It's like, all right, you big show-off, you don't have to go on and on about it. Many of my classmates had made me feel inferior when I was a child – even my imaginary friend got better exam results than I did. They ought to create another site called *Imaginary Friends Reunited* – it would be nice to see what he was up to. I expect he's in computers as well. Everyone else seemed to be.

Arabella from the *Sunday Times* would have almost defied me to deceive her – she generated resentment on more fronts than I could count. She was a successful journalist on a national newspaper; an appallingly provocative piece of behaviour in itself, made worse by the fact that she seemed to take it completely for granted. She was obviously privately educated, again her fault and grounds for entirely justified major bitterness, since this meant that she only had to speak a few sentences in that special accent of hers to be instantly appointed Head of the BBC. She said 'two cappuccini' not 'two cappuccinos', and to cap it all she lived in London. I realized that I actually resented the entire population of Greater London, approximately ten million people, all because they happened to live in a place where the beer was too expensive and everyone presumed that you must live there too in what they thought was the centre of the bloody universe. Even the beggars sleeping on London's pavements would have been included in this malevolent generalization. 'Ooh no, you wouldn't beg on the streets of Seaford, would you? Not good enough for you, I suppose.'

If I had drawn a Venn diagram of my grudges I would have had to create resentment circles for all the following groups of people: people who were important, people who knew people who were important, posh people, rich people, famous people, people with personalized number plates, people who described themselves as living 'in London and Gloucestershire', people with fake tans, people with real tans, people with swimming pools, people who got laptops out on the train, people who had letters after their name, people who had titles before their name, people who wore suits, people who wore uniforms, people in any position of authority, be it policeman, traffic warden or librarian receiving overdue books. Bouncers, bishops, bank managers, any sort of umpire or referee in any sport and any person who was president or prime minister of a major world power (except Boris Yeltsin, who was pissed the whole time so he was forgiven). If an individual occupied the area where my grudges overlapped, then obviously I resented them twice or three times as much accordingly. Prince Edward, for example, was in so many overlapping circles it would have needed a three-dimensional Venn diagram to fit them all together. Who else prompted indignant contempt? People who got taxis, people who played golf, people who wore significant ties, people who gave their kids stupid names, people who had an initial in the middle of their name, people who pretended they liked sushi (i.e. everyone who ate sushi), people who were members of any kind of club (particularly health clubs), people who went to raves, people who wore sunglasses indoors, people with silly facial hair (pointy sideburns, tiny goatees, etc.), people who printed or broadcast their personal opinions, businessmen who appeared in their own adverts, families who sent Christmas cards with a photocopied sheet recounting what an incredibly successful year they'd had and, most of all, people who wrote bestselling books about their bloody holiday homes in Southern Europe.

But apart from all of the above, I generally felt a benevolent sense of love and goodwill towards all mankind. Oh, hang on, I forgot everyone in the United States for thinking that theirs was the most important country in the world, just because it was. And everyone from Canada for minding that you'd presumed they were from the United States.

But I hadn't *wanted* to resent anyone; in fact, I would have much preferred it if lots of people resented me. And the wonderful thing about the article in the *Sunday Times* was that I could almost feel myself becoming warm-hearted and generous towards the whole world as I re-read it. 'Do you know Arabella from the *Sunday Times*? Lovely woman, very thorough journalist.' 'Oh you must read *Scorpions in the Swimming Pool*; he's spot on about all the hilarious problems of having your own villa in Tuscany.' At last I could look everyone in the eye as an equal, now that I deserved the respect and admiration of everyone out there; I was Jimmy Conway the celebrated comic.

On the morning the article came out I walked along the

front at Seaford with a 'yes-it's-me' cod modesty that presumed everyone in the whole town had already rushed out to buy the *Sunday Times* and turned straight to the review section. But people were walking straight past me as if nothing was different. Couldn't they see how the whole world had changed? Were they going to carry on as normal? It was quite unnerving. Now look here, I thought; I'm quite prepared to behave as if I'm just an ordinary member of the public, but that doesn't mean you have to believe that I am.'

Because I was so enjoying the immaculate fit of this celebrity costume I was modelling, I didn't want to do anything to remind me of the darker reality of my situation. I had told a massive lie about myself which had been printed in a national newspaper and before long my friends would be asking for an explanation. Though it felt extremely risky, the only thing I could possibly do would be to tell them the truth. I'd present it as a trick against all those clever London media types; an elaborate wind-up by one of the little people. I imagined my friends laughing at how gullible this journalist had been to believe the ludicrous idea that I could be someone. And the more I thought about this, the more I wished the article was true.

I did a quick ring round and suggested we meet up for lunch; since Nancy was giving up smoking I suggested the café rather than the pub. I knew they'd never have bought and read a Sunday broadsheet, so I didn't give them any clues on the phone. We met up in Mario's café in the High Street, the only place in town greasier than Norman's hair. We often ate there together because there was nowhere else you could get such an excellent and reasonably priced fry-up. Admittedly, you may not have ordered a fry-up, you probably asked for the shepherd's pie, but Mario was so convinced of his amazing powers of memory that he refused ever to write his orders down.

'I'll have double egg, sausage, bacon and tomatoes, and a slice, please,' I said to him optimistically, as he nodded wearing the smile of a man whose mind was a million miles away.

'Egg, sausage, beans and tomatoes. No problem.'

'No, not beans; bacon.'

'Oh, you want bacon too, now. OK, no problem.'

For Mario the words 'no problem' were an involuntary verbal tic he stuck on the end of any sentence in which he had, in fact, just created a problem.

'Bacon instead of sausage, no problem.'

'No, *as well as* the sausage. Double egg, sausage, bacon and tomatoes, and a slice.'

Similar versions of this routine were then repeated with everyone else's order and we sat back and waited to see what would appear.

'Somehow I feel Mario is not in the right business,' said Nancy.

'Well exactly,' I replied. 'His wife told me she'd asked him to buy a little shoe repairers but he hadn't been listening.'

'Really?' said Nancy, and everyone laughed and she hit me lightly on the arm and said I was funny, and it was the perfect opportunity to tell them about the story in the paper. So I can't explain why I didn't take it. Suddenly the conversation had moved on. Norman was telling us about something exciting that had happened to him. Everyone has some talent hidden away inside and Norman had been fortunate enough to discover his gift. Norman was a great air guitarist. If miming a musical instrument was your thing, then you would look up to Norman as one of the masters. And after years of developing his hobby in private, he announced that he had reached the finals of British Air Guitar championships.

'That's fantastic news. So if you win, do you pretend to pick up an imaginary cup?'

I couldn't help feeling that playing air guitar must fall slightly short of the satisfaction you get from playing a real live guitar; that *imagining* you are producing brilliant guitar solos, impossible riffs and elaborate chord sequences can't be quite as fulfilling as doing it for real. Maybe I was just jealous. My parents were too straight to let me do air guitar. I had to do air cello.

'Can we come and see you play?'

'No way. You might put me off and then I might play a bum note or something.'

We had often asked Norman to perform a bit of air guitar for us and he had always refused. 'Couldn't we just listen to a tape then?'

'No, that wouldn't work,' pointed out Chris, astute as ever.

The conversation moved on and almost immediately there was another obvious opening for me, but I couldn't now dive in there and share my own news because it might look like I was just doing it to go one better than Norman. Then Nancy talked anxiously about Tamsin and I felt a little guilty for keeping our conversation secret from her. I reassured myself that if my course of action was the most likely to prevent her daughter from getting pregnant then Nancy would thank me in the long run. Tamsin had apparently been feeling a little unwell.

'What, in the morning?' I said, panicking.

'No, it was last night. It's just period pains.'

'Oh thank God,' I said. 'I mean, thank God it's nothing more serious . . . I mean, they're such a worry, aren't they?'

My friends stared at me with a little concern and I thought that since I now at least had their attention I might as well confess about the story in the paper.

'Anyway, there was a reason I suggested we all met up for lunch,' I announced. 'I've got something to tell you,' and my formality seemed to make them sit up.

'Jimmy Conway!' yelled Panda, throwing open the door of the café. 'You're a bloody dark horse and no mistake! Has he shown you today's *Sunday Times*, everyone? Jimmy, why didn't you tell us?'

'What? Tell us what?' said Dave.

'How long have you been reading the *Sunday Times*?' said Norman to his girlfriend.

'Oh, um, the motoring section does bike reviews, doesn't matter,' she said making an extra effort not to pronounce the 't's. 'Jimmy here has only been secretly going off and appearing at cabaret clubs in London and that. He's famous. Jimmy's famous!'

'What are you talking about, Panda?'

'Don't take my word for it. It's all here. The *Sunday Times*, no less. The one time I buy it!' She tutted and slapped down the paper, and there was my face staring up at them, with Steve Martin and Billy Crystal no doubt adding to the impact. There was a loud crash from the kitchen, or it might have been the sound of their jaws dropping, I'm not sure. It was the moment when Clark Kent first lifts up a truck or the expanding muscles rip through the shirt of the Incredible Hulk.

'Oh my God, Jimmy!' exclaimed Nancy.

'So that's why you were mates with Billy Scrivens,' said Dave, 'because I thought it seemed a bit unlikely at the time.'

'Bloody hell, Jimmy!' said Norman, looking at it in amazement. 'You mean, you're a celebrity.'

Panda continued: 'Look, there's a photo of him in the Comedy Store.'

Nancy rubbed my arm proudly. 'Well done, good for you. I knew you'd achieve something like this one day.' She seemed genuinely pleased for me, as if she knew this was what I'd always wanted. 'Maybe you'll be on *This Is Your Life*,' she added.

'Why do you mention that?'

'It was in those teenage letters, remember? And admit it, you'd still love it, wouldn't you? Was this what you were about to tell us when Panda came in?'

'Er, yeah,' I heard myself say. 'Yeah, it was . . .'

And I tried to take a casual sip of my steaming tea but winced as I burnt my tongue.

'So, are you any good?' said Chris.

'Er, well, I dunno, I haven't seen me.'

'He's bloody brilliant according to this,' said Dave, scanning the text.

I could feel myself going red. 'Well, they have to take an angle, you know – it's either "I love it" or "I hate it".'

'Bloody hell, Jimmy!' said Norman again, still in shock.

'It's incredible, well done!' said Nancy.

'I can't believe it!' said Dave. 'You're *not* a nobody!'

And I tried not to enjoy the attention too openly, and then thought it might be a nice gesture to change the subject and ask them what else they'd been up to, but it was too obvious an attempt at modesty, like Neil Armstrong saying to his wife, 'But enough about where I've been – how was the shopping mall?'

Panda ordered herself a greasy fry-up, all washed down with a big mug of Earl Grey, while the others crowded around the page, fighting for space to be able to speed-read the article.

Having allowed this lie to take hold, I felt increasingly power-less to prevent it growing ever larger. As my friends re-read the feature, they started to ask more questions.

'Hang on, when were you in America for two years?'

'Oh – typical journalist – she's got that all wrong. I said I was in America two years ago.'

Nancy looked a little perplexed as to how such a thing could have slipped her mind. 'But this whole piece is based on the fact you've just come back from having made it in the States . . . it doesn't make sense.'

'Look, I went over to America for a few weeks a couple of years ago, you probably don't even remember; I kept it quiet in case it all went horribly wrong. I tried my luck at stand-up and it went quite well.'

'But they say you've made it really big there over the past couple of years! How can anyone get something as basic as that so wrong?' said Norman in astonishment, and for a second I was tongue-tied.

'Eggs, beans, sausage and chips,' announced Mario, provid-ing an answer as he plonked down a spectacularly incorrect combination of fried food in front of me. 'Mario, have you ever thought of going into journalism?' I said, as he followed this up by placing various random mix-and-match orders before the others. We apologetically pointed out that these dishes were not exactly what we'd ordered and Mario rolled his eyes in disbelief at the incompetence of his kitchen staff. He whisked the plates away, all the while maintaining an utterly charming exterior, but once he'd kicked open the swing doors into the kitchen we could hear him shouting, 'No fuckin' beans, I said! I fuckin' told you fuckers, double fuckin' egg, bacon, sausage and chips, you fuckin' fucks!' and this was followed by the sound of smashing crockery.

'Oh no, he just told them chips instead of tomatoes,' I said. 'Is this the best moment to put my head round the door and point that out?'

'Probably not,' ventured Dave.

Once my friends had accepted that they had an important and successful creative person in their midst there were all sorts of incisive questions they wanted to ask about this most modern of art forms. 'So how much do you get for a gig?' 'What's the most you've earned in one night?' 'How much does that make a year?'

I did my best to answer them as evasively as possible and I'm sure I noticed Chris starting to laugh at my jokes just a little bit more than before. They shared the news with Mario, who showed his other customers the front of the newspaper and pointed me out to them. And then he brought a white coffee for Nancy who'd asked for tea without milk, and an espresso for Norman who'd asked for a cappuccino. But when he took my pudding and coffee order he remembered it exactly. Apple pie with cream not custard, and another cappuccino with no chocolate. Perfect, thank you, Mario. 'Oh, Mario, actually my friend here wanted a cappuccino as well.'

'Oh, terribly sorry, sir, coming right up, sir.'

I was enjoying this now, starting to really play the part. 'Yeah, so that was two cappuccini.'

It just slipped out. I was feeling a little bit cool and I over-reached myself.

'Two cappuccini?' sneered Dave. 'Since when has the plural of cappuccino been cappuccini?'

'Well, er, it just is, that's all.'

'It might be in bloody Tuscany, mate, but round here we say "two cappuccinos".'

'Or "one cup of chino, please" if you're my mum,' added Nancy.

We each paid for what we'd eaten, except Mario would not accept any money from me. He insisted that my meal was on the house. Norman and Dave looked suitably disgusted.

'So are you coming for a pint or two tonight?' said Chris.

'Oh I'd love to, but I can't – I'm playing the Comedy Store.'

'The Comedy Store?'

'Yeah, so I've got to head into town.'

'What town's that then?'

'Well, London, obviously. Sorry – yeah, gotta head up to London. So I can't make tonight.'

'Hey, can we come and see you?' said Nancy.

'Er, not tonight. Trying out some new material, you know.'

'Oh. Is that clothes material or comedy material?' said Dave.

'Comedy material. Oh, I see, you're joking. Right. Hey, that's my job!'

But they didn't laugh at that. Dave just said, 'Well, don't forget to have a couple of *cappuccini* while you're *in town*.'

Already it had started. Already there was a gap between me and them. I was treating my best friends slightly differently, and they had markedly altered their behaviour towards me. Honestly, there's so much petty resentment in this country. Why can't we just applaud and admire people who are doing well in life? It's like, you stick your head slightly above the parapet, and all the whingers and embittered losers have to start resenting whatever you do. It's pathetic, it really is. Tall poppy syndrome, they call it, except I suppose I was more of an opium poppy, a big white, escapist, trip-inducing poppy. I only stood out because I'd persuaded everyone that my hallucination was the reality.

*

It was on the Monday morning that I had my first call from an agent wanting to meet and talk about possible representation. His name was Viv Busby and he sounded like a bad actor playing 'second East End gangster' in *The Bill*.

'No bullshit, Jimmy, you're the guv'nor, you're the main man, and I respect totally what you're sayin' about not wantin' an agent an' all that, but let's have a chat an' see if I can take some of the hassle out of arrangin' gigs an' that' so you can concentrate on the comedy . . . 'cos that's what you do best, mate.'

'Oh, thank you very much. Have you seen my act then?'

'To be totally honest with you, Jimmy, not for a while, mate, not for a while. But I've always loved what you do. That fish routine – bloody funny, mate! Comedy classic that is.'

This agent had read that I did not want an agent and his immediate reaction was to suggest that he became my agent. I suppose that's the sort of person you want on your side. He was very persuasive about meeting up. I got the feeling that promoters and broadcasters would always find themselves forced to agree with him for fear of ending up inside one of the concrete pillars of the Channel tunnel rail-link. He attacked his half of our conversation, or rather his seven-eighths of our conversation, with such missionary zeal that it left me nowhere to go other than polite acquiescence. To question a single assumption would have involved going, 'Whoa! Whoa! Back up there, you are not listening to what I am trying to tell you. Now just stop talking for five bloody seconds and hear what I am saying. I DO NOT WANT TO MEET UP WITH YOU, OK?' But being rude to strangers on the phone is not something I was brought up to do and so a date was made for me to come to his office. His company weren't 'in town', they were 'up west'. By now I was sufficiently savvy to understand that 'up west' did not mean Lewes or Peacehaven. That night I left a message on his office voicemail saying that I couldn't make that date after all. I was doing a gig 'out of town'. And then I called three other agents that had rung me during the course of the day and left similar messages for them as well.

The article in the *Sunday Times* seemed to have precipitated a thousand private panics for all those people who thought they were in the know. I was suddenly the new fashion that nobody had foreseen, like text messaging or foot and mouth disease. What the feature had proclaimed was, 'Hey, everyone, here's a famous person you really ought to have heard of by now! You might think you're in the in-crowd, but if this new star isn't in there with you, then maybe you just became the out-crowd.' And just as everyone had seen the emperor's new clothes, a surprising number of people claimed to have seen a Jimmy Conway set. One person wrote to me anonymously c/o the *Sunday Times* just to say how much they'd enjoyed my show. What is going on inside that person's head? I asked myself. If they had given a return address I might have been able to ponder some possible motive, but why should somebody send me an anonymous thank-you letter for a gig they had never seen? It was insane. But no one was behaving rationally. In Seaford, a solicitor and his wife I'd passed on my road a couple of times suddenly invited me to dinner. If my diary hadn't been so full of fictitious gigs I might have said yes.

For fear of appearing out of touch, a number of other newspapers and magazines were soon doing little diary items or features on me. Some of them involved brief phone interviews; some of them used Jimmy Conway quotes from other pieces as if I had spoken to the journalist writing the piece. My mobile phone number seemed to become public property very quickly, as if there was a central register where researchers and journalists logged useful information, and I was now chalked up on the 'latest additions' board.

Even without the assistance of agent and probable horse decapitator Viv Busby, I got a number of requests to perform at various comedy clubs or at universities. One student union wrote: 'Although we appreciate that you are one of the top performers in the country, I'm afraid we can offer you only £1000 for thirty minutes.' A grand! For half an hour's work! Imagine that, several nights a week! I had a ready-made career as a stand-up all lined up before me, if only I knew how to do it. It was as if all my life I had wanted to be a pilot and then suddenly the airlines said, 'No problem! There's the keys, take that jumbo jet there.' However much you wanted it, the knowledge that you were going to crash the plane into a mountain was always going to be a fairly compelling disincentive.

More letters came my way via newspaper offices over the next few weeks. My favourite was from someone a few years younger than me who felt he had been aimlessly drifting along for too long now and wanted to know how to get where I was today. 'I'm afraid there's no substitute for hard work and experience,' I wrote back. As well as the predictable requests from charities and students, there were also a handful of letters addressed in green ink. These were the rather disturbing appeals from people who wanted me to use my 'access to the media' to tell the world that their house had been bugged by Brussels bureaucrats or that Cecil B. de Mille had stolen their idea about doing a film based on the Bible. One correspondent believed that not only were our senior politicians all reptiles in disguise, but Jewish reptiles at that. In my reply I urged this man not to jump to conclusions. 'OK, just because all the prime ministers and the American president and the other world leaders happen to be Jewish reptiles in disguise, I still think we should judge them on their record in government. It doesn't automatically mean there's any great conspiracy going on. Let's judge these lizards on their actual policies . . .'

But everyone seemed to have gone insane for a while. When somebody marketed an astrology chart for cats, I was asked to go on the radio and talk about it. 'We just thought you might have something funny to say,' said the dippy researcher on the phone as if I was so desperate to publicize myself that I would go on Radio 5 Live to talk about feline star signs. Although when I listened back to the tape I thought I was mildly amusing about it: 'Sagittarians are known to be good with money, stubborn and always licking their bum.' It seemed that I had become appointed the first person producers and researchers thought of when they needed a sound bite about anything vaguely silly. 'That new comic – Jimmy Wotsisname; get his take on it, put him on the panel/in the paper/in the radio car.'

Each interview or booking seemed to spawn another and for me these little media appearances became my raison d'être. They weren't in order to sell my book or my hit single because there was no product to be promoted. They weren't to raise money for a good cause or to draw people's attention to an injustice, they were simply to publicize myself. Indeed, the fact that I wasn't wasting all my time doing what I was famous for freed up far more time to publicize it. I was becoming the celebrity equivalent of Nike or Gap. I didn't produce anything myself; I just focused on marketing the brand.

There is a clever trick of the brain by which you can

immediately spot your own name on a whole page of newsprint. I expect Hugh Grant couldn't help his eye locating his own name on the front page of the tabloid that said 'Hugh Grant Arrested With Vice Girl'. But sometimes I would be flicking through a newspaper or magazine (not particularly looking out for references to myself; I bought *Hello!* for the recipes), when I would turn over a page and spot my name and then go back a few lines to see what was being said about me. I had this experience reading an interview in the *Guardian* with one of the major suits-in-chief at BBC television. 'Agents are the enemy of talent,' he said audaciously. 'Every time some new comedian comes along, for example, they're snapped up by this new breed of aggressive promoters, who then price their talent right out of the market. That's why Jimmy Conway is such a breath of fresh air. Real talent doesn't need pushy agents shouting down the phone about how brilliant their clients are. You mark my words – Jimmy Conway will go further than any of them.'

I was interviewed for a feature in one of the colour supplements called 'What's In My Fridge?' in which minor celebrities talked about their beliefs, their career, their lifestyle and how all this was reflected in the contents of their fridge. Jimmy Conway had some milk, eggs and a raspberry yoghurt. That's just what happened to be in there. Of course, if I'd been really uncool and preoccupied with how I came across, I would have spent hours walking around the supermarkets and delicatessens trying to select exactly the right balance of foodstuffs to convey the image of a creative yet busy single man; modern enough to cook interesting dishes just for himself, yet so in demand socially that he had to plan his catering well in advance. Some exotic pasta sauces, perhaps; a few unusual salad ingredients, a home-made salmon quiche, a little Parma ham and half a summer pudding with a big tub of fresh cream. But none of these appeared in Jimmy Conway's fridge. I hid them all in the cupboard under the sink when I lost confidence in the whole gourmet image thing just before the photographer called. Still the raspberry yoghurt said something about me I think. I'm the kind of guy who likes yoghurt.

The journalist who did the 'What's In My Fridge?' interview described the little house in Seaford as my holiday home. I suppose this was technically true; I had spent most of my holidays here because I'd usually been too skint to go anywhere else. 'Jimmy Conway clearly values the peace he finds away from it all in his holiday cottage on the South Downs. His love for this part of the world is something he used to share with his good friend Billy Scrivens.' My friendship with Billy had gone from strength to strength since he'd died. The vacuum created by his absence forced journalists to find other ways to refer to him and so they often mentioned this new comedian Jimmy Conway as if I was some sort of surviving disciple.

When I walked Betty up on the cliffs I would find myself going back to the spot where I had passed Billy, like a criminal returning to the scene of the crime. I could see his old holiday cottage in the distance and wondered if his widow Stella had any idea of the level of my deception. Since our brief conversation at the funeral I had thought about her often and wondered if our paths might cross again. Strange that I only ever walked the dog on this side of town these days.

It was her dog I saw first. Max was something of a celebrity-by-association himself, but as he came over the hill I feared there was no guarantee that it would be Stella walking him. I stroked him as he wagged his tail around me, then he tried to run on, but I held his collar tight and patted him some more until his owner came into view. It was indeed Stella. Her extraordinary good looks still glowed around her like luminous fairy dust. When Billy Scrivens had set out to get himself a trophy wife, he had to have the Champions League trophy wife, the Jules Rimet trophy wife, and frankly I was the Rotherham United reserve team and was never even going to make the play-offs. But despite her dazzling good looks and infectious smile, there seemed to be some sort of sadness about her. Maybe I am just gifted in this way, but I'm sure I detected some inexplicable distant sorrow in the woman who had very recently lost her husband while he was in his prime.

'Hello again. Jimmy Conway – we met at Billy's funeral.' It wasn't the best opener for someone who needed cheering up. But the dogs gave me an excuse to walk alongside her for a while and she commented on how much coverage I suddenly seemed to be getting.

'I see you did "What's In My Fridge?",' she remarked as she threw a stick that was grabbed by both our dogs. 'Billy agreed to do that once. When the photographer opened the fridge door he was confronted by a midget dressed as an Eskimo sitting there reading the paper. He shouted, "Get out of my house!" and the photographer apologized and shut the door again. Then he realized he was the victim of a *Gotcha!* and the Eskimo midget came out and turned to the hidden TV camera to tell children watching at home never to hide in fridges.'

'Yeah, I remember watching that, it was a great one,' I said, admiring the way she was still able to talk about her husband's career with a smile.

There was a pause while I wondered if it was acceptable to carry on talking about Billy's show now that she had raised the subject.

'Did you ever worry that any of the *Gotchas* went too far?' I asked.

'Oh yes, all the time. I mean that famous one of the old lady on the Portaloo. She was furious at first.'

This particular stunt was the stuff of television legend. An unsuspecting old lady entered a temporary toilet in the middle of Trafalgar Square. But once she was sitting down, all four walls were whipped away by an overhead crane, revealing her to everyone with her knickers and tights around her ankles.

It turned out to be a pivotal moment in the story of British television. A row about 'dumbing down' ensued in which the infamous prank was criticized by the culture secretary in the House of Commons. However, the look of indignant shock on the old lady's face, followed by the hopeless action of reaching for a toilet-roll dispenser that was no longer there, had made this scene an incredibly popular TV moment, a national family joke that was on the front page of every tabloid. Downing Street were apparently furious that a minister had criticized the toilet lady stunt without first clearing this with Number 10 and the culture secretary ended up having to do a complete U-turn, saying it represented the best in ground-breaking and innovative programme-making.

'Nobody *has* to sign the consent form so it's always up to them,' said Stella in defence of Billy's show. 'But you're always going to upset somebody when you try to push back the boundaries. But that's what Billy was all about – he was always searching for the next television first.' And then she paused and did her brave face and I wanted to give her a con-soling hug but I stopped myself because I knew my kindly motives of caring sympathy were mingled with rampant lust and desire. My dog brought back the stick so I threw it over the fields once more.

It was good to talk to someone about celebrity and show business who knew a great deal more about them than I did. I felt celebrity was something Stella and I had in common. My friends didn't react as well as I had hoped to hearing about my latest radio interview or newspaper feature, but to Stella it was perfectly normal, it didn't seem like showing off. She talked about the strange customs of the Planet Fame and I nodded and agreed while taking careful mental note of everything she said. Sometimes I wondered if I was struck by Stella because she fitted this new image I had of myself: the flashy comic with the exciting career who should have a beautiful model on his arm. A lot of today's male celebrities had once had long-standing girlfriends whom they'd dumped the moment they started to get well known. It wasn't that these men were shallow; it's just that they didn't feel comfortable speeding along in their new red sports car beside a woman who worked in the public sector. I felt sure that I could never be so callous, so vain and calculating. The fact that I didn't have a long-standing girlfriend to dump in the first place was nothing to do with it. There was still Betty, my Border collie, of course. Maybe she worried that I was planning to swap her for the Scrivenses' showbiz Labrador.

'I read an interview with that old woman from Trafalgar Square the other day,' I continued. 'It was for a "Where Are They Now?" slot in some TV listings magazine. They called her "Toilet Lady".'

'She did very well out of it. Became a bit of a minor celebrity herself after the clip went into the opening titles of Billy's show. For a while she made a living opening super-markets and doing adverts for toilet paper.' Stella asserted that being on Billy's show was the probably the highlight of this old lady's life. That most people's lives were quite mundane and meaningless, with every evening spent slumped in a chair staring at a television. So for an ordinary person to be transported to the magical world on the other side of the screen gave them status and kudos of which they could previously have only ever dreamt.

'Actually, the article said that she'd had quite an interesting life. She worked as a midwife in India in the 1950s and had campaigned for the rights of low caste pregnant women or something.'

'Who, Toilet Lady?'

'Yeah, what was her real name? Began with a T.'

'Toilet Lady,' confirmed Stella.

Max snapped aggressively at Betty and wrestled the stick away from her. Stella made a token attempt at telling her dog off. I knew there was some truth in what she had said. That you could discover a cure for cancer or bring peace to the Middle East but you were never really anybody until you had appeared on television. That was the modern definition of status.

'Is that right, though? Is that what we want?' I said.

'Says the man who's not on television yet,' she smiled.

Was my unease prompted by a concern about the values of our society or vain indignation that all my publicity so far counted for so little?

'Yeah, but what about all the other media?' I said. 'Things definitely changed for me after that feature in the *Sunday Times*.'

'Well, they all contribute a little bit, obviously,' she conceded. 'But without wishing to demean your standing, Jimmy, no one ever got mobbed by fans because of a particularly interesting discussion on Radio Four. Your name is known in certain circles, but that doesn't make you famous.

You're not on television. People don't see your face and think, Oh look, there goes Jimmy Conway.'

This presented a problem for me. I'd only got as far as I had by apparently being the one performer who wouldn't do television. This had been my Unique Selling Point, the thing that marked me out from the crowd. So to go to the next level of fame, to go on telly to do my 'I won't do telly' line, might arguably be seen as a little bit hypocritical by one or two eagle-eyed pedants. As I wandered home towards Seaford I thought about what Stella had said. Down in the town below me, every chimney had a television aerial or satellite dish. Every home was endlessly consuming TV; thoughtlessly breathing it in and exhaling it just as quickly. My one appearance on the TV news was already forgotten. It wasn't just a case of appearing once on the telly. You had to be on that screen over and over again for it to count for anything. Deep down I knew that Stella was completely right about my own status. Before I talked to her I'd thought that I must seem quite important, that everyone else had been just as aware as me of this supposed new comedian's arrival on the scene. On reflection it was a fairly safe bet that the rest of the British population was not endlessly re-reading each newspaper feature about me or listening to my every minor radio appearance. Billy Scrivens had been a supernova, but I was barely visible with a telescope. And without the means to keep shining brightly, I'd never count for very much. One brief artificial glimmer of light in my mid-thirties and that would be it. I'd be famous for fifteen minutes like that bloke said, oh, what's his name? I can't remember. He's not famous enough any more.

— 7 —

27 Elms Crescent,
East Grinstead,
West Sussex,
England

Dear James,

Well, who would have thought it!! You were hoping for an MBE,
but you got a knighthood as well! Congratulations — and you
can take it from me as a semi-neutral outsider that it was most
definitely deserved. Obviously these little accolades don't
really mean anything to you, it's all rather embarrassing, but
it might seem rude to refuse them and anyway if you turned
them down you might not be offered any more. Although John
Lennon gave back his MBE, but you don't have to worry about
that because the Vietnam war is over now and so you shouldn't
feel like it's selling out if you accept it. Anyway, Jimmy
Savile has OBE on the end of his name after his programme and

that looks very impressive indeed. I don't think it would look like you were copying if you did that when you get yours.

Of course, these honours don't just belong to you. They are also for all the ordinary people behind the scenes who have worked so very hard on your behalf and have been paid much less. How nice it must be for them that all their hard work has now been recognized with your knighthood. Perhaps it would be a nice gesture to send some of them a little present as a thank-you. Nothing too flash, but not too cheap either. A box of Matchmakers, or a Chocolate Orange maybe.

At this time it is important that Nicholas is not made to feel inferior by all your success. Hard to imagine that he was once the high achiever of the family! You should be sensitive about how you break this happy news to your sadly rather embittered and jealous older brother. Perhaps it would be better coming from someone else and they could sort of just mention it in passing – e.g. your secretary could ring him up and say, 'Could you hold, please? I have your younger brother, Sir James Conway MBE, on the line for you.' Though if you wanted to hear his reaction you'd have to listen on the extension.

I hope you enjoyed meeting the Queen. Some people criticize the royal family, which isn't fair because they can't answer back. In any case they do a lot of work for charity and it's much better than having a dictator like Adolf Hitler. You are now the second person in your family to meet the Queen; a few years before you were born, Mum handed her a posy of flowers from the other side of the railings when she did a walkabout in Royal Tunbridge Wells. But I think you were right not to mention it. Her Majesty meets a lot of people like that and she probably wouldn't have remembered it even if you'd shown her the photo from on top of the telly. Congratulations once again, and it just goes to show

that if you really work at something, you'll get there in the
end.

Mine sincerely,
Jimmy

When I was a child an MBE must have still meant something. I suppose I had regarded those awards as the ultimate accolades because they were given out by the Queen. I was now struggling to imagine exactly what benefits you got from being a Member of the British Empire when that particular club had been closed down some years earlier.

The reason all those old-fashioned awards have lost their appeal is they are no longer marketed correctly. They're still handed over at a stuffy private ceremony at Buckingham Palace, with maybe one quick snapshot afterwards for the *Daily Telegraph*. No wonder the public has lost interest. Who's going to get excited by a photo of some anonymous civil servant holding up his medal and being completely upstaged by his wife's enormous hat? As Stella said, if it isn't on television it hasn't happened. If the British establishment wanted people to care about the official honours system they should do a proper glitzy awards bash and put it out on ITV after *Coronation Street*. Five minutes of funny topical stand-up from Her Majesty before she introduced her first guest to read the nominations for the opening award of the night: 'A big hand for His Royal Highness the Duke of Edinburgh!' And the band would play a couple of jazzy bars of the national anthem as Prince Philip skipped jauntily down the steps clutching a gold envelope. A little bit of scripted light-hearted banter between the Queen and her husband for good measure: 'Phil, I like your medals . . .'

'Thank you. This one here is for outstanding courage when confronted by the enemy.'

'Yes, though to be fair, not many pheasants ever fired back at you!'

And the laughter of the studio audiences would provide a little break in the tension over who'd won the phone vote for the coveted title of Commander of the Order of the Bath.

In the twenty years since I had imagined that the ultimate prize was a medal from the Queen, a whole new royal family had emerged, bringing its own new honours system with it. A few letters after your name counted for nothing compared to the glamour and kudos attached to the glittering prizes regularly dished out on national television by the new kings and queens of British celebrity: the rulers of the House of *Hello!*

I could never resist the drama and excitement of a televised awards ceremony. My attitude towards them always followed the same pattern. I would begin by attempting to appear cynical and knowing. 'The Soap Awards!' I'd exclaim in appalled disbelief. 'What will they think of next? I'm not watching this. It's just an extended trailer; an excuse to show a load of old soap-opera clips!' An hour later I was still shouting at the screen: 'How can you give "Soap of the Year" to *Emmerdale*?! Oh come on; it's got to be between *Corrie* and *EastEnders*, surely?'

I always ended up caring because I could not help but identify myself with one programme over another, with this actor rather than that one. That is how celebrity works, I suppose. It's a process of associating yourself with various stars and then vicariously enjoying their successes and lifestyle.

All these thoughts had been prompted by one small rectangle of cardboard that had landed on my doormat before being half destroyed by Betty. In the grandest of loopy royal writing it informed me that the pleasure of my company was requested at the British 'Biz Awards. And at the bottom of the gold-edged card, just above the teeth marks and doggy saliva, a solitary word proclaimed the grounds on which I had qualified for this invitation:

Nominee.

When I finally prised the accompanying letter out of Betty's jaws, it informed me that I had been nominated for the category of Best New Stand-up. I shouted such a triumphant 'Yes!' that Betty jumped clear off the ground in excitement. I think she imagined I was so happy because of the excellent job she'd made of opening the envelope. I re-read the letter and then rang Nancy to tell her the incredible news.

'I can't believe it – me, nominated for Best Stand-up. It's just ridiculous!'

'Why's it ridiculous?'

'Well, er, because I'm not. Erm, probably.'

I had wanted her to be happy for me, but she was curiously reserved about it.

'So when are you moving to Hollywood then?' she said.

'I've already bought a place.'

'Really?' she said in amazement.

'Nancy! How can you be taken in by your own joke?'

Famous people had this line they always trotted out when they were interviewed on telly. 'I've been very lucky,' they would humbly admit, forcing the interviewer to contradict them and assert that their rare talent and hard work were much greater factors in their enormous success. I'd always thought that the 'I've been very lucky' mantra was fairly transparent false modesty, but now I began to realize what a huge part luck must really play. A screen goddess could never guarantee her next film would not be a turkey; a great band might emerge only if their type of music happened to come into fashion. Often the people who made it were no more talented than the next contender. Like myself they happened to be in the right place at the right time. Everyone in society is spinning around like a load of lottery balls in the drum; it's luck who ends up rolling out and becoming someone special. And now it seemed that fate or some other more powerful force beyond my understanding was about to give my phantom career another big leg-up.

Around this time I read a story in the newspaper about the unmasking of a bogus doctor. A man had been treating patients and prescribing drugs in an NHS hospital with no qualifications whatsoever. I presume he must have had some sort of medical knowledge. People would surely begin to notice if you were bluffing your way through open-heart surgery.

'Er, right, let's remove this big gristly lump here.'

'But that's the heart, doctor.'

'The heart? Blimey, it doesn't look like that on the Valentine's cards, does it?'

Over the years I had read about various bogus professionals, phoney aristocrats, refugees claiming to be Russian princesses, criminals impersonating police officers. It occurred to me that I had become the show business equivalent – I was a bogus celebrity. My fame was forged, I had risen without trace, I was a nobody-somebody, a plastic VIP. But the thing about fame is that either you are well known or you are not, and before long that's all that counts. 'Are you famous, then?' is a question that answers itself. You wouldn't say to Madonna, 'Are you famous?' If you have to ask, the answer's 'no'. Unless you were my dad, of course. Then you'd definitely ask Madonna if she was famous, before boring her for an hour about how much rubbish there was in the hit parade these days.

The invitation to the award ceremony said 'Black Tie', which is a sort of euphemistic shorthand because there isn't enough room on the invite to put 'Dress Code: Look Like a

Twat'. Since I'd never played the part of Mr Hudson in *Upstairs Downstairs*, I didn't own a black bow tie or a pair of trousers with that shiny stripe down the leg, so I had to hire a complete outfit from a shop in Brighton where a rather camp man asked me if I would like a cummerbund. 'Hmm, a cummerbund,' I pondered out loud, hoping he might help me out, 'do I want a cummerbund?' while thinking: Is it a) a type of fruity bread; b) an item of clothing; or c) a bizarre gay sex act? Since at the time he was kneeling down in front of me with a load of pins in his mouth, I thought I'd better say no, just to be on the safe side.

Unfortunately the clown's trousers I had hurriedly said were fine turned out not to have any slots for a belt and since I didn't own a pair of braces I ended up shuffling into the Grosvenor House Hotel with my jacket obscuring a row of safety pins where my trousers were hooked to my shirt to prevent them from falling down. I handed my invitation to one of the girls with the lists of names and when I said 'Jimmy Conway' she remarked, 'Oh, you're a nominee, aren't you?' and the other guests who were arriving all looked in my direction.

'Er, yeah. Best New Stand-up . . .'

'Good luck!' and she gave me a smile. A large man with his own frilly shirt said, 'Hi, Jimmy, Matt Margerison, Total TV. I'm producing a comedy-clips show for Sky One called "When Plastic Surgery Goes Bad" – I'd love to have lunch with you some time,' and he gave me a card.

'Oh, thank you very much, um, well, I'm busy on Wednesday and I'm going to see my parents on Monday although I could move them to Tuesday . . .'

'Gimme a call,' he shouted back as he headed off into the throng, already catching someone else's eye.

I walked into the bar and a man presented me with a tray that offered a choice of champagne or orange juice. This time I was not going to do anything as embarrassing as ask how much the drinks were. In fact, I thought I'd forgo the champagne and request a glass of beer from the curiously deserted bar. I got myself a lager and turned to survey the setting when I heard the barman calling me back. 'Oi – that's three fifteen.' I'd never understand how this all worked. The really expensive drink was free, but if you wanted an everyday beverage you had to pay wildly over the odds. The extra fifteen pence was a touch of genius. They must have thought, Look, if we whack the price up to three quid it'll be obvious we're taking the piss, so let's call it three fifteen and everyone will think it's been carefully costed.

I stood alone and sipped my drink, wishing that Nancy or another of my friends could be here to share it with me. Nancy would have loved all this glamour. No, on second thoughts, she would have hated it. She would have felt self-conscious and enormous just because she was a normal size fourteen and did not have the figure of a nine-year-old child. Actually Nancy described herself as a 'fourteen-stroke-twelve', the latter figure added on as a permanent aspiration. I had entered this hotel by walking on a red carpet. Nancy would have said, 'We can't walk on that. Come to the side.' At the end of the meal she would have stacked up the dirty dinner plates to make it easier for the waiter. It would have been as much as I could do to stop her offering to help with the washing-up.

'Hello, stranger,' said a woman's voice behind me, and I turned to see Stella looking stunning in a tiny dress made by sewing some sequins onto a handkerchief.

'Oh my goodness! Hello there!' I said, and for the first time

I gave her a kiss on the cheek, which went slightly wrong as she went to give me a second kiss on the other side and I realized this too late, leaving her craning her neck towards my retreating head.

'You never said you'd be here tonight,' I stammered.

'Last-minute decision,' she whispered. 'But I told them to put me next to you on the table plan. Come on,' and she took my hand and led me through to the dining room. Everyone stopped their conversations and stared at us open-mouthed. Who is that with Stella Scrivens? everyone seemed to be thinking. I followed her, offering a polite smile to the staring guests as the men tried not to let their suppressed envy cause them to snap their champagne glasses in two. She must be interested in me, I thought. To suddenly come along and get herself seated next to me, it's because I'm really starting to make it, that's what happens . . .

The dining hall felt roughly the size of Shea Stadium, and was packed with large white circular tables brimming with flowers and bottles of wine and glistening cutlery. They had invited about a thousand people for dinner, which was probably just as well. I mean, with a dining room this size you wouldn't want to invite a couple of friends round for a bowl of pasta; it wouldn't feel right. On every seat was a fancy carrier bag stuffed with presents: a T-shirt promoting a new cable channel, a soon-to-be-released comedy video, a box of cigars, aftershave and perfume, a disposable camera – all sorts of treats and surprises that were handed out free to everyone attending. As I arrived at my designated place, all the privileged overpaid people of the show business industry were greedily rifling through their goody bags like spoilt children on Christmas morning. The champagne was free, the food was free and obviously you'd expect a grown-up party bag as well to take home in your courtesy car. As far as I could work out, the richer you got, the less you had to pay for; they had taken 'to each according to their need' and turned it on its head.

As I toyed with my cold starter I attempted a conversation with the man on my other side, a slightly drunk Scouser who had an uncomplicated analysis of the evening's proceedings, though it was one he expressed quite emphatically. 'These awards are a load of bollocks. It's all bollocks, all of it. These people: bollocks; this whole industry: complete bollocks; these prizes: meaningless bollocks; all these free gifts: marketing bollocks; this food: pure bollocks.'

At which point I think I pushed away the small plate of half-eaten pâté and popped a bit of gristle out from my mouth into a paper napkin. It seemed perverse that the people who were at the ceremony had less interest in the event than the people who'd be watching at home. We looked at the list of nominations and Stella seemed to know a fair bit about it all.

'Who's getting the Lifetime Achievement Award?' I asked.

'Benny "Bonk-bonk" Bullivant.'

'For lifetime achievement?' said the man on her other side. 'But he's only mid-forties.'

'Yeah, but he's got AIDS; didn't you know?'

'Oh, fair enough, then.' He shrugged. It turns out that the Lifetime Achievement Award is the last rites of the showbiz industry.

The second course was a chicken leg with new potatoes. Everyone got a leg. There was no breast. That's a thousand chicken legs but no white meat, the sort of order that would really annoy my butcher in Seaford. I ate mine slightly too quickly and noticed that, just as with her starter, Stella didn't even pick up her knife and fork. She didn't even pretend to push stuff around the plate for a while. Some people didn't eat

171

wheat; some didn't eat dairy products. Stella didn't eat food. I sat there longingly eyeing her untouched roast chicken, but I guessed it wasn't correct form here to help yourself to someone else's leftovers.

Stella had a lot of people to whom she wanted to go and say hello and I watched her confidently flit from table to table. Everyone watched her cross the room. They all knew who she was and I felt proud that she'd been sitting with me. Finally she plonked herself in an empty seat beside an old friend, while the chair's original occupant returned and patiently waited for her to finish. I sat at my table, now feeling a little self-conscious and increasingly nervous as the awards ceremony proper was about to begin. I decided to slip away to the toilet just to get a break from it all. But they had even contrived to make the act of relieving oneself into a luxurious five-star experience. Standing to attention by the washbasins was a short old man in a ridiculous maroon bell-boy outfit designed to be as demeaning to him as possible. He was employed to hand everyone a little towel as they finished washing their hands. Thank God for that – otherwise they might have had to pick up the towelette from the pile themselves and then where would they have been? The towels were passed from the pile with a pair of gleaming tongs, just in case the old man didn't already feel completely worthless. 'Right, Stanley, on Saturday night, there's a big awards ceremony at the Grosvenor House Hotel in Park Lane. A five-course meal, free champagne, funny speeches, the lot. And you're going to be there . . .'

'In the banqueting suite?'

'No – your job is to stand in the bog all night passing hand towels to everyone. Oh, and use these disinfected tongs because we don't want any of the guests cringing at the thought of catching your filthy germs, you disgusting little leper.'

I pushed open the toilet door and was relieved to see there was no one employed to squeeze into the cubicle with you to tear off little pieces of toilet paper and pass them across with tweezers when required. I locked the door and sat down. I didn't need to go to the toilet. I kept my trousers done up and sat down on the toilet lid for a break. I just needed somewhere to hide for a few minutes, somewhere to get a rest from pretending to be relaxed. What was I doing here? It was ridiculous. I must be insane to have let it come this far. It was all going to come out this evening. The compère was going to announce the shortlist and then reveal that they had tried to find anyone who'd seen Jimmy Conway, and discovered that he'd never been on a stage in his life. At which point I would try to bolt for the door only to be grabbed by two ex-SAS bouncers who'd march me to a cashpoint machine and make me pay hundreds of pounds for my three glasses of champagne and chicken leg with new potatoes and cherry tomato.

I tried to calm myself down. It was all right; this evening was just a bit of an adventure. My old showbiz chum Mike Mellor would win best new stand-up. I would applaud and try not to look disappointed or jealous and that would be that. I would drop this ridiculous charade and disappear out of sight after my hour in the sun. I should just enjoy tonight like a society fairground ride.

I heard the door swing open and voices braying and echoing off the tiled walls.

'So whose table are you on?'

'Oh, Penny Webster; directed *What Are You Laughing At?*. You know, the comedy-clips panel show on E4. It's up for Best Comedy Quiz.'

'Oh yeah, I taped that but I haven't watched it yet. I'm here with Mike Mellor – he's up for best new stand-up.'

'He must be in with a chance, isn't he?'

'Well, they reckon it's between him and Jimmy Conway. Conway's been very clever . . . not doing telly, being so selective about where he plays. Makes him seem special from the outset.'

'Yeah, well, the papers love him. Did you see that *Sunday Times* spread?'

'Yeah, though I'm not sure the journalist really got to the heart of him.'

'Have you seen his act then?'

'Er – well, not recently. I saw him ages ago, you know. When he was just starting out. But I could tell he was going to be huge even back then. That fish routine. Bloody hilarious.'

'Was that at the Banana Christmas Cabaret a couple of years ago?'

'Er – might have been actually, yeah.'

'God, that's amazing – I was at that gig as well. I thought he looked familiar. Yeah, he was really good, wasn't he?'

'Yeah – although, um . . . I've seen him do better than that.'

'Where was that?'

'Catch a Rising Star in New York. He brought the house down.'

Game set and match to the biggest liar. Well, second biggest liar after the bloke sitting on the toilet lid anxiously lifting up his legs in case he was identifiable from his shoes and trousers, even if they were the same black shoes and black trousers that everyone else was wearing. If these two poseurs could convince themselves they'd seen my act, were others going around saying how good I was? Was it possible that the jurors deciding on the award might fail to admit to each other that they'd never actually seen me? Would they all bluff and jump on the Jimmy Conway bandwagon to avoid the risk of looking hopelessly out of touch? A couple of years before I'd been approached in a bookshop and asked to take part in a literary poll. When they asked me for my Novel of the Century I went all pensive to hide my panic and then said solemnly, '*Ulysses*, by James Joyce.' I'd never got beyond page bloody one of *Ulysses*, but it just felt like the right sort of answer to give the clever girl with glasses. And indeed *Ulysses* went on to win the poll. Had everyone who'd given that reply been bluffing just like me?

I sat in the cubicle for another few minutes, but my visit to the toilet had not been successful. I had not flushed any of my worries away. I had anxiety-constipation. It wasn't just the nomination that made me nervous. It was the easy self-confidence of all the beautiful people around me. I was a fish out of water, I thought. No, worse than that: a fish that had been taken out of water and expected to play centre forward for Manchester United in front of 60,000 people. Hmm . . . was this the beginnings of that legendary fish routine? I think not.

I unlocked the cubicle door and realized I ought to flush the toilet to keep up appearances. And having pretended to use the lavatory I then felt obliged to wash my hands. As I did so, I was handed a towel by the man with the least rewarding job in the world.

'Um, thank you, thanks a lot.'

'You're welcome,' he said with a routine courtesy as he stepped back into position beside his pile of clean folded towels. I wiped my hands for slightly longer than normal, demonstratively making thorough use of the little towel, hoping he might feel that little bit more appreciated. 'Do you know what, dear?' he'd say to his wife that night. 'There was one man who genuinely relished the towel I gave him this evening. He made sure he got every last drop of water off his hands – it's moments like that that make my job worthwhile.'

I considered unbuttoning my shirt and giving my armpits a quick wipe but decided that might be overdoing it, so I just did the backs of my hands and wrists once more.

As I did so, my eye caught a bowl of coins next to the soap. For a split second I thought this was such a luxurious venue that they left bowls of free money lying around like complimentary sweets; handy amounts of loose change to which you could help yourself if you fancied a pound coin or two. Then I realized that I was supposed to tip the towel man. The bowl contained mostly pound coins, with a couple of fifty-pence pieces pushed to the bottom to discourage anyone from leaving such a paltry amount. A tip? I thought in astonishment. For giving me a towel?

I have never thought of myself as a particularly mean person but I couldn't help feeling that a pound was rather a lot to pay to someone for handing you a flannel. In the Mr One Pound shop in Seaford you could get a set of three screwdrivers for a pound. Or a plastic football. Or a framed picture of a little girl holding a kitten. Here you didn't even get to keep the flannel. And it's not as if I'd been presented with any choice – I mean, I wouldn't have minded picking up my own little towel, rather than pay a pound to have someone do it for me.

If there was any moisture on my palms now it was from anxiously sweating over what I should do next. I quickly realized that I had no choice but to add to the pile of gold coins that the towel millionaire was extorting from all the foolish famous people. No, no, no, stop! I had to put such petty parsimony out of my head; he probably relied on these few tips to feed his wife and disabled sister-in-law. What could I have been thinking of, being so mean as to hesitate over the price of half a pint of lager? I handed him the used towel and with a confident smile reached into my pocket and took out the only coin in there. Shit. A two-pound coin. Two quid. That was an absolute fortune. In the Mr One Pound shop in Seaford, that could buy – well, two of anything.

'Oh, erm – I haven't got any change, sorry.'

'Beg your pardon, sir?'

Damn, he was going to make me repeat it.

'I haven't got any change – you know, to pay for the towel. Sorry.'

'There's no charge for the towels, sir – and any tip is at sir's discretion.'

'That's what I meant, sorry about the tip. I've only got a two-pound coin.'

'Very good, sir.'

Aargh! Why did I say that? 'A two-pound coin' like it was a fifty-pound note or an American Express Gold Card. During this exchange another satisfied customer had taken a towel, quickly dried his hands and casually hurled a pound coin into the bowl with the expertise of Michael Jordan throwing a basketball.

'Um, how about if I put my two-pound coin into the bowl but took a pound coin back in change?'

'Beg your pardon, sir?'

'I was just thinking, because two pounds is a bit too much, can I put in this two-pound coin and take out a one-pound coin, leaving you with a pound? Which is still quite a lot after all.'

'Thank you, sir. Much obliged.'

Wow – was I classy! James Bond move over, there's a new ice-cool player in town. Sophistication, casual understated generosity, that certain *je ne sais quoi* – some of us are just born with it, I suppose. A man standing at the urinals had been listening to this exchange. He looked across at me taking my change from the little plate and then glanced down at the appendage in his hand and then back at me as if there was no discernible difference between the two. As I went to push the door to go, I told myself I might have handled the tipping business with a little more dignity and poise. But I discovered too late that the door opened inwards and I headbutted the wood panelling in my eagerness to leave. I did a double-take and then pulled the handle towards me, attempting a faint long-suffering smile at the towel man who switched his gaze away from me immediately our eyes met. I had begun by wanting him to feel better about himself, and after encountering such a total prat he must been eternally grateful to be the person he was.

I had been intending to get another beer from the bar on the way back but decided to switch from paying for the beer to drinking the free wine. I had to cut down on the volume of liquid. It was bad enough forking out £3.15 for a half of lager without paying another quid on top to siphon it off again at the other end. Before I had come along this evening I had thought I was only there to make up the numbers and there was no chance of me winning the award. I had not thought up an acceptance speech or worried about how much I was drinking. I tried to tell myself I still believed this, even after the conversation I'd overheard in the toilets. But when I went to fill up my wine glass a strange thing happened. I put the bottle down again and switched to water. Just in case, I said to myself; just in case.

The plates were being cleared away and the ceremony proper was about to begin. There must have been something not quite right with that chicken because an ache was growing in my stomach. Stella had returned and I talked to her about all the times Billy had been nominated. He loved collecting prizes. Stella said he'd often volunteered to collect awards for showbiz colleagues who were unable to make the ceremony and then he'd simply refuse to pass them on. Stella still had one of Hugh Grant's BAFTAs on her mantelpiece.

'Do they ever tell you beforehand whether you've won?'

'Well, they used to have to tell Billy because he'd only turn up if he was collecting a prize,' said Stella. 'His agent demanded to know beforehand. But, no, a lesser celebrity wouldn't normally know until the same moment that everyone else does.'

The guy next to her chipped in. 'One time I was up for this award and so was the producer with me. And just before they opened the envelope the cameraman shoved me out of the way to get a really good shot of the nominee sitting beside me. That sort of gave me a clue.'

I tried to smile but my nerves must have made it seem very false.

'Usually you know you are not going to win it,' he said; 'that Joe Bloggs is going to win it. You are convinced it is impossible that you could win it, this is so clearly Joe Bloggs's year, but then they open the envelope and for a split second you think, maybe I can win it, maybe she's about to read out my name.'

'And then she does read out your name?'

'No, she reads out Joe Bloggs's name. And then you feel disappointed and stupid for even briefly deceiving yourself that any other outcome was possible.'

'Jimmy's up for the award after this one,' said Stella, squeezing my arm.

'Oh well, good luck,' he said, marginally impressed, and we sat back to watch the proceedings begin.

The first award was for the Radio Personality of the Year and was decided by a *Radio Times* readers' poll. The winner was generally the radio presenter who did the most telly. A while back a former DJ had won it for three years in a row without ever performing on the radio once. Roving cameramen picked out the nominees whose faces were then transmitted on huge monitors beside the stage as their names were read out. The winner was announced and he gave a slightly too shocked expression before kissing his partner and leaping up to collect the statuette, giving a word-perfect impromptu speech.

My category was up next. I felt myself physically shaking. The host made some joke about this room containing the biggest collection of comedians outside the House of Commons, which got only a small laugh so they applauded instead to show they at least appreciated the sentiment. A cameraman kneeled right down beside me and stuck a big lens in my face. Occasionally you come across people you sense are a little bit too intrusive into your personal space, but this bloke was ramming the door down and barging right in there with a live television camera. Apparently the trick is to behave as if you are completely unaware that a camera or anyone was even looking at you, but I was buggered if I was going to pick my nose and wipe it under the chair. I adopted a sort of benign smile that I imagined was relaxed yet confident, interested and yet enjoying myself. I casually reached to take a sip of water and discovered slightly too late that it was a small vase of flowers.

The host was looking out towards a camera but from where I was sitting I could see his script scrolling past on an autocue. 'Previous winners of this award have gone on to create some of the finest lager commercials ever made,' he quipped. The shadow chancellor of the exchequer had been invited on to read out the nominations for best new stand-up, and did so with such fluency that at home millions of voters must have thought, Well, he read those names off that card pretty well; he'd clearly do a fantastic job running the economy. The little red light on the end of the camera came on as they read my name out – and then it was off again as the faces of the other nominees momentarily filled the screens. But for that split second the camera on me was live; my face had been beamed into millions of homes around the country. In nearly every road in every town, in every block of flats in every city, some-one will have been looking at me. People in the pub in Seaford, old school friends in East Grinstead, all of them would have sat up and gone, 'Bloody hell, that's Jimmy!'

The shadow minister opened the large gold envelope and read the name on the card to himself before sharing it with the expectant crowd. And in that split second I noticed the little red light on the television camera that was pointing at me had come on again and I couldn't understand why that should be and then he leaned towards the microphone and proclaimed: 'And the winner is . . . Jimmy Conway!'

I didn't move or react for a second or two. Stella kissed me on the cheek and said, 'Go on, Jimmy.' A thousand people were all looking directly at me as I tremulously rose to my feet, stunned and terrified and totally elated. I was the Best New Stand-up Comic in Britain, though with my knees weakening beneath me the 'standing up' bit was in question. I weaved my way between the tables vaguely aware that the band was playing an instrumental version of 'Make 'Em Laugh' that could just be heard over the applause. I realized I was probably rushing too much, so I slowed down to make the moment last longer. For those few seconds that evening I was Robbie Williams coming out for an encore, I was Adolf Hitler approaching the podium at the Nuremberg rally, I was Ronaldo walking up to collect the World Cup. The chairs magically parted for me as I walked and the applause and adulation built, and it flashed through my mind that millions of viewers at home would be watching my progress to the stage. I was totally the centre of attention, everyone was focused on me; it was like nothing I had ever experienced. Being third donkey in the Infants nativity didn't even come close.

I stepped up onto the podium. What could I possibly say? I recalled Gwyneth Paltrow's speech when she won an Oscar. She said she would like to thank everyone she had ever met in her whole life. Maybe I could do that and then go one better and name them all? I wished I'd been prepared for this moment; had even half a witticism up my sleeve to throw to staring masses.

'Well done,' said the shadow chancellor, managing to sound patronizing in only two words.

'Thanks,' I said accepting his handshake. The host gestured to the microphone for my speech and I could feel my legs shaking behind the lectern. How I would have loved to ride that tiger and wow them all with hilarious in-jokes of the TV world and give little waves to familiar faces in the crowd as I thanked all my friends in the biz. I wished I could have fulfilled all their hopes for me. They were so ready to laugh, but I just didn't have anything funny to say or even the air in my lungs to say them. All these thoughts raced through my head as I stared out at the ocean of smiling faces in front of me. I hadn't said anything for several seconds now and my nervousness was clearly visible. If I'd been prepared I might have been able to sustain the deceit, but the way I was visibly cracking under this pressure left me only one way to go. Confession.

'Look, there's been a terrible mistake,' I blurted out, my voice cracking like a teenage boy. 'I've never done any stand-up in my life!'

The anticipated collective gasp never materialized. Instead a huge wave of laughter swept across the hall, mutating into applause, and I saw guests turning to nod to each other about what a true comic genius they had anointed. 'This is the first time I've even spoken in public,' I went on. 'I teach English as a foreign language in a small town in Sussex.'

The laughter increased, and the host patted me on the back as he wiped away the tears of laughter. 'Brilliant, Jimmy,' he whispered. 'Tell you what, that'll probably happen for real before too long!' and he indicated the route off the stage towards my table as the applause and cheers continued. One or two people were actually trying to lead a standing ovation.

'Thanks, thanks a lot,' I said as various portly television producers shook my hand on the way back to my table.

'Well done, Jimmy,' shouted across someone pretending to know me. And the people on my table who had earlier declared these awards to be of no value or significance now demonstrated this opinion by enthusiastically associating themselves with me and waving to friends at other tables who looked impressed to see them sitting with an award winner. A couple of them even picked up my statuette and used their free disposable cameras to have their pictures taken clutching it.

The rest of the evening was a completely different experience. And obviously it was out of pure necessity that I walked around so much clutching my award. Suddenly I was everyone's best friend. Well almost everyone's. Towards the end of the evening Mike Mellor came over to say there were no hard feelings, and quickly demonstrated that in fact there were. I had my suspicions that he might have drunk slightly too much because he seemed to be struggling with the fairly minor challenge of leaning against a wall.

'So you won then?' he slurred.

'Yes, thanks a lot.' I don't know why I was thanking him; because I'd been anticipating him saying congratulations, I suppose.

'Pretty impressive considering I don't know a single comic who's ever seen you perform.' He tried to stare at me but his eyes kept missing the target.

'Oh well, you should get out of London a bit more,' I said.

'You know why they gave it to you, don't you?'

'Er, because they thought I was the best new stand-up?'

'No, because that's me,' he said, as if this was generally accepted fact. 'No, it's all showbiz politics, innit? It's like a warning shot to the agents – don't price your guys out of the market because there's always this new talent coming along.'

It was true that the chair of the jury had been the BBC chief who had praised me in the *Guardian*. I attempted a wan smile as he continued.

'Especially people who reckon they don't even need agents, like Jimmy Fucking Conway.'

'How did you know my middle name?'

'I know a lot of things about you,' he ploughed on. Although his aggression was alcohol-induced it still scared me that I might have been found out. What exactly did he know?

What were people saying? A smug smile ran across his face as he prepared to lay down his ace of trumps.

'If you're such a great stand-up comic, come down and close the store, right now.'

'I beg your pardon?'

'Come and do the last set at the Comedy Store tonight. Then we'll see how good you really are.'

'Ah no, not possible I'm afraid. I have to stay for the winners' photo call. Another time maybe?'

'Yeah, right!' And he weaved across the room delighted that I'd been unable to rise to his challenge.

I probably would never have stood up to Mike Mellor if I'd been completely sober, but by the end of the evening I was only slightly less drunk than him. With over a dozen other awards to sit through after mine I had found myself excitedly glugging back the wine and then overemphatically applauding every winner in order to demonstrate just how extremely worthwhile I considered these awards to be. I smoked one of the free cigars from my goody bag and every time I emptied a bottle of Chardonnay the wine fairy would magically replace it with a full one. By the end of the night, I think they must have changed the angle of the floor or something, because it never seemed to be under your feet when you expected. I seemed to have lost Stella, but at least I was still looking where I was going, unlike that big pillar with the plant on top that just stepped out in front of me. I went and sat down in the toilets once more and this time closed my eyes for a moment or two. When I came out again it was very confusing because everyone had gone home and the cleaners were sweeping up broken glass in the enormous empty hall. I vaguely remember asking an elderly Asian lady if she had seen a goody bag hanging on the back of a chair at table number 97, but her English was poor and I suddenly felt a little embarrassed to be describing all the luxury gifts the privileged guests had received earlier.

And then I remember wandering through central London to get the night bus back to my parents' house, my bow tie suitably wonky as I clutched this metal figurine as though it were my drunken pal. The night bus was parked up at the bus stop, but the driver wouldn't open up the doors just yet. 'Don't you know who I am?' I thought momentarily. Only when he was ready to set off did he finally press his magic button and I stepped up and announced my destination with the confident air of Mr Success.

'One ninety,' he grunted. I reached into my pocket for the two-pound coin, but then realized that I had rather unwisely invested half of it in a tip for the man who'd passed me a flannel. With people waiting behind me I went through the motions of searching through my pockets knowing full well that I didn't have any other change. I made what I thought was a constructive enquiry, but the driver just looked at me and said, 'Of course we don't take fucking MasterCard.' You would have thought that on seeing my award he would have been so delighted to have me on board that he would have let me travel for free; that he might have even made an announcement to all the other passengers telling them about the special guest who was sharing his journey home with them that night. But apparently not. In today's Britain if you haven't got the bus fare you are not allowed on the bus. Really! You try to brighten up people's lives, to bring a little laughter into this troubled world, and that's all the thanks you get.

And so with a refreshing drizzle fizzing in my face, I began the three-mile walk back to my parents' house. Perhaps it was my guardian angel's way of making sure I didn't leave my award on the bus or fall asleep and wake up in Zone 7, but anyway I didn't care, because my head was still spinning with all the excitement of the night that had just been. It was without doubt the greatest evening of my life. I felt a sensation so alien and so intoxicating, a feeling of being someone special and interesting, someone people wanted to know and talk to.

About a mile from home a police car slowed right down beside me, coming rather dangerously close, I thought, and the officers peered through their windscreen at this strange lonely figure walking through the night.

'Excuse me there,' said the police officer through the car window. 'Could you walk on the pavement, please, not down the middle of the road?'

'Oh sorry, I didn't realize,' I said, hoping they would ask me about the unusual object I was carrying.

'And where've you been this evening then?'

'I've been to the British 'Biz Awards at Grosvenor House in Park Lane,' I said, which I thought was guaranteed to prompt more interested questions.

'OK, sir, take care now.'

What? Were they going to leave it at that? I was shocked at the lazy inadequacy of their detective work and felt obliged to provide answers to the sort of enquiries I felt it their duty to make.

'Yes, so if you're wondering what this is in my hand, it's an award. My award, which I won. At the awards ceremony.'

The driver leaned across. 'Was that the thing on the telly this evening?'

'That's right. BBC1.'

'I watched most of that before I came on duty. What did you win then?'

'Best New Stand-up.'

'Oh yeah, I recognize you now,' he said, seeming more impressed. 'Well, why don't you hop in the back? We'll give you a lift home.'

'VIP in the car – let's give it some blue!' said the driver and they put on their flashing light and sped me through the empty streets. 'Tell me,' he said as he pulled up outside my parents' house, 'where do you get your ideas from?'

'Oh, there's a little shop in North London called Just Ideas of Hampstead. I buy them all there.'

They had a good laugh at that. In fact, they laughed at everything I said. And as the car pulled away and they waved goodbye, I imagined the chat in the police canteen the next day. 'Yeah, we gave that Jimmy Conway a lift home last night. You know, that comic who won the award on the telly last night. Yes, very funny bloke he was. Very funny bloke.'

— 8 —

27 Elms Crescent,
East Grinstead,
West Sussex,
England

Dear James,

It is important to remember that being a star is not all having
fun and going to parties. It is also a great deal of jolly hard
work. That's partly the reason why I'm quietly confident that
I will make it. Hard work is something I have never been
afraid of. As long as the work is not too difficult and I really
enjoy doing it, then I'm prepared to do whatever it takes. As
long as it's not too physical and it's indoors and in the dry
and it's not algebra or clause analysis or anything, then I'll
just stick with it and keep on going until the job's done. Like
when I start my summer project on the History of the Tudors,
I'll probably end up going mad and doing a whole page on
Elizabeth alone!

But although you work hard, Jimmy, you play hard too. I

mean, it wouldn't look too good on This Is Your Life if everyone said, 'Well, we never saw much of him – he was always at
home working.' So you should work hard, but not so hard that
you just want to go to sleep when you have finished working.
You should leave some energy for playing hard afterwards. I'm
not actually sure what 'playing hard' really means, but I'm
sure you will by the time you read this. I think it involves
going to a lot of parties and things and sometimes staying up
till one in the morning. If it means heavy drinking remember
that it's not actually very clever or grown-up to get drunk
and lose control. In fact, it's rather pathetic (e.g. Dad at
Midnight Mass). And if there are any people on drugs at these
parties, well then you just say, 'I'm sorry, there are drugs
here, I'm leaving.' And then you leave. But apart from that,
you will probably have developed a reputation as a bit of a
wild one! Like at midnight or whatever you might suddenly
suggest that everyone just runs out and jumps in the swimming
pool! Obviously having checked that the pool area is well lit
and that everyone is a competent-to-strong swimmer, say up to
Bronze Award standard.

If you are going to be on This Is Your Life, it will of course
be totally unexpected, but that doesn't mean you can't
practise your surprised look in the years running up to it.
It might be worth working out exactly what you are going
to say when they jump out at you as well, because if you
start off by going 'Oh Bl**dy H*ll!' or something
unbroadcastable like that, they might decide to stop there
and then and go and do a lady sports star or something
instead and that would be a disaster. I mean, it would be
such a shame for all your fans who would have so liked
to hear all about your early life and how hard you had to
work to make it to the top.

I think I shouldn't start my project on the Tudors until I've done a proper study plan. I've discovered that Henry VIII only had two of his wives beheaded, although that's still too many. In fact, it is actually 'sexist', but they didn't think about things like that in history.

I'll write again soon,
Jimmy

'Award-winning stand-up Jimmy Conway and Stella Scrivens share a joke with camp comic Graham Norton and his mystery companion.' This was the caption beneath the photo in *You* magazine the following week. There I was, holding up my award for the camera while Graham Norton looked at it rather suggestively. I was interesting and famous enough to feature in the Party People section of *You* magazine. I had really arrived: I was an official Party Person. Which is more than can be said for the shadow chancellor. You had to feel sorry for him, really: twenty years as a member of Parliament, working his way up to become a leading opposition spokesman who might soon be running the national economy. It was quite an achievement when you thought about it and, all right, so he wasn't as well known as some politicians, but you would have thought that *You* magazine would have checked before describing him as camp comic Graham Norton's mystery companion.

Nancy wasn't as pleased for me as I'd hoped. 'You looked like you were enjoying yourself on the television,' she said curtly.

'Er, well, it was quite an exciting evening.'

'Did Stella Scrivens kiss all the award winners or just you?'

'She was just pleased that I'd won. It was a showbiz party, everyone kisses everyone.'

'Yes, she seemed to be squeezing your arm or laughing at your jokes all evening.'

'Nancy, you and I split up nearly a decade ago. Why should it concern you that Stella Scrivens or any other girl should happen to kiss me?'

'Yes, but we're still *friends*, remember?' she said. 'And as your *friend*, I just don't think you should be flirting with that bloody walking Barbie doll. It's only six months since her husband died.'

'I wasn't flirting with her. I was "comforting" her. It said so in the *Sun*.'

'I just think you could do a lot better than her, that's all. Speaking as a *friend*.'

I had wanted to buy all my old mates a drink to celebrate the award but the whole evening fell a bit flat. When Dave said, 'Statistically speaking, there are not very many people in China,' everyone just nodded and agreed with him. An hour later Norman said to me: 'I lost my air guitar final, in case you were going to ask.'

'Oh sorry, Norman. God, it had completely slipped my mind.'

'It doesn't matter,' he mumbled, though clearly it did.

'I bet you were the best.'

'No, it was my fault. I just went to pieces under the pressure. I must have looked ridiculous.'

Apparently Panda had thought Norman deserved a second chance and asked the judges for a viva. Chris laughed and said, 'What does he want one of them for? They were crappy cars.'

After I won the award all kinds of exciting new things started happening for me but now I felt increasingly unable to tell any of my friends. There were more interviews, more photo sessions and more features. The papers didn't just want to know what was in my fridge; they wanted to know where I ate, to see a room of my own and hear about my kind of day. TV producers all simultaneously had the same original idea of putting Jimmy Conway's name on the proposed cast list for their sketch-show pilots. Various heads of development invited me out to have lunch with them. If nothing else I saved a fortune in food bills and put on about eight pounds in a couple of weeks. None of them could understand why I would not make one exception just for them and secretly reveal where I would be performing my next stand-up set. I was quite principled about this and nobody was ever informed; such was my determination to uphold the principles of guerrilla comedy. The result was that a number of TV executives were forced to start regularly going to comedy clubs in the hope of finally seeing my celebrated act. Unfortunately it seemed they just weren't going to the right venues; on the plus side, several other promising young comics got noticed and were offered their first break in television.

One or two of the producers tentatively raised my resolution not to do television, and I explained that this only referred to my stand-up material. If they wanted me to appear on a make-over show or a celebrity survival challenge then I would be more than happy to oblige. I was interviewed for a nostalgia clips show called *Weren't The Old Days Like, Soooo Embarrassing?* and after some footage of David Soul singing 'Don't Give Up On Us Baby' there I was telling a nostalgic anecdote about the summer of punk. As it happens I was too young to remember punk rock but they still wanted me on because the people who really could remember it turned out to be too old to appeal to their target audience. So I sat in front of the camera and trotted out a prepared line I had thought was quite funny. 'Pop music today . . .' I sighed. 'It's not like the punk rock we used to listen to. I mean, these days, well, you *can* hear the words. And the songs *do* have a proper tune . . .'

The producer, who was interviewing me from behind the camera, didn't react to this joke at all and just glanced at her clipboard and said, 'Erm, yeah, Jimmy, when you look back at that time, would you say it was almost as if there were no more heroes?'

'Er, well, a bit, I suppose,' I replied, slightly disappointed that my preparation seemed to have been a waste of time.

'Remember my questions won't be in the final edit.'

'Oh yeah, sorry,' and then I took a breath. 'When I look back at those days, it's like there were no role models left, there was nothing to believe in, it's like, there were – no more heroes.'

And in the broadcast version they cut from me saying that line straight to 'No More Heroes' by the Stranglers and that was the only appearance I made. She had attempted to get me to idly muse that we had felt that we had No Future and that Something Better Change and that Teenage Kicks had been so hard to beat, but then she became suspicious that I was onto her when I attempted to tell an anecdote that ended with the line 'And so I said to him, "Yes, Sir, I Can Boogie".'

I watched my appearance on the programme and decided that at least I wasn't as underwhelming as most of the other 'celebrity' contributions on the show. Who are all these people? I kept thinking as I fast-forwarded through the tape they sent me; I've never heard of half of them. I decided that the way to avoid being one of these anonymous rent-a-quotes would be to make as many appearances as possible and then I'd be a slightly famous rent-a-quote.

I took part in a live discussion on breakfast television. The depletion of cod stocks in the North Sea had caused several tabloids to do features on the possible extinction of the traditional British fish and chips and they decided this was the sort of thing that demanded my particular expertise. On the phone the researcher explained to me that since they had three serious pundits, they thought Jimmy Conway with his famous fish routine might be able to add a lighter note to the proceedings. So I found myself sitting in the green room with a Conservative from the House of Lords, a desperate trawlerman who'd come down from Hull and a Green MEP from Holland. All the guests for the various other items were in there too, flicking through that morning's newspapers or sipping endless cups of coffee. The Ethiopian ambassador was asked if he was the skateboarder, and then another researcher said, 'No, he's famine – skateboarding's in make-up.' 'Are you HRT?' they said to the Dutch MEP before adding, 'Oh no, sorry, you're all fish aren't you?' Our microphones were clipped on and during the news and weather we were quickly ushered onto the sofas by a floor manager, and then the presenter said, 'Has cod had its chips? With me are four people to discuss the end of a great British tradition.' I sat there waiting for her to ask me something while the two politicians talked non-stop and then finally she said to me, 'Jimmy Conway, what's your take on all of this?' and I looked skywards and said, 'Cod! I mean, what a stupid fish that is! They keep swimming into trawler nets and they taste delicious. All those millions of years spent evolving, you'd think they would have had the sense not to taste so nice, wouldn't you? So, cod, you're going to be extinct. Well, whose fault is that then? Just accept it and move on!'

The presenter looked a little shocked and when she realized I had stopped suddenly faked slightly too much laughter before adding, 'Thanks very much and now here's Kelly with business breakfast update.' I have a feeling I may have said 'dodo' instead of 'cod' by mistake but either way it suddenly didn't feel very funny with the environmentalist and the trawlerman sitting there beside me. He'd come all the way from Humberside and hadn't said a single word. He'd been asked a couple of questions that had both been answered by the politicians and he never got his chance again. 'Yeah, I wondered if four guests might be too many for this item,' said the researcher to him nonchalantly when he complained that his entire crew had avoided putting to sea so they could watch him stick up for their industry. 'Never mind, hopefully you'll get longer next time,' she said as if there would ever be a next time for him. So the poor fishing industry never got defended but hey ho, not to worry, at least Jimmy Conway found out that he still didn't have a fish routine.

Because very few of Britain's broadcasting organizations, national newspapers, PR companies and media players seemed to be based in Seaford, I found myself regularly having to stay in London for several days at a time. My parents seemed delighted to have me there and Betty didn't seem to object to eating organic dog food. Although Mum was always exhausting, there was a definite shift in my parents' attitude towards me. Previously when Mum began her monologues you never knew where that hurtling train of thought might end up, but now when I overheard her conversations with her network of friends I could guarantee that the success of her youngest son would always somehow be incorporated into the narrative.

'Oh, hello, Marjorie, it's Val here, we had a wonderful day at the Eden Project, Brian Lacy was very brave and walked all the way round which is very hard when you've got one shoe built up two inches higher than the other, people do tend to stare of course I suppose it wasn't so bad when platform shoes were all the rage, even if it was just the one, mind you I always thought that was such a dangerous fashion, I'm surprised Ben Elton didn't keep twisting his ankle, not Ben Elton, I mean the other one who sang 'Crocodile Rocker', you know he did the song at Diana's funeral, I do think it's good the Queen is finally accepting Camilla, poor Charles has to be allowed to get on with his life it's so hard being in the public eye, but

Jimmy seems to handle it very well, did you see him on Breakfast Television this week, a very interesting discussion about fish, a big Mercedes picked him up from the house with a proper chauffeur and everything although he didn't have a hat, six o'clock in the morning he rang the doorbell, I must do you my cod mornay before they're extinct, John Elton that's it, not Ben Elton, John Elton I knew I'd get it in the end, I wonder if they're brothers.'

Now my mother's stream of consciousness would always incorporate my latest appearance or interview. It wasn't so much a stream of consciousness, really, more of a torrent, a Niagara Falls of consciousness.

Mum had spent the past year planning the party for their golden wedding anniversary – an event I had been dreading because of the amount of defensive self-justification it would have involved on my part. 'Are you still working part-time at that language school Jimmy?' 'No plans to settle down and have children yet, Jimmy?' But the change in my fortunes meant that in the event it was my brother Nicholas who seemed to be thrown on to the defensive.

'So, Nicholas – what is it like to have a famous younger brother?' he was asked while standing right beside me.

'Yes, he seems to be doing quite well at this comedy lark,' he said through gritted teeth. 'Shame he won't let any of us come and see him.'

The party went off very well and I managed to remember which elderly family friend was suffering from which fatal condition. Brian Meredith said hello and I said, 'I'm very sorry to hear you've got – er, Parkinson's, is it?'

'That's right.'

Yes! I thought to myself, delighted with my excellent memory. I correctly matched the illness to the pensioner throughout the evening until I thought Ray Dowie had Huntingdon's when in fact he and his wife had just moved to Huntingdon. He only had a hiatus hernia. Damn!

Now they had seen me on the television they all imagined I must be some sort of millionaire. 'So, are they paying you well, these TV people?'

'Oh well, mustn't grumble,' I replied evasively.

'What car are you driving these days?'

'Well, I don't do much driving to be honest – they tend to send chauffeurs to pick me up,' I parried, determined not to reveal that I was still driving the same rusty Nissan with its own in-car pond under the carpet.

'So are you still renting the house in Sussex, or are you thinking of buying somewhere, maybe something a little more substantial?'

I sometimes think it would be simpler if we all walked around with our incomes tattooed on our foreheads so that people didn't have to play this elaborate game of twenty questions to place us on the salary scale. The television appearances did pay, however, and often a lot more than I would have got for a whole week's work at the language school.

My hours at the school had always been fairly flexible but I was stretching Doreen's patience with the number of times I was arranging for other teachers to cover for me. We were sitting in Doreen's office. Unlike most people, her desk was not covered with hundreds of scraps of paper. There was just a lamp, a telephone and a large wicker basket containing two panting miniature schnauzers.

'Peckish, Jimmy?' she asked, unwrapping a couple of Walnut Whips.

'Ooh, yes please.' I loved Walnut Whips.

Then she took the walnuts off the top and passed them over

to me as the dogs wolfed down the remaining chocolate and lightly whipped marshmallow filling.

'They don't like the nuts,' she explained. 'It's funny how things go, isn't it, dear? Before you started this comedy lark I'd had you in mind to possibly teach at a new language school we're setting up in Kuwait.'

'Kuwait? Didn't that end up being part of Iraq or something?'

'No, dear, there was quite a big war to ensure that it wasn't part of Iraq, if you remember. My nephew's found me some premises and the pay would be more than double what you're getting now. But I don't suppose you're interested now you're an up-and-coming comedian.'

'Er, well – that's very flattering, Doreen, but um . . . to be honest, Kuwait, I mean, you know if it was the United Arab Emirates that might be different.'

'Really?' she said.

'No, I was joking.'

'Oh, right, well, that's your main job now, I suppose. Are you planning to stay on here part-time at the school or will you finally be moving on to better things?'

The dogs on her desk were staring at me. They expected a straight answer to this question.

'I dunno. I hadn't really thought about it. But don't worry. I'll give you plenty of notice.'

My wages at the language school depended on the number of lessons I taught, but my regular income was just enough to keep me in dog food, even if dinner guests often expected something nicer. Of course, I had various other investments. My foreign currency reserves would have been worth a small fortune if any of those drachma coins or lire notes had still been legal tender in their respective countries. The success of my other investments was dependent on the correct six balls falling out of the machine on a Saturday evening. So when I was asked if I was interested in meeting an advertising agency who'd had the idea of getting me to do some stand-up comedy for a television commercial and when I was told how much money would be involved if I became the face of the campaign I had to give it very serious consideration. The ad would involve two days' filming. To earn the same amount of money at the language school would take sixty-two years and three months.

'Half a million pounds' was the figure I had heard on the phone. There were all sorts of other words and phrases, such as 'residuals' and 'dependent on repeats' and 'if the contract is renewed', but none of them had lodged in my brain quite as firmly as the phrase 'half a million pounds'. I tried to imagine what on earth I could buy with so much money. My imagination knew no bounds: that amount could buy me half a million of anything in the Mr One Pound shop. In fact, I could buy Mr One Pound outright, except that as a long-term investment it was probably a bad idea because in a few years' time you'd have to change the name to Mr One Euro, which didn't have the same ring, quite apart from having to cut your prices by forty per cent.

It was so much more money than I could ever possibly spend that I thought I'd probably just give a lot of it away. All my friends were so short of cash all the time it would be great just to share it out among us and see all our problems simply melt away. I tried to picture the faces of Norman and Chris and Dave and, most of all, Nancy; it could so transform her life if she wasn't always struggling to buy Tamsin everything she wanted. I didn't need much money. I'd just get myself a nice house and a decent car and that would do me. Just a house and a car and some new clothes. And a laptop computer, and maybe an MP3 player, but not a flash one or anything. And a CD writer – it would be great to do compilation CDs of all your favourite songs. But apart from those few essentials for myself, I'd just give the rest away. I certainly wouldn't waste it on anything vulgar or extravagant. I mean I know a jet ski might seem like a rich boy's toy and, sure, we always used to sneer at the yuppies who whizzed up and down the coast on them, but in practical terms it would probably be a really quick way of popping over to Brighton, so in many ways a jet ski would be a sort of investment.

No, no, I had to tell myself, I didn't want any of that rubbish. If I was going to do this commercial I'd do it for my friends. Nancy had had Tamsin at the age of nineteen and not spent any money on herself since. What was two days' work to me? I'd spent longer than that trying to put up a curtain rail for her. Anyway, I hadn't even landed this commercial yet. I was getting carried away. The producer from the advertising agency wanted to meet me to discuss their idea. 'Do you know the Savoy Grill?' he asked me. Unsurprisingly I didn't know the Savoy Grill, although it sounded very expensive. I hope the cost of this lunch won't be coming off my fee, I thought. As it turned out he wasn't talking about us having lunch together but a 'working breakfast'. This is like a normal breakfast but instead of feeling guilty about sitting in the café before going to the office, you get to feel self-righteous about what long hours you're working instead. I did actually have plans for eight o'clock on Tuesday morning: I'd planned to be in bed asleep, but I feared they might not consider this a sufficiently important appointment to justify moving their meeting.

I turned up embarrassingly early and found myself sitting

alone at a table waiting for the posse from the agency to arrive. Glancing around at the other diners I realized that the Savoy Grill did not have as strict a dress code as I'd imagined, so I propped my big menu up on the table and slipped off my tie.

'Jimmy, hi – you beat us to it,' said a tall man in jeans and a T-shirt, holding out his hand for me to shake. 'I'm Piers,' he said as I stuffed my tie into my jacket pocket and surrendered my hand to a vigorous squeezing. There were six or seven of them who introduced themselves to me and then proceeded to order coffee and croissants.

'Coffee and croissants, Jimmy?'

'Er, sorry, I was a bit early, I've already ordered,' I said as double egg, bacon, sausage, black pudding, mushrooms, tomatoes, baked beans and two slices of fried bread were plonked down in front of me. 'Er, I decided against the croissants. Trying to cut down on my wheat intake, you know. Excuse me, are these fried slices rye bread?'

'No sir,' apologized the waiter. 'We can do you some rye bread if you prefer.'

'Oh not to worry,' I said magnanimously.

With nobody else eating and the focus so completely on me, I did my best to carefully time the moments when I popped a big forkful of food into my mouth. Somehow I got it wrong every time. So when Piers said, 'What did you think of the show-reel we sent you, Jimmy?' I just raised my eyebrows and mimed an enthusiastic 'pretty good actually' sort of face while inside frantically chewing away at large pieces of sausage and bacon. Six faces were staring down the table at me to see what their guest was going to say about their edited greatest hits and I worried that it must look as if I was deliberately stalling for time because I hadn't liked it. I tried to mime a more detailed response combining a seriously impressed expression with vigorous nods but my repertoire was soon exhausted and I was reduced to having to do an apologetic point at my bulging mouth. This managed to elicit a rather forced smile from the woman who'd brought her own herbal tea bag.

Finally I managed to say that I thought it was really good and hoped that would be the end of the matter, and they seemed reassured as they all popped sweetener into their black coffees. 'You didn't think it was at all a bit same-y?' said Lucy. The bastards! They had got me a second time – a whole slice of fried bread folded over a large piece of egg was working its way around inside my mouth. I managed an outraged surprised grunt at the very suggestion that it was all a bit same-y, then shook my head vigorously, furrowing my eye-brows in a serious emphatic way. I was communicating like Guy the Gorilla, though with slightly worse table manners.

It transpired that they had sent me their show-reel because it was they who were trying to impress me. I had gone along imagining that I'd be trying to persuade them to put me on some sort of shortlist but it turned out that the agency were on a charm offensive. They were desperately trying to con-vince me that I really ought to do this advertising campaign and be paid hundreds of thousands of pounds for a couple of days of work. Boy, did they have to twist my arm.

'The idea, Jimmy, is that the ad opens with you on stage in this comedy club, and you're getting laughs, you know, and then we reveal that you're surreptitiously writing a text message on your mobile phone at the same time. And the strapline is: "Visit the bank while you're at work today. Text message banking from the C and P."' A forkful of fried egg was hovering in midair, waiting to see if he was going to ask me a question or begin another monologue. 'I know what you're thinking,' said his assistant, though this was unlikely because what I was thinking was: 'Phew! Managed to eat my egg in time!'

'. . . you're thinking, which bit of my stand-up do they want me to use?'

'Er, yeah, well, that is an issue I suppose,' I conceded.

'Is there any particular routine of yours that springs to mind?' asked Lucy. I placed my hand on my chin and feigned an exaggerated 'thinking hard' expression while staring into the middle distance. 'Ummm . . . well . . . well . . . let me see.'

'What about the fish stuff?' ventured Piers.

'Ooh, I dunno about that,' I said. 'I'd never be able to do it in a club again.'

'What's the fish stuff?' said Lucy.

'That's one of Jimmy's most famous routines.'

'Oh, I love animal jokes, tell us the fish routine, go on,' and there was a murmur of agreement around the table.

'You can't expect him to perform an entire stand-up comedy set sitting down to breakfast at eight in the morning,' said Piers, coming to my rescue. I let out a huge sigh of relief. 'Just give 'em the best bit, Jimmy,' he added, and all the heads along the table leaned inwards in anticipation of this hilarious routine that everyone talked about. They were grinning in a 'this is going to be really good' kind of way and the only way out seemed to be to give them what they wanted. I cleared my throat. 'The thing about fish,' I began, hoping that a well-observed, yet surreal, word-perfect monologue on the subject of fish might suddenly pop into my head from nowhere. There was a chuckle of anticipation from the end of the table. 'The thing about fish is . . .' and then unsurprisingly the words dried up. There was a moment of awkward silence.

'Can I get anyone more tea or coffee?' said the waiter, and

there were groans all around the table. Isn't it always the way? You're just about to tell the punchline of a joke and the waiter interrupts and shatters all the tension. 'Oh no, I can't do it now, the moment's gone,' I said, and then I deflected the attention by asking about why they thought I was right for the job.

'Because we can't afford Elle MacPherson!' said a wag on the end of the table who wasn't there at any subsequent meetings.

'What is precious about you, Jimmy,' said Piers, casting an annoyed look down the table, 'is that you are well known to our target audience around the country but *not* via the television screen.' Privately I wondered whether they needed to fire their market researchers, but I nodded modestly as if I was flattered but unable to contradict them.

'Everyone who's been to your gigs in all those little clubs around the country, they're suddenly going to see you telling them to switch to text banking and because subconsciously they already trust you, it makes the message far more potent.'

At this point I wondered if what I was now involved in could possibly be construed as some sort of commercial fraud. This agency were prepared to pay a lot of money because they valued the reputation I had built up in the provincial comedy clubs. They would be paying me for some unquantifiable aura that I didn't actually possess; they were prepared to shell out for a fame that I had invented. That meant I would be trading under false pretences. You could go to prison for fraud. Unless you were famous, of course. Then you generally got let off. So if I was found guilty, the jury would have also decided that I wasn't much of a celebrity. I tried to imagine the judge passing sentence in the packed courtroom. 'James Elliot Conway: you are a duplicitous con artist who deliberately undertook an elaborate and perfidious fraud in order to swindle this poor defenceless advertising agency out of hundreds of thousands of pounds. Furthermore, millions of television viewers, many of them pensioners, were also taken in by your pathological lying and may have lost their life savings by mistakenly sending their money to someone else's account while they were attempting to master text message banking. I therefore have no choice but to pass the maximum sentence for this offence. You will taken from this courtroom, thence to a place of execution where you will be hanged by the neck until you are dead. And may God have mercy upon your soul.' And throughout this speech my useless defence lawyer would be shaking his head in disappointment because he'd just coloured in the wrong bit of the animal silhouette in his copy of *Puzzler* magazine.

I pushed the remainder of my fried breakfast away and resolved to dissuade the assembled company from this crazy course of action. 'Look, Piers, I don't know what your focus groups or whatever are telling you, but I don't think I'm as famous as you think outside the narrow circles of Medialand. I mean, some of these provincial clubs only hold about a hundred people and I've not been gigging that long,' I pleaded.

Piers was reassuring. 'Jimmy, it's not all focus groups and market research, you know. I want you for this advert because I think you'd be the best person for the campaign. I don't know how you do it but you just have an "ordinary bloke next door" quality about you. You're smiley; you're appealing.'

'And you're very good looking!' blurted out Lucy and then immediately turned red.

'I was in the audience for the 'Biz awards,' continued Piers, 'and when you did that gag from the stage, I thought, Yup, we've just found the person we are looking for. The fact that you're a popular stand-up and have just won an award re-assures the client, but sure, this campaign will obviously still have to work for those viewers who don't know who you are. Yet.' And the word 'yet' was left hanging there meaningfully; the bait of greater fame that this repeated exposure would bring was dangled tantalizingly in front of me.

Piers wanted Jimmy Conway and no one else for this advert. He was a very persuasive person, so confident that when he asked for the bill he didn't even do a mime of scribbling on a little pad. He tried to get me to agree in principle there and then. I said I would sleep on it, but I didn't sleep at all. Deceiving people is one thing, but deceiving people and getting large amounts of money for it suddenly felt like a far more dangerous game. I realized that it wasn't the principle that was keeping me awake here; it was the price. If the advertising agency had shoved three twenties into my hand I would have thought, Brilliant, what a result! The trouble with their offer was that it was too high. Was I nervous about all this money because I still considered myself to be of so little value? If I was really going to become a celebrity shouldn't I force myself to try and start thinking like one? This money might seem like a fortune to Jimmy Conway, the part-time TEFL teacher from Seaford, but to Jimmy Conway the top club comedian – well, it was barely enough to keep him in jet skis. And then I considered the morality of what I was about to do. I thought how Nancy's life could be changed if she could afford a few things for herself once in a while, if she could have a little car and maybe move out of that oppressively cramped flat she shared with her mixed-up daughter. She needed the money more than this agency. I got out of bed and went downstairs to ring their office. I left a message on their answerphone saying I would be delighted to be the public face of text message banking.

'The thing about fish . . .' I mused at the mirror over the mantelpiece. 'The thing about fish . . . is that they can breathe underwater,' I sighed. It needed work.

My contract for this job must have been written by James Joyce after he decided that *Finnegans Wake* was not sufficiently challenging. Joyce is what they call a stream of consciousness writer, meaning that as soon as you read a couple of sentences your mind wanders off into its own in-dividual stream of consciousness, remembering that you were supposed to take the Nissan in for its MOT, and then wondering if a car could fail for having moss growing along the window rims. This contract that I was supposed to read posed an even greater challenge to my level of concentration. In what was perhaps an obscure reference to the artist formerly known as Prince, they dubbed me 'Jimmy Conway, hereafter known as the artist', but beyond that first line all I can remember is a couple of the individual words such as 'pursuant' which I think is a term from heraldry, and *sine qua non* – which I'm sure was Spain's entry in the 1987 Eurovision Song Contest.

I rang the agency and one of the women who'd been at the breakfast was very reassuring about it all and informed me it was a 'standard contract'. She tried to press me on which section I was unsure about, which reminded me of my German teacher asking me precisely which part of the prose comprehension I didn't understand. 'Well, um, just generally. I'm not quite clear what it's saying in general terms.'

'Which paragraph in particular?'

I glanced at the contract in front of me. 'Er, well, you know the bit where it says, "This is an agreement between . . ."'

'Yes.'

'. . . and then at the end, where it says, "Signed on behalf of the artist"?'

'Yes.'

'Well the thirteen pages in between those two sections – that's the bit I don't understand.'

I had come to realize that the figure of half a million pounds was an optimistic forecast of what I might potentially earn if the ad ran and ran and they continued to film subsequent commercials along a similar theme. But it was still more money than I could have imagined earning a few months earlier. The most bizarre aspect of it was that I got one lump sum of money for doing these ads, and then about twice as much on top of that for promising not to do any other commercials for anyone else. Someone said celebrity was the new royalty, and now I was being paid a fortune not to work I was beginning to get an idea of what they meant. I quickly scanned the contract one last time and when I was confident that I wasn't committing myself to a time-share apartment in Lanzarote, I signed on the dotted line.

A car picked me up from my parents' house very early on the first day of filming. Obviously if I'd got there any later we'd only have been able to film the advert one hundred and twenty-seven times rather than one hundred and twenty-nine. I was shown into a bustling studio on an industrial estate in north-west London. It was like the inside of a huge aircraft hangar with people hammering sets, putting up lights, cameras on overhead booms swinging in from above; everywhere people were busy and knowing what it was they had to do. And all this activity was centred round me: Jimmy Conway, the 'I' of the storm.

There is a fairly predictable sensation that develops when everyone starts to behave as if you're really important. It is very tempting to completely agree with them. Like any human being, I'd spent my entire life seeing everything from my point of view, but now it seemed that everyone around me had come round to realize the merit of this perspective. 'Jimmy, you must be wanting some breakfast?' 'Don't worry about that drilling noise, Jimmy, we're getting that sorted.' 'That was a great result for your team last night, Jimmy!' Although I was well used to being the centre of attention at home, one Border collie watching my every move had never felt as gratifying as this. And when it is everyone's job to make you feel special, it seems churlish not to cooperate. If the runner wants to know if he can get you another coffee, you sense that it is only polite to say yes please. You could jump up and say, 'Oh no, let me get you one!' but it would only create embarrassment on both sides. You just have to play out the role of exaggerated importance that has been allocated to you, like the bride on her wedding day or the captain on a cruise ship.

The runner who brought me a coffee said, 'Actually, it's a bit of a coincidence, we have a slight connection.'

'Oh really?' I said, wondering if I ought to recognize him from somewhere.

'Yeah, my ex-girlfriend went to the same school as you, though you weren't there at the same time.'

There was a slight pause while I struggled to find anything to say about this.

'Oh. That's, um, quite a coincidence.'

'Angela Mullery – I don't suppose you knew her?'

'Er, no. Doesn't ring any bells.'

'No, well, she was there about ten years after you.'

'Yeah, well, I was only held back a year nine times in a row, so we must have just missed each other.'

I know he was employed to pander to my every whim, but he didn't have to laugh quite that much.

What a pointless piece of information, I thought as he left me with my cappuccino. And yet he had relayed it with such excitement – we were connected because he had gone out with a girl who went to the same school as me a decade later. 'Jimmy Conway – oh yeah, we worked together and he went to school with my ex-girlfriend . . .' But everyone was finding excuses to come and have a word with me. The assistant producer knocked on my dressing room door to ask if the big basket of fruit was OK, and I said it was fine, and then she pressed me again. 'Are you sure – because we can change it if you're not happy with it.'

So I tried to imply that I was just an ordinary person, that they needn't make quite so much fuss. 'Actually, all those fancy fruits are a bit exotic for my liking, you know, kiwis and kumquats and all that – I couldn't just have an ordinary apple, could I?'

'Of course, Jimmy, that's no problem at all. I'll get you an apple right away,' she said sweetly.

'Only if it's no trouble.'

'It's no trouble at all.'

As my dressing room door swung shut I heard her shouting angrily: 'Who put a fucking fruit basket in Jimmy Conway's dressing room with no fucking apples?'

The setting for this commercial was a small tatty comedy club, so obviously rather than go to a small tatty comedy club the agency had gone to great expense to recreate one in a film studio. While I was up on stage I would be holding the microphone with my left hand and discreetly writing a text message on my mobile phone with my right. Except, for the close-up, it wasn't actually my right hand, it was the hand of Simon the hand model. I was introduced to him and we chatted for a minute or two while I tried not to stare at his hand too obviously. It was OK, you know. It was perfectly fine as hands go, but nothing to write home about if you ask me. I mean, it's not as if my right hand's got seven fingers covered in warts and boils or anything. I saw a horror film once where a zombie ripped out the priest's internal organs. I wonder if that was the actor's own pancreas or they used a professional pancreas model for the close-up. I didn't care for Simon much. At lunch he wore gloves and then he was very angry that there was no pudding left and I heard him saying to the caterers, 'Do you know who I am?' How could they be expected to recognize him when he was wearing gloves?

After much careful deliberation I had finally informed Piers that there was nothing really suitable in my stand-up set that I wanted to use on television so they talked about hiring a couple of gag writers to provide the jokes I'd do at the top of the advert. And then it was decided that with the time available they would only show the end of a routine, without any set up, but my audience would laugh and the viewers at home would just have to take our word for it that it was a great punchline, if only they'd been at the club to hear the rest of it. So I found myself endlessly having to repeat surreal phrases like 'Talk about floppy disks!' (huge laugh) or 'So that's why Mr Spock's ears were so pointy!' (big laugh and applause).

It had started as one of the most exciting days of my life. A few hours later it had become one of the most excruciating. It was as if someone had said, 'Right, Jimmy, we want you to make love to Marilyn Monroe in this speedboat riding the crest of a fifty-foot wave off the coast of Hawaii.' And then they say, 'Right, now can you do that another hundred and twenty times?'

You see people saying things on the television and it looks easy and you think anyone can do that. But there were marks on the floor that I had to hit the moment I said a certain word, but I had to say it slightly differently for this take and remember not to look into the camera lens, and the first time I said my line I had taken sixteen seconds and at the second attempt I had taken fifteen seconds and Piers was asking if I could split the difference.

So I tried to say the line taking exactly fifteen and a half seconds and after three more goes, the girl with the stopwatch said the timing was absolutely perfect and I felt pretty smug for a second.

'No, Jimmy, you ended up about six inches ahead of your mark then – you'll be completely out of focus.'

A couple of the producers mumbled quietly to each other and looked in my direction. Although it was clear that Piers was the person in charge, there were all sorts of other chiefs around to give me notes that contradicted the previous instruction I'd been given. The clients in particular seemed to go out of their way to give me impossible notes that Piers was in no position to dismiss. During the morning I received instructions such as, 'Can you say it slightly more quickly but make it sound less rushed?' and 'Can you try and make the word "and" more comedically interesting?'

Although the instructions were impossible to fathom, they were at least presented to me with the utmost courtesy and caution, as if I was some unexploded bomb that might be detonated by the merest raised voice or unobsequious tone. 'That was really fantastic, Jimmy. What might make it even more stupendous would be if you could just say the words in the right order like you did in the run-through.' I can't imagine there are many other jobs in which people are constantly addressed in this grovelling manner. You don't get sergeant majors on the parade ground saying to their new recruits, 'That was really, really super, I simply adore the way you're all marching in the same direction now, but it would just be to-die-for if you could try a teensy-weensy bit harder to remember to march in step as well.'

It was only because I was the star that they indulged me like this. The 'supporting artists' who were to play the part of my 'audience' were processed like refugees in a detention centre. The second assistant director couldn't have treated them with less respect if he had herded them onto set with an electric cattle prod. Because they were supposed to be in a little comedy club, they all had glasses of beer placed in front of them. It was decided that the simplest thing would be to use real beer poured from cans, which the supporting artists had to sip occasionally, and which would then be topped up to the same level for reasons of continuity. You would have thought that somebody might have spotted the flaw in this plan. I know the advertising people were all on diets and didn't smoke or drink or anything like ordinary folk. But they might have realized that if you force a group of poorly paid extras to sit all day in front of self-replenishing beer glasses, then several hours later they are going to be pissed out of their heads.

Just before lunch I eventually said my line perfectly, the timing was right, I hit the mark on the floor at the right time and the word 'and' was sufficiently comedically interesting. And then one of the extras let out a huge guttural belch that echoed across the set and ruined the perfect take. 'Oops, beg pardon!' he giggled and this set the others off tittering. Piers tried to be cross with them but the person he was shouting at fell off his stool backwards and then lay there giggling.

'Just how much have they had to drink?' he asked angrily.

The girl in charge of filling up their glasses pointed to a carrier bag full of empty beer cans.

'Oh well, that's not too bad,' said Piers.

And then she pointed out the two bulging bin liners brimming with empty beer cans as well.

'This is bloody ridiculous. Whose idea was it to give them real booze?'

'Yours.'

'Was it? Well, you didn't have to give them so much.'

'I was just told to keep the glasses at the same level for continuity.'

'Well, they were sober for the first take and now they're completely rat-arsed, so what sort of continuity is that?'

'I want to go to the toilet,' said the extra still lying on the floor. By now a group of them had started singing. Others had forgotten that they were supposed to be working and were getting up and helping themselves from the stack of distinctive gold cans.

'Special Brew!' shrieked Piers. 'I don't believe it! I thought you were only allowed to drink that in the park. Why don't we give them a meths and paint-stripper chaser while we're at it!' he muttered as 'I'm Forever Blowing Bubbles' echoed tunelessly around the room.

The extras were eventually herded off the set and Piers could barely believe how reasonable I was about the whole thing.

'Honestly, Jimmy, I'm so sorry about all that,' he kept saying.

'It's fine, don't worry about it.' I shrugged, relieved that I was no longer the reason we were running behind schedule.

'God, I've never known a performer be so understanding. We'll have to change things around a bit. Do some close-ups after lunch, and some hand shots. Get Simon's hand to Make-up please!' he called out, and Simon went with it.

The adverts were recorded in two days as scheduled and were due to go out later that month. The first time I saw one was a Tuesday night at eight-twenty. It wasn't a big deal or anything, but I thought I might as well switch the telly to ITV at around that time just to see it. And then everyone else in the Red Lion said: 'Great, Jimmy, can we switch back to the football now?'

One initial transmission didn't change very much. But it's like a hit record: the first time it comes on the radio you barely notice it, but then you hear it a second time and the chorus stays with you. And then it's played again, and now you remember some of the words and notice the saxophone solo in the middle and you find yourself humming along, until with repeated exposure you discover that the whole song has got under your skin and you know every note. The first time my advert went out was like any other television appearance. But it was the cumulative effect of its repeated transmission that really changed things. Jimmy Conway the comedian was repeating the same punchlines on television over and over and over again until the whole nation knew them off by heart. It wasn't an advert for text message banking, it was an advert for me.

Strangers would recognize me and have to stop themselves laughing when they thought about how funny I was. Even though there was no whole joke told on the screen – you just heard a punchline and saw the audience's hysterical reaction – the subconscious association was still 'that face equals funny guy'. People I had barely spoken to over the years would see me coming down the street and grin from ear to ear, nodding as if to say, 'Here comes the joker, what's he going to say now!' Lorry drivers would spot me from their cabs and shout out, 'No wonder Mr Spock's ears are so pointy!' and giggle to themselves as they sped past. I knew things had really changed when I walked past a building site and all the men on the scaffolding called out after me: 'All right, Jimmy?', 'Wotcha, Jimmy!' and 'Oi, talk about floppy disks!'

Blimey! I thought. Finally I am truly famous! Either that, or I'm being harassed by a load of gay scaffolders.

At last I was somebody. Great punchline, no joke: that's me.

— 9 —

27 Elms Crescent,
East Grinstead,
West Sussex,
England

Dear James,

They say that fame makes a man attractive. The more famous
you are, the more attractive women find you. By that logic,
they must think the Pope is drop-dead gorgeous. Not that
that's a great deal of use to him. He can hardly cruise around
in his Popemobile picking up hitch-hikers and suggesting they
pull up for a bit in the car park of the woods behind the
Vatican. The Pope is a celebrity who is celibate. They should
coin a special phrase for it. He could be called a ~~'celebaty'~~
~~'celibatatery'~~ a celibate celebrity.

   For most other stars it must be very tempting to sleep with

every gorgeous girl who throws herself at you. However, it would be morally wrong to take advantage of your fame in this way. By now, Jimmy, you will probably be having to resist this kind of temptation on a daily basis. Like, you'll just be at some party and a beautiful blonde model will grab you and take you into a luxury bedroom and lock the door and she'll take off her clothes and let you see everything. You will just have to politely explain that yes, you find her attractive, both physically <u>and</u> intellectually, but it would just not be right for you to engage in sexual relations. Even if she's really sexy and has long hair and a silky black bra which is slipping off her shoulders and she wants you to tug it free because she's really desperate to have full sex with you right away and she'll even let you feel her bosoms and everything. You'll have to firmly say, sorry, but you aren't interested. That you have absolutely no intention of squeezing those full rounded breasts with the erect nipples that she would let you rub and jiggle about as much as you wanted, even while she is sitting on top of you and you are really doing it, up and down, up and down, up and down.

Where was I? This is a while later now, I got distracted by something and had to break off for a bit. Oh yes, the point I am making is that a real star should not go to bed with some stranger he has never met before. That gorgeous model might be a tabloid journalist under cover. Well, I suppose she can't be under cover if she's completely naked. Though you could argue it's a disguise of sorts, since she wouldn't be in the nude when she was in the offices of the Sun, unless she was also a Page 3 girl of course, but I don't think many of them are journalists as well. Anyway, what I am saying is that I bet she wouldn't tell you she was a tabloid journalist <u>until after you had done it</u> and she would end up writing embarrassing things about you not being very experienced in bed, and having a small penis and not lasting very long, and silly tittle-tattle like that which really is irrelevant and ridiculous and anyway not at all true.

The good news is that you won't be tempted by all the girl fans who want to sleep with you all the time because you will have such a full and loving relationship with your beautiful wife. I won't actually go as far as predicting that my wife will be Jennifer Barrett because she doesn't even seem to notice me at the moment. Even though I made a deal with God that if I got triple twenty on the dartboard in my bedroom she'd definitely kiss me, she still hasn't come near me yet.

But if it isn't Jennifer then it will be someone even lovelier and Jennifer will look back and wish that she'd taken her chance when she had it. She should have recognized me as the go-getting high achiever I'm going to be. Right, I'd better go and start my history project. We're back to school in a week.

Mine sincerely,
Jimmy

The 1980s were a terrible time, although not for the reasons they show in all those documentaries. They get the emphasis all wrong. They go on about the Falklands War and the Miners' Strike, the unemployment, the corporate greed and all that political stuff, when in fact the overriding burning issue of the 1980s was: 'When am I going to lose my virginity?'

This was the crucial topic of the age. When will Jimmy Conway get to do it with a girl? was the question to which no politician or newspaper editorial ever gave a satisfactory answer. But what a momentous event it would be when it finally happened! Mrs Thatcher would emerge from 10 Downing Street where the assembled pack of journalists and photographers had gathered having heard that something really big was about to break. And then she would step up to the microphone to introduce the minister she was permitting to relay this wonderful news, even if she had to be there just to be associated with such a momentous announcement.

'I would like to hand you over to the Minister for Having Done It, who has got some news I think you might like to hear.' And then the Minister for Having Done It would step forward as the cameras flashed and whirred, trying to look statesman-like but succeeding only in looking smug.

'At approximately twenty-three hundred hours this evening, we received the following communiqué: "Be pleased to inform Her Majesty, that Jimmy Conway has just done it with Jennifer Barrett in his parents' bed while they were stay-ing the weekend at Grandma's. Let it be known that consequently from this day, the fifteenth day of August 1983, Jimmy Conway is, no longer, a virgin. God save the Queen!'

This would be the cue for the news hounds to shout excited questions.

'Minister! Minister? Are there any plans for them to do it again?'

'Do all of Jimmy's school friends know that he has done it?'

But then the PM steps in to cut them off: 'Just rejoice at that news, and congratulate Jimmy Conway and Jennifer!'

And then the two of them disappear back inside the door of 10 Downing Street as television programmes on all four channels were interrupted with a news flash to show the historic announcement once again.

But as the decade wore on, the likelihood of any such proclamation seemed to be getting no closer. It didn't have to be Jennifer Barrett. I wouldn't have minded having sex with any female, really. My maths teacher Mrs Slough, Kim Wilde, Nancy Reagan, Mother Theresa, Auntie Jean; I didn't feel I was in any position to be too choosy. It seemed to me to be the greatest injustice that there were two billion females on Planet Earth and I had not so much as touched one breast of a single one of them. That's four billion bosoms in the whole wide world, give or take. They couldn't all be completely out of bounds.

Although I did eventually lose my virginity a few brief centuries after writing the above letter, the anticipated golden age of constant sexual activity never seemed to materialize. But once I became a celebrity, suddenly everyone wanted to flirt. In fact, I even received a letter from now mother-of-three Jennifer Barrett, delighted that I was doing so well and confessing that when we were teenagers she'd always rather fancied me but had never had the courage to do anything about it. For God's sake! I thought. Now she bloody tells me!

Everything had changed. Suddenly I was an attractive and interesting person for the opposite sex because they recognized me off the television. It's all so shallow, isn't it? So phoney, so demeaning. I mean, what sort of man wants to walk into a room and suddenly find attractive women flirting with him just because he happens to be on the telly? Answer: me.

This is how I came to meet Tanya. She was so amazed to find herself in the same room as Jimmy Conway, she kept talking and blushing and saying how she'd never met anyone famous before. She thought my adverts were 'brilliant' and that I was really funny and brilliant and she'd heard me on the radio ('brilliant') and seen me reading the nominations at the British Soap Awards and it was brilliant and then she said she'd give anything to be a celebrity. She had gone along to the auditions for *Pop Idol* but she reckoned they were prejudiced against people who couldn't sing. She was going to try and get on *Blind Date* next, she said, because she thought if she was spotted on that, it might lead to a job as a weathergirl or a presenter on *Crimewatch UK* or something.

'What it's really like being famous?' she asked me longingly. Her question crystallized it for me: I had finally reached the destination I had always longed for. Now I was recognized wherever I went; waiters never kept my table waiting; security men didn't ask for ID but jumped up and opened the door for me. That week the *Sun* had a picture of a buxom starlet meeting Prince Andrew and his eyes were momentarily focused on her cleavage and the headline read 'Talk About Floppy Disks!' Wherever I went people demanded that I utter these four words and then they would fall about laughing when I did.

'Well, it's very exciting,' I said to Tanya. 'You know, interesting and frightening and exhilarating all at once.'

'Hmmm. Say "Talk About Floppy Disks!"'

'Er, I'd rather not.'

'Go on. Here, Janet! Come and listen to this: he's going to say it!'

An expectant hush fell over the whole room.

'Talk About Floppy Disks!' I said and everyone burst out laughing.

There was one sensation I didn't report to Tanya. Celebrity status didn't make me feel fulfilled. Obviously my quality of life had improved as everyday barriers were whisked away and money was easier to come by and people treated me with respect, but I still felt that same indefinable emptiness inside. On the homely set of the breakfast TV show on which I'd appeared, there was a grand flight of stairs leading to an ornate door at the top. When I'd watched that show at home I'd always wondered what was behind the door. But then I got to appear on the show and afterwards I got to walk around the set, to climb to the top of that showbiz staircase and see where it led. I opened the door. There was nothing behind it. It led straight back down to the studio floor again.

But like me before, Tanya thought fame was the answer to everything. She wanted to know how she could get into show business and what various other celebrities were like 'in real life' and I took care to answer all her questions as best as I could, as if this was somehow now part of my duty. I talked to her for ages. It was all very selfless of me. I did her that courtesy at the party where I met her and I did her that courtesy in the taxi on the way back to her flat.

Joseph Kennedy said that 'sex was an itch that needed to be scratched'. As the weeks since my last scratch turned into months I had found myself itching all over. I had invisible rashes all over my legs and arms. I had imaginary chicken pox and virtual eczema. The last time I had woken up beside a woman I had to apologize for snoring and dribbling throughout the flight.

As I paid for the taxi and Tanya apologized for the unglamorous location of her home, I sensed that some unspoken contract had been drawn up between us in which we had already agreed to go to bed together. 'I, Tanya Callaghan, do hereby undertake to engage in sexual activity up to and including full intercourse with Jimmy Conway for one evening only on condition that I may tell all my friends that I had it off with that comedian off the telly, you know the one who says Talk About Floppy Disks. I undertake not to become a demented stalker and will not break into his house and stab him for failing to talk back to me from my television screen.'

Tanya was undeniably attractive, short and slim with a tanned midriff that was exposed because her T-shirt seemed to have shrunk in the wash. She poured me a glass of wine and we sat down on the sofa together. Then before I had even taken a sip she leaned across and began kissing me as if I was in urgent need of mouth-to-mouth resuscitation. Her eyes were closed while mine surveyed this stranger's flat. On her television were photos of her with her family. One of them featured her and her sister posing next to Goofy at Disneyland Paris *and there were no kids in the photo*. All of us have had sexual encounters we've regretted, but could I really go to bed with the sort of woman who went to Disneyland *without children*? Her bookshelves featured several videos, a spider plant and a collection of soft toys of which I recognized only Snoopy and Garfield.

I jumped slightly as she began to grope my crotch. I had never known a woman be so direct before, and while I can't deny that the predatory male side of my character was excited at the obvious imminence of sex, another part of me couldn't help feeling that this was all rather bad manners. Normally before the outbreak of all-out war there's a little bit of diplomatic tension, a couple of border incidents, increasing hostility until the troops are eventually mobilized and the explosions begin. This was straight in there with Pearl Harbor. She wasn't exactly keeping me guessing about where I stood. *Hmm, now she's squeezing the bulge in the front of my trousers, what can this mean? It must be some sort of subtle coded signal, but you could interpret that in a number of ways, couldn't you?*

'Have you got a condom?' said Tanya, momentarily releasing my exhausted mouth. There she goes again. Another cryptic half-clue to leave me guessing just how far this girl was prepared to go on this first date. Oh, if only women could just be a bit more up front about everything instead of forcing us to go through this elaborate dance, all this second-guessing 'does she want to or doesn't she?' stuff.

'Erm, a condom? No, no, I haven't.'

'Doesn't matter. I've got some by my bed,' she said, launching her face against mine once more. A bed? She's talking about a bed now. I wondered if that had as many soft toys on it as her bookshelves had.

It was true that I didn't have any condoms. I hadn't gone to that party with the deliberate intention of casually seducing someone just because I was now recognized wherever I went. Besides, I couldn't buy condoms any more because now I was recognized wherever I went. What does Prince Charles do if he needs some contraceptives? He can hardly wander around the chemist and hope to sneak it past unnoticed with a comb and a toothbrush.

I think by this point I must have been expected to be fiddling with Tanya's bra strap or squeezing her breasts through her turquoise crop top or something, because she suddenly broke off.

'What's the matter?' she said.

'Nothing, what do you mean?' I said, slightly too defensively.

'You seem a bit – you know, not very relaxed?'

She was right, of course, although I was embarrassed that it was so obvious. I was in two minds about going through with this. Actually, it wasn't so much 'two minds': my brain was against it, it was another part of my body that was lobbying hard in favour of proceeding. She only wanted to sleep with me because she thought I was a celebrity. Yet I knew that I wasn't the genuine article, that I was deceiving her, tricking her into bed just as if I had laced her drink or had dishonestly promised the chorus girl the lead part in the musical.

'Tanya, I'm sorry but I don't think I should go to bed with you.'

'What?' she said indignantly.

'Sorry, it just feels wrong, you know, a bit sudden.'

'Is it because I'm a nobody; is that what it is?'

'No – it's because *I'm* a nobody. It's all wrong. I'm here under false pretences.' I stood up. 'Look, we've only just met. Maybe it's different for you because you recognized my face right away and felt like you knew me. But I'd never seen your face before until a couple of hours ago, and I don't know the first thing about you.'

'Oh,' she said dejectedly. 'So it is because I'm not famous then.'

As I walked home in the drizzle, pointlessly hailing taxis with their lights turned off, I wondered what a real star would have done. They probably wouldn't have gone back to her flat for a start. An experienced TV celeb would never risk sleeping over at some complete stranger's house. Imagine it. In the middle of the night, tiptoeing out of the toilet in a skimpy ladies' dressing gown only to bump into some astonished flat-mate in the hallway. 'Bugger me! It's the bloke off *Antiques Roadshow*! What the bloody hell are you doing here?'

'Oh I was just trying to flush a used condom down the lavvy, but it won't go down.'

'Right. Listen, er, my grandma's left me these antique porcelain figures, and I was wondering what they might be worth . . .'

I finally got a taxi and slumped back in my seat still wondering if I had done the right thing. Perhaps a real celebrity would have had sex with the fan and then forgotten all about her. Maybe I lacked that ruthless, selfish drive, the killer instinct needed to get to the very top. Perhaps I should be attempting to emulate the sexual psychology of today's showbiz stars. The trouble was I didn't fancy being tied up by transsexual prostitutes while out of my head on cocaine. I attempted to be as positive as possible about the evening. Tanya had thought I was 'brilliant', and had wanted to sleep with me because I was famous. People at the party had nudged each other and pointed in my direction; everyone wanted to talk to *me*. I had achieved everything I had ever dreamt of. I was a star, members of the public were impressed by me, at last I was recognized wherever I went. As these self-satisfied thoughts glowed inside my head, the taxi driver put his hand over to pull back the glass screen between us.

'I hope you don't mind me saying, but you're that bloke off the telly, aren't you?'

'Yes, yes I am.'

'I expect you get fed up with people recognizing you all the time, don't you?'

'Oh well, I don't really mind. In my job the time to start worrying is when people stop recognizing you!' I quipped.

'That's true, you've got a point there!' he chuckled. 'So how come the bloody weather forecast is always completely bloody wrong then?'

'I'm sorry?' I said, slightly perplexed.

'Well, they pay you all that money to say whether it's going to rain or not and you never bloody get it right.'

Now that he'd said this I suppose I did look a tiny bit like that weatherman, even if I didn't wear beige polyester. The fact that this cabbie and I had just agreed how important it was for me to be recognized made me reluctant to point out that I wasn't the celebrity he was thinking of.

'I mean, when you say it's going to be sunny, I make sure I put on my bloody raincoat, know what I mean!' he went on. I felt slightly irritated.

'Yeah, well, we tell you the wrong weather deliberately,' I told him conspiratorially. 'The government forces us to.'

'Really?'

'Yeah. If we say it's going to pour with rain, all the people who work outside are going to phone in sick and all the foreign tourists are going to cancel their holidays, so we are under strict instructions from the spin doctors in Downing Street to say the weather's going to be much better than it really is.'

'You know, that doesn't surprise me,' he replied. 'That doesn't surprise me one bit.' And he shook his head in dismay about how even the weather was being spun these days.

'But you'll keep that to yourself, won't you?' I said as we pulled up.

'Oh yeah, of course I will,' he lied. I paid him for driving me home and recognizing me, even if I was a little insulted that he thought I was someone else. Obviously you can't blame an ordinary member of the public for something like that; I wasn't that vain and petty and mean. I just didn't have any loose change for a tip, that's all. He really is a tight bastard, that weatherman.

I was distressed to discover that this sort of mix-up happened more frequently than I would have imagined. I was also variously confused with a daytime TV quizmaster, a presenter on the Shopping Channel and on one occasion a man wanted in connection with a series of armed raids in the East Midlands whose photo had appeared on the news. The only group of people who never got me mixed up with any other celebrities were the celebrities themselves. The very people who had stared right through me at Billy Scrivens's funeral were now inviting me to their book launches and after-show parties and welcoming me to their bosom like some long-lost friend.

Nothing motivates a star like the fear of their own fame fading. I think I was invited to parties by VIPs I'd never met because they needed to bolster their own fame by surrounding themselves with the latest arrivals at the celebrity ball. I sensed that they didn't feel any more secure than I did. I suppose fame is so precious because it's so intangible. If you buy a new car, it's there, gleaming; an undeniable physical presence. You can drive it around, park it in the street and glance around too many times as you are walking away from it. But fame is in the air, an invisible, one-step-ahead will o' the wisp that you can never be sure is going to stay around or just flit away to glow around someone else. So the stars I met were constantly seeking to become more famous. Even if they were Oscar winners and major film stars, it still wasn't enough; they didn't feel they'd arrived yet, they couldn't see the Hollywood for the trees. Would my own nagging sense of frustration be lifted if only I could get more famous? Was the problem with this drug that I hadn't got a big enough shot of it?

Or was my insecurity different because my fame had been all smoke and mirrors in the first place? Every time I hoped I might be becoming a bona fide star I found myself having to lie again. My fancy costume was a mass of safety pins underneath. If *Hello!* magazine ever wanted to do a feature on me, I'd never be able to show them my house in Seaford.

For comedian Jimmy Conway, home is a one-bedroom rented terraced house in Sussex. 'The wonderful thing about living in a seaside town is that I can look out of my window in the morning and gaze out upon the vast expanse of the Safeway supermarket car park,' says Jimmy, proudly showing us the view though the very off-white net curtains. Every room is full of memories. A large brown circle on the ceiling reminds Jimmy of the time the phone rang when he was running a bath. The large modern radiators remind him of a time when the central heating worked. The woodchip wallpaper that undulates across the bathroom walls was personally chosen by Jimmy from Do-It-All's famous economy range. The distressed lounge carpet is a mottled brown and its chaotic textured pattern features all sorts of unusual shades that Jimmy describes as 'vindaloo' and 'tikka masala'. Throughout the home the decor has been carefully chosen to reflect Jimmy's hectic lifestyle. As well as scatter cushions, there are scatter newspapers, scatter pants and scatter takeaway pizza boxes.

The homes you saw in *Hello!* and *OK!* magazines all seemed pretty much the same. They had tables you couldn't put things on and cushions you would never dare to sit upon. I think it must be a precondition of them photographing a star's home.

'Um, hello there. Look, we just have to check – you do have big puffy yellow curtains, don't you?'

'Of course I do.'

'Jolly good. Sorry we had to ask but you can't be too careful.'

My home could not have been more unsuitable and yet when *OK!* did finally contact me and ask if I would be interested in appearing in a photo feature, I couldn't resist it. 'Yes, I'd be delighted!' I said. I couldn't help myself, I was just so flattered to be asked. It was another step on the show business ladder, another medal in the war against anonymity. I knew I didn't have a home I could ever possibly show them but a voice in my head said, Let's cross that bridge when we come to it. And then another panicky voice screamed: There is no bridge, you idiot! THERE IS NO BRIDGE, the ravine is completely bloody bridge-less! It's 'Let's step off that cliff and fall to our death when we come to it!'

The only solution was to use someone else's house. If I was to be cross-examined by the celebrity police, my only chance was to give a false address. I had the perfect location: my parents had keys for the London flat of their Korean neighbours who were often out of the country. I'd been in there once with Mum when she'd gone to water their plants, and she was always saying it was like something out of *Ideal Home*. This place really looked like a star's home. Expensive ornaments were carefully placed in backlit alcoves, full bottles of lotions and bath oils were neatly arranged around the jacuzzi. These people had shelves with just one item on! At no point had this little figurine been gradually joined by some old paperbacks, piled-up videos and a couple of cracked empty CD cases.

Why shouldn't this be my London pad as far as the general

public were concerned? The Korean couple were the least likely people on Earth ever to buy *OK!* magazine. It would be a very straightforward operation. I would give a very specific time to the photographer, I'd be in there waiting for him, I'd let him in to take a few snaps and he'd be on his way again in half an hour. And all right, after the deed was done I might have to confess to Mum and Dad and persuade them to keep this little secret to themselves, but other than that it was quite plausible that 'one of Britain's most exciting new comics' (*Daily Telegraph*), 'the fastest rising star on the comedy circuit' (*Time Out*), should have an opulent flat like this in West London.

The arrangement was made and one quiet Wednesday morning I let myself in through the front door, entering the code to silence the beep on the burglar alarm. When I had previously accompanied Mum around the apartment it had felt legitimate, but now I felt like an intruder; a style burglar who was there to filch a little bit of this couple's opulent lifestyle for myself. I put a pint of milk in the fridge so I could confidently offer a cup of tea and then I spread a couple of that day's newspapers across the coffee table along with a scuffed paperback copy of *Carrot – How One Root Vegetable Changed the History of the World*.

I sat on the sofa and lay back. 'Yah – this was originally three rooms but my architect did a wonderful job with it.' I crossed my legs the other way and placed my hand on my chin pensively. 'Yah, of course this building was originally an old clock factory – it's such a shame there's no real industry left in the capital—' then the door buzzer went off and I leapt up in shock. 'Hi there, come on up!' I said to the intercom, pressing the button to release the main door downstairs. I had a last glance in the mirror to check that I was completely happy with what I was wearing. The casual, just-thrown-on-a-few-old-things look had taken me ages to get right.

I suppose if I'd stopped to think about it I'd have realized that a professional photographer was bound to turn up with more than just a little camera. His arrival was like the D-Day landings. He and his young assistant carried in metal boxes, light stands, tripods, a big white umbrella, electrical leads, a reflective silver circle, more metal boxes. I was worried that by the time he had unpacked everything a whole month would have passed by and the flat-owners would arrive back from New York just in time to see me perched on the end of their double bed with a big hairy photographer leaning over me.

He introduced himself as Carl while his assistant didn't even bother. Almost immediately it seemed as if Carl was testing me to see if it really was my flat. 'Sorry, do you mind if I use your toilet?' he said. He was never going to catch me out with a question like that. 'Down the corridor, second on the left!' I said confidently.

'Got it!' he shouted back.

'Yup,' I said to his assistant proudly. 'That's where the toilet is all right.'

'So have you lived here long?' quizzed Carl as he returned.

'No, no, well, yes. I mean, it's just a London pad, you know. I have a place down in Sussex as well.'

The assistant and Carl seemed to have some private joke which they were not about to share as they both tried to stop themselves sniggering.

'Nice pictures!' he said.

'Thanks,' I replied, and the assistant let a brief laugh slip out. I looked at the pictures and saw that they weren't nice at all; they were a bit gaudy.

'Er – actually, they're not mine. A friend asked if he could store them here. Not really my kind of thing.'

'Oh right,' smirked Carl. 'Tell me – doesn't that little fountain with the angels get on your nerves, bubbling away in the hall all day?'

Now the assistant was biting his lip, nearly exploding with suppressed hysterics. I glanced at the fountain. It was awful. In fact, although the whole flat was tidy and large and expensively done out, seeing it through their eyes I realized that it was full of the most extravagant and vulgar furnishings imaginable. While I was in the kitchen making them a cup of tea, I could hear them pointing things out to each other and giggling at my appalling taste, and the penny dropped that I would now be exposing all of this to the entire nation.

'Look at those bloody curtains – they're disgusting!'

'Shhh . . . Not so loud.'

'Sorry.'

'Not you. I was talking to the curtains!'

And they collapsed into more hushed giggles at my expense.

When I returned with the tea I attempted to claim that I'd recently employed someone to furnish the house for me but I didn't really like it and was going to change it all again.

'Oh well, as long you as you don't throw out the zebra pattern sofa,' said the assistant and Carl sniggered and I consoled myself with the fact that at least they didn't suspect anything. And then the phone rang.

Carl looked at me expectantly and I smiled benignly back at him. 'Sorry, do you want to get that?' he said.

'Er, no, not really.' I shrugged. 'Your time is precious.'

'Oh, that's OK – we're going to be a while setting up so please don't mind us.'

The phone continued to ring insistently.

'OK, well, er, I think I'll still leave it . . . I'm sure they'll ring back if it's important.'

At that point an answering machine cut in. I froze in terror that the instructions to the caller would be transmitted across the room, thereby exposing my fraud when it had barely begun, but thankfully the outgoing message was relayed in silence and I was safe. And then we all listened to the amplified incoming message. It wasn't so much *what* was said as the fact that my caller was talking Korean that made Carl raise his eyebrows.

'Annyong hashimmikga,' she said. 'Kanapsummida. Olma imnigga Halggi han-guk aradmddupta?' Her message went on and on while I stood there nodding contemplatively at what was being said. 'Interesting . . . interesting . . .' I mumbled to myself. Carl looked like he was about to say something but I solemnly raised my palm as if prevent him interrupting my concentration.

'Annyong-i kyeseyo!'

Finally the message ended and I shook my head in annoyed irritation at what had been said.

'What language was that then? Japanese?'

'Korean.'

'Blimey, you speak Korean, do you?'

'Well, you know . . . Un petit peu. I get by. They want me to go and do a gig out in Saigon.'

'In Vietnam?'

'Not Saigon, sorry, what's it called? Seoul. I was always get those two mixed up, because they both had wars, didn't they? I mean Korea and Vietnam, except it's not called Seoul any more, is it? Hang on, that's not right. Seoul is still called Seoul but Saigon is called something else, isn't it?' My nervous blabbing was making me look guilty so I felt forced to put any doubt out of his mind. 'I'd better deal with this now,' I announced and I picked up the phone and dialled a number and then angrily chastized the speaking clock in my best version of made-up oriental gobbledy-gook. 'Ning-dai sorne waidonga noy niee dawii blioni dwing noee singa hyundai daewoo noi Daewoo,' I said and I slammed the phone down. They both stared at me. 'I had a Daewoo,' said the assistant after a moment's silence. 'But I changed it for a Honda.'

The piece when it appeared was very flattering. The decor was still appalling so I fitted in perfectly between the premiership footballer and the former TV impressionist. A journalist from the magazine had come about an hour later and talked to me about my busy life and like all hacks I had encountered distorted what I had said or simply made things up. Only this time blatant lies were published to give the impression I was much nicer than I really was. My words were twisted and used in my favour. This wasn't muck-raking as much as 'perfume-raking'. Somebody should take them to the Press Complaints Commission.

My mother saw the piece and asked if I had bought the flat belonging to the Korean couple in their road without telling her. In unnecessarily hushed tones I explained I had been dared to pose in a house that wasn't my own as a bet to raise money for charity, but this secret mustn't get out or the injured seabirds wouldn't get the cash. She was delighted and promised not to breathe a word. Then she probed me on which charity and how much I had raised and somehow I ended up having to write the cheque out there and then before handing it over to her to send off.

It was hard to measure whether the *OK!* piece had moved me up another little notch in the eyes of my peers but the various invitations and requests for public appearances seemed to arrive at an ever greater rate. I said yes to all of them. Something told me this vacation on Planet Fame might not last very long and I wanted to make the most of it while I was there. It meant that I was hardly seeing anything of my old friends in Seaford. This wasn't a deliberate policy. It was merely that there was always an exciting new invitation or event I didn't want to miss. I knew what going down the Red Lion for Dave's birthday was like. I'd done it many times before, but I could hardly turn down a free ticket to the opening night of a new musical based on *Apocalypse Now*. They had a full-size helicopter on stage and real Vietnamese food at the after-show party.

Having sat through the whole of *Napalm!*, I made casual chit-chat with the other stars whose invitations had probably pushed out some of the people who'd actually worked on the production. Where I had once stood on the edge of circles hoping someone would introduce themselves to me, now the circles magically opened and other famous faces greeted me as if we were European explorers meeting in darkest Africa. There was a pecking order, of course, and there were certain megastars you knew you had to wait to be introduced to. I couldn't exactly go up to Robert de Niro and say, 'Hi, Rob. Jimmy Conway. You probably recognize me off the text message banking advert. Honestly, isn't filming a dreadful bore sometimes?' But for the celebs who were feeling nervous that their careers might have peaked or for those who were a couple of rungs behind me, Jimmy 'Talk About Floppy Disks!' Conway was exactly the sort of person to be seen with.

I found myself sipping champagne beside some cravat-wearing luvvie and he gushed so enthusiastically I could feel my face turning red.

'Oh, Jimmy, can I just say I saw you do a turn a few months ago and you were absolutely brilliant.'

I didn't know what to think when people said things like this to me. Were they completely deluded or just so full of showbiz bullshit they went round casually lying to everyone they met?

'Oh, thanks very much. Glad you enjoyed it.'

'Yes, you were very funny, really. I think the words "comic genius" would not be overstating it.'

'Golly. Thank you.'

I was embarrassed now. I wanted to talk about something else.

'Where did you see him?' cut in a voice behind me. It was Mike Mellor, the skinhead comic who'd failed to graduate from charm school. He was wearing a T-shirt with his own picture on it.

'Ooh, now – it was a while ago and they're all so similar, aren't they?' said Malcolm. 'But what I do remember is that he was very very funny. I mean, that fish routine, well, it's just a classic, isn't it? An all-time comedy classic. Up there with the greats, darling!'

'Was it in London?' he persevered.

'Um, yes, I think so. Was it in North London somewhere maybe?' he said, hoping to be provided with the name of a comedy club.

'Jongleurs Camden?' I suggested.

He clicked his fingers and pointed at me.

'Jongleurs Camden! That was it! Yes! Brilliant, really funny. I nearly came up and introduced myself afterwards but time and place, darling, time and place . . .'

'Yeah, it was a good gig, that one.'

'You've never played Jongleurs Camden,' said Mellor.

'Sorry?' I said, though I'd heard him perfectly.

'You've never played Jongleurs Camden.'

'Haven't I? Oh I dunno, like Malcolm says, these clubs all merge into one, don't they? Maybe it was Jongleurs Battersea then.'

'You've never played that either. My missus works for Jongleurs. You've never played either club or at any gig I've ever been to in the past five years of doing the circuit.'

I stammered for a moment, unsure how I might defend myself from Mike Mellor's knowing accusation.

'Yeah, well, I mean . . . You know, I've never seen you either, Mike, but what does that prove? Malcolm here enjoyed my set, didn't you, Malcolm?'

'Very funny, you must try and catch him, really.'

'Sorry, I should have introduced you. Malcolm, this is Mike Mellor. He's a stand-up as well. Maybe you've seen him. Mike was runner-up for Best New Stand-up at the British 'Biz Awards . . .' I gabbled and then kicked myself for provoking him further. Mellor bristled uncomfortably to be reminded of this.

'No, I can't say I've had the pleasure. But congratulations. That's still very good. Who were you runner-up to?'

'Er, Jimmy was best newcomer,' sneered Mike to his shoes.

'Sorry, I can't hear you, darling. Who was it?' insisted Malcolm.

'It was Jimmy here,' he was forced to repeat. 'Jimmy Conway.'

Mike Mellor had seemed to hate me from the first time he saw me. A month earlier he had come up to me at a Comic Relief football match and said, 'That gag you do in the advert about Mr Spock's ears – you're going to have to drop that because *I* do *Star Trek*, that's my patch, you're trespassing on my material.'

I sighed and said, 'Oh beam me up, Scotty!' and that didn't seem to endear me to him any more. 'What, so Gene Roddenberry has given you exclusive rights to make jokes about his characters, has he?' I went on.

'No, but it would be like me doing stuff about fish. You just don't nick another comic's subject matter; that's how it works on the circuit. Not that I'd expect you to know that,' he said pointedly.

'What if there was a creature that was half fish and half Vulcan? Could I make jokes about that?'

He thought about this. '*Not* if it was on *Star Trek*,' he said earnestly. 'But if it turns up at the fish counter at Sainsbury's, then it's yours – I'd steer completely clear.'

Mike Mellor always reminded me what a fraud I was. If my advert had featured me just talking to camera as myself then I might have felt I was now justifiably famous, but because I was clearly being shown at work, doing what 'Jimmy Conway' did for a living, the lie that I was a top stand-up comic was being amplified. I never felt completely at ease whenever Mike Mellor and I were at the same event. He Knew. I could feel it every time he was near me. I don't understand how he came to know, or whether he had just had some inspired hunch, but I just sensed that He Knew. I learnt that he was asking other comics if Jimmy Conway had ever appeared at a gig they were doing; I saw him chatting with a promoter and pointing in my direction, and while he was out there actively compiling evidence against me I felt that my great secret was in danger of being exposed.

I had known for some time there was only one way out of this. Soon I would have no choice but to go out there and do it. If I wanted to sustain my celebrity comic persona, eventually I was going to have to tell jokes in front of a live audience.

And the prospect completely terrified me. But it was to happen sooner than I expected. Stella Scrivens was at the same party. I'd wanted to talk to her but I was waiting for the tabloid photographers to move away so that I didn't have to spend half an hour justifying myself to Nancy.

'Hi, Jimmy,' she said, giving me a big kiss as flashbulbs exploded. 'I've got a big favour I've been wanting to ask you.'

Mike Mellor was eavesdropping from where he was skulking beside the vol-au-vents.

'I'm organizing a big charity gala at the Palladium, all the top stand-ups, music acts and everything, raising money for Star Appeal in memory of Billy. Would you be up for doing ten minutes of your set for us?'

'Er, yeah, sure,' I shrugged. 'I'd be delighted. Is ten minutes all you want? Because I can do more if you need . . .'

'That's great. I'll see how we go – I've still got a couple of slots to fill.'

Both of us could feel Mike's glare boring into us.

'Er, what about Mike here?' I blabbed out of sheer embarrassment.

'Er, well, I've sort of got my full quotient of comics now,' she stammered.

'Not to worry,' said Mellor, staring directly at me. 'I'll make sure I'm in the audience.'

So that is how I came to agree to perform in front of two thousand people. I was to make my stage debut at the highest-profile comedy event of the year. I felt like someone who'd been going around claiming he was a black belt in judo and had suddenly been confronted by a gang of terrifying attackers and now everyone was looking at him to beat them all up. I was informed that the event was going to be filmed for a video release, then it was going to be televised, and then I learnt it was going to be transmitted live on BBC1. Each piece of news was presented to me like some fantastic new development that would do so much to help the charity, but all it did was make me want to have a sex change and become a nun in remotest Paraguay.

The date was set. The middle of September. A whole year since I'd first pretended I had known Billy Scrivens, I was now going to attempt to follow in his footsteps for real. Live on stage in front of two thousand people. Millions of TV viewers watching live at home. 'I can do it!' I said out loud at home in Seaford. 'I am going to be a bona fide star at last!' I said to the dog. 'I'm going to be huge! I'm going to be a great success, I'm sure of it!' and she snuffled and panted and turned her head on one side and wondered why I was lying on the floor underneath my bed.

— 10 —

27 Elms Crescent,
East Grinstead,
West Sussex,
England

Dear James,

Oh God, oh God, oh God. It's the last day of the holidays and I
haven't done my history project on the Tudors and I'm really
going to be for it and I'm scared of going back to school
tomorrow.

   By now, James, you will probably laugh at the things you
used to worry about when you were thirteen. Like the fear you
once had of getting into trouble or making a fool of yourself,
or anxieties about whether people liked you or not. You will
have probably learnt that you can only overcome your fear of
something by doing it. Like if you have a terrible fear of
heights, for example, and you made yourself jump off a tall

building then you might overcome — actually, no, you would die, so that is not a very good example, but generally speaking if you are scared of something you should try and force yourself to do it.

Like last year when I was being bullied by Kevin Fraser. My teacher talked to me about it and said, 'You have nothing to fear but fear itself.' And then he gave me a smile and said 'All right?' and I nodded and that was that. I had nothing to fear but fear itself. Oh, and Kevin Fraser punching me hard in the face, I thought, I did still have that to fear. And being kicked by him when I fell over. I couldn't help feeling that was still quite a frightening prospect as well. And him bending my arm up my back and nicking my dinner money and chucking my PE kit on top of the bus shelter. In fact, the more I think about it, I don't think Mr Stock could have been listening, because it wasn't fear itself I was frightened of, it was definitely Kevin Fraser.

But if your fear is of something that's actually not very frightening or genuinely dangerous, in that case you should force yourself to do it. Unless you have a genuine phobia or something, that's different. That's a recognized medical condition and those people need sensitive counselling to help them snap out of it and pull themselves together.

Most people don't achieve their dreams because they just never plucked up the courage to give it a shot. It's like that song: 'You've got to have a dream, if you don't have a dream, how you going to have a dream come true?' Although my main dream is being in the Arndale centre with no clothes on, and I'd rather that one didn't come true, thank you very much.

Mine sincerely,
Jimmy

'Imagine if they had a *Star Trek* character that was half Vulcan and half fish . . .' I declaimed into the microphone, a little laughter in my voice, shaking my head in disbelief at the foolishness of such a notion. 'He'd be, like, totally logical most of the time, except when you put a little worm on a hook right in front of his nose . . . Then that little fishy side of him wouldn't be able to resist it, would it? "Hmmm, interesting, captain, I appear to have a giant rusty hook piercing my cheek causing me immense agony and massive internal haemorrhaging".'

With one hand on the flex, I lowered my microphone and took a well-earned bow. This particular microphone doubled up as the shower attachment from my bath and admittedly the only audience was my own reflection in the large cracked mirror above the sink. It was impossible to know whether this routine was hilarious or stupid made-up nonsense. I mean, there's no such thing as a Vulcan and fish can't talk. Surely the audience will spot both of these basic flaws in my premise half a mile away. I'd thought this new material was quite funny when I'd first written it down, but then I had to consider the other possibility, which was that I was quite probably going insane. And wasn't *Star Trek* all a bit passé now, a bit of a comedy cliché? Up and coming young comics of the twenty-first century didn't do routines about *Star Trek*. They did routines about *Star Trek, the Next Generation*.

I had changed my entire set half a dozen times and this particular script was not made any easier to read by the fact that it had been torn into pieces and then sellotaped back together again. A psychologist might say that I was having a panic attack, but that suggests a short period of intense anxiety and my permanent state of terror wasn't like that at all; I was having panic sieges and panic marathons. Even though the gig was still over a month away, my pressure-cooker head felt that it could stand the worry no more and that I should abandon the whole idea. In fact, I had been close to doing this when I had stumbled across my name in an article in a Sunday newspaper. A critic writing a negative piece about the general state of comedy in Britain had casually added as an aside: 'Even Jimmy Conway is not as funny as he used to be.' What? How dare he! I thought. Who does this bastard think he is? 'Jimmy Conway is not as funny as he used to be.' I was exactly as funny as I used to be, which is not funny at all. He had absolutely no right to write that about me without seeing me first. It was a moral outrage of the first order. I'll show him, I thought. He'll eat his words when I storm it at the London Palladium. And then I sat down to try and work out exactly which hilarious and original jokes would ensure that I stormed at the London Palladium and a wave of fear and paralysis came over me once again.

It was the balmy month of August and the celebrity social calendar seemed to be suspended. Seaford was full of grockles trying to extinguish the raw glow of their sunburnt bodies by throwing pints of cold lager down their throats. It became an effort to walk out of my front door. I'd be recognized and forced to be friendly and cheerful towards endless strangers who knew me. The holidaymakers' resolute determination to get drunk gave a dangerous edge to their overfamiliarity. One night on the way home I was stopped by a kebab-eating drunk with a huge beer gut under his Chelsea shirt, which made me think it unlikely that he actually played for them. He kept grinning and pointing at me as he searched hard for the precise words to describe my exalted celebrity status.

'Oi! You're that fucker off the wotsit!' He had grabbed my

arm so that I could not get away until he had shown me to his friend.

'Oi, Terry, look – it's that fucker off the wotsit!'

'Fuck me, so it is! Oi, mate, say it. Go on, say, "Talk About Floppy Disks!"'

'No thank you.'

'Fuckin' say it!'

'No, I don't want to.'

And then his excitement flipped into anger that I had broken the terms of my celebrity contract.

'You think you're fucking great, don't you, you stuck-up twat!'

And he hit me in the mouth with such force that I fell clumsily to the ground and cracked the back of my head on the pavement.

'And he's soft as shite! Talk About Floppy Disks!' and they laughed and left me there tasting the blood between my teeth.

For a while after that I felt besieged inside my little house, just grubby, unshaven me, a stir-crazy dog and endless blank pieces of paper in front of me. It doesn't take long to go mad. Tamsin was my only contact with the human race, if indeed she qualified. By now she had so many rings through her lips you could hang a pair of curtains up there. I had started employing her on a daily basis to walk Betty to save me going out at all.

'How's your mum?' I asked her.

'Fine,' grunted Tamsin, perhaps irritated that I should want to talk about Nancy rather than her.

I could tell she wanted another session with the doggy psychiatrist. She was patting Betty as if she hadn't seen her for ages and they'd just spent an hour together. Betty really ought to have got out a notebook and put her glasses on.

'Good dog, what a good dog,' said Tamsin, plonking herself down on the sofa.

'Betty, what do you think your daddy would say I asked him a favour?'

'Well, I can't say until I know what it is.'

She wrestled with the dog some more, allowing Betty to lick her face so much I worried the dog might get tetanus.

'I was wondering if I could take Kelvin to one of your comedy gigs,' she said, still looking at the dog. 'Then if you like came over afterwards and said hello and chatted to me and I introduced you to Kelvin, then he might be more interested in me after that.'

'I'm sorry, Tamsin, that won't be possible.' Her face fell as if all her hopes had been built up on this one idea, as if it was her last chance to hold on to the boy she thought she loved.

'You know I never say where I'm going to appear. And besides, it's you Kelvin should be interested in, not me.'

'But I know a celebrity!' she implored. 'That's the only interesting thing about me.'

This was about the most depressing thing I could think of. Apart from the fact that she didn't.

'Don't be ridiculous! There must be plenty of blokes who'd be attracted to you,' I said, trying to think of someone who worked in a magnet factory. 'No, I'm sorry, I can't help you. Sorry.'

'But what else can I do?' she pleaded and then she went quiet for a minute or two before finally reaching for the nuclear button once more.

'Betty, would you be jealous if I had Kelvin's baby?'

'Oh, not this again!' I snapped, angry that she'd resorted to blackmail. 'Get pregnant then, you stupid child. Ruin your life if that's what you want. I can't stop you.'

I tried to go back to my work but the only words I wrote down were 'Ring Nancy about Tamsin'. I put this note by the phone, but I still felt guilty that I'd never told Nancy about her daughter's ludicrous pregnancy idea. The shame I felt at losing my temper with a fourteen-year-old girl kept coming back to me as I attempted to think up jokes. It didn't help me feel funny.

Tamsin stopped coming round to walk the dog and after a few days I finally made the call I should have made months ago. The phone seemed to ring for longer than was feasible in Nancy's tiny flat and then there was a beep and her recorded voice informed me (and any burglars who happened to ring) that she and Tamsin were on holiday in Normandy. That was the holiday we'd always had together. I rang Chris and Norman and Panda; no one seemed to be around, until finally I got a reply from Dave's mobile.

'Hello?' he shouted, sounding surprised.

'Dave? It's Jimmy.'

'Hello, stranger. Don't you have a PA or someone to make your calls for you now?'

'Where are you?'

'We're in France, where do you think? It's August bank holiday.'

In a clipframe on the wall were various photos of holidays from years gone by. There we all were on the ferry from Newhaven or struggling to put up tents or waving on the beach with bottles of cheap wine in our hands.

'Oh. I didn't know it was happening this year.'

'What, because you're too busy, everyone else cancels their holiday?'

'No, I just didn't know you were all going away . . . I might have come along maybe, for a few days.'

'What, a celebrity on a walking holiday? And who'd carry the bloody sedan chair?'

In one of the photos I noticed Dave with his arm around Nancy. That had never bothered me before.

'Is Nancy all right?'

'Hang on, Jimmy. *L'addition, s'il vous plaît*,' I heard him ask, exaggerating his Yorkshire accent. 'We're in a *crêperie*. Panda said that was a crêpe restaurant. But I thought it was quite good.' I could hear everyone laugh in the background. 'You can have that if you want, Jimmy, you know, for your comedy act.'

'Thanks. So everyone's all right, are they?'

'Yup, we're all fine, Jimmy. Tamsin's gone off for a sulk, but it's quite useful having someone who keeps spare barbecue skewers through her nostrils.'

And I could hear everyone laughing again and I said I'd see them when they got back. *I'd* started the Tamsin jokes. Nancy would be playfully slapping Dave on the arm now.

I didn't even attempt to work for the rest of that day. They must have made a decision not even to tell me they were going on holiday; there must have been a conversation when someone said, 'What about Jimmy? Shall we invite him?' and they'd agreed there was no point or that they'd rather go without me. The final photo I'd put in the clipframe was from last August, a picture of me way out at sea waving from the water. Waving goodbye, lost, presumed famous.

The next day I took down the photos. Every morning I went through the charade of sitting at my desk, in the hope that the invisible joke-writing pixie might turn up at the same time and put down the magic words for me. Whenever I decided I was stuck I'd take this as my cue to walk Betty up to the cliffs. The poor dog was pressganged into three or four walks a day. But she always threw herself into her task with far more enthusiasm than I managed for mine, and today as I followed her route over the cliffs and away from the sea I envied her enthusiastic optimism.

Oh brilliant! Here's a big bit of grass! I'm going to run and run and run, oh no, stop! There's a big branch, I'll have that, God it's heavy, I'll just lift the end up and half drag it round and round in circles, ooh, hang on, there's something else, an insect just buzzed near me, I'll have that! Snap! Snap! Snap! Missed it, never mind, charge over the hill, roll on my back, leap up, charge down the hill, this is brilliant, this is fantastic, this is the most fun you could possibly have in the whole wide world!

When I had bumped into Billy Scrivens up here on the cliffs, I had been so excited and honoured just to be in his presence, flattered to be breathing the same air as someone so incredibly famous. Now that precious currency had been devalued. Having seen so many celebrities close up and observed their faults and foibles, for me they'd turned back into mere mortals. They weren't all the wonderful people with the perfect lives portrayed in the magazines, any more than they were all self-obsessed megalomaniacs. I'd learnt that they were as different as any group of people, with the same number of insecurities and anxieties as the rest of us. Some seemed fairly balanced and self-aware, while others had had their idiosyncrasies magnified a thousand times until a slight human failing became a hideous neurosis. I'd seen multimillionaires taking home all the free boxes of tissues from their dressing room. I'd heard a slightly shy actress in the back of a limousine calling her agents to ask them to phone her driver to tell him to turn down the air conditioning. Real life, it was not.

There was, of course, something else they possessed that I had been hoping I might be able to get by without. Talent. Ah yes, that endless supply of gold that I had been attempting to weave from straw for the past few weeks. The fact that I felt I could no longer sustain my life as a celebrity without getting up there and doing the very thing for which I'd become a star seemed to have provided a conclusion to my unwitting experiment. Although it was indeed possible to be famous for being famous for a short while, eventually talent, or lack of it, will out.

In the distance I could see Stella Scrivens's cottage. All I had to do was go round there now and explain that I was unable to appear in the charity gala on account of the fact that it was my grandmother's funeral that day. No, I was having a testicle removed, but I didn't want to talk about it. It was my grandmother's funeral *and* I was having a testicle removed, so I definitely wouldn't be able to make it.

The alternative was going back home and trying once more to write a funny routine and such a prospect made me quicken my pace towards the cottage. I was giving up. It was over.

The gate was heavy with entwined honeysuckle. The path up to the front door led me through a dark pergola tunnel sagging with fading roses and overgrown Virginia creeper, just starting to turn red as the summer came to an end. The front door was slightly ajar and yet when I rang the old-fashioned bell there was no response. I pulled on the rope a second time, but it failed to prompt any approaching footsteps or a barking dog. I had tied Betty up at the gatepost because, like its former owner, Billy Scrivens's Labrador had a reputation for attempting to mount any female that crossed his path and this was not something I felt would assist me in the awkward conversation I was about to have. I wondered if Stella was somewhere in the garden so I walked around the entire house before finally pushing the front door open and shouting a quizzical 'Hel-lo?' Breakfast things were still on the kitchen table and a newspaper was cast to one side. There was a picture of Stella and Billy with Prince Charles on the mantelpiece, and another of Billy just fooling around on some exotic beach. There were shelves of books about television and comedy and the great performers of the past. Things seemed to have remained exactly as they were since Billy had died. Stella had obviously not found it in herself to start clearing out his books and videos or replacing his pictures.

And then in a scruffy old armchair I noticed a large cardboard box full of papers and photos and important-looking documents. I could not resist flicking between the files. I saw a camera script from one of Billy's old shows, some boring receipts and a few meaningless scraps of paper before I spotted a copy of a contract with the BBC, which I carefully lifted out of the box and nosily scanned. The document revealed that Billy had been earning £75,000 a show before he died. I remembered how there'd been something of a stand-off between Billy's agents and the BBC in the weeks before his death. The Beeb had criticized Billy's management company for being greedy when they had demanded even more. Then a couple of days later the corporation had found themselves rapidly going into reverse gear as they paid emotional tributes to this wonderful performer so tragically cut down in his prime.

Suddenly there was a loud noise behind me. I panicked and guiltily shoved the documents back in the box until I realized it was the chimes of a grandfather clock in the hallway. Even more nervous now, I none the less tentatively flicked through the box again, but I was about to leave it and go when I noticed a few sheets of paper packed with closely typed words in an unusually small font. I pulled the document out of the box and glanced over the dense printing that had caught my eye. I understood immediately that I was looking at a comedy routine. My hands were shaking as I clutched the script and yet I could not prevent myself from smiling at the opening joke. It was so completely superior to anything I could ever have written and I knew I'd never heard it before. The second line was even better, the punchline catching me completely by surprise, and as I read on I found myself laughing out loud.

I could almost hear Billy's voice delivering this comic monologue and yet I didn't recognize any of this material. There was a date printed at the bottom of the first page – two days before Billy had died. The enormity of my discovery suddenly struck me: this routine must have been penned by Billy himself – possibly the last thing he ever wrote. It was priceless; it was a piece of comedy history and yet it would never be performed. I put it back in the box. And then I glanced around furtively before picking it up again and slipping the sheets of paper into my inside pocket. At that moment there was an explosion of gushing water in an outside drain, like the adrenalin that was suddenly rushing through my veins. Upstairs, feet were moving about on creaking floorboards. I hurriedly tiptoed towards the door. From an old photo on the wall, Billy's face smiled knowingly at me as I slipped out. Tripping slightly on a flagstone, I dashed along the pergola tunnel and untied Betty, glancing back at the house as I did so. The curtains were still drawn upstairs. Stella must have been having a bath while the dog was being walked. She should be more careful – anyone could have walked in and stolen something.

This comedy routine could not have been more perfect for me. It matched the voice and technique I'd adopted for the television commercials, although I guessed this was probably because I'd been subconsciously aping Billy Scrivens's style of delivery. The monologue was fantastic: there were back references and running gags and a building narrative all climaxing to a brilliant punchline that I was certain would bring the house down. There was even another half page of stuff for the inevitable encore. There was no hilarious fish routine but you can't have everything. But now I was armed. Now I believed I could do it.

When I was a child there was a comic-strip story called *Billy's Boots* in which a young boy played like a brilliant footballer whenever he wore the enchanted old boots of a great soccer star of days gone by. I would be playing the London Palladium with *Billy*'s *Jokes*. I'd be protected by this magical routine, this hypnotic gag-packed mantra that would cast a comedy spell on any audience exposed to it. Nothing was going to stop me now. After weeks of fear I couldn't wait for Saturday night. I strode around my living room performing the material with a swagger and a confidence I'd never felt before. The night was billed as a gala concert in memory of Billy Scrivens a year after his death and what greater tribute could there be than for me to perform his final routine? Obviously I'd be the only person who knew it was Billy's routine, but it was the principle that counted here.

My mobile rang but I refused to be distracted. I finished delivering my final joke before taking another bite of toast and nonchalantly answering the phone.

'Yeah?' I said, perhaps slightly too cockily.

'Hi, it's Stella Scrivens here.'

I dropped the toast. My heart was suddenly pounding so

hard that I was worried Stella might hear it on the other end of the phone.

'What? What is it?' I said panicking.

'Are you all right?'

'Yeah? All right? Of course I'm all right, why shouldn't I be?' I replied far too aggressively.

'Nothing. I'm just checking you've been fully briefed for Saturday?'

'Oh. Is that all?' I said, watching Betty wolf down the slice of toast that lay at my feet. 'Sure. Of course. In fact, I think I've got some pretty good material together, actually.'

'Great. It's just the researchers said you hadn't replied to their emails with all the details.'

'Oh, sorry, I'll have a look,' I said, covering up the script on the table as if she might be able to see it with some new special phone attachment at her end.

'And thanks very much for doing this,' she said in that special flirty voice she always used when she talked to me. 'It really means a lot to me, George . . .'

'George? This is Jimmy Conway.'

'Oh, sorry, Jimmy. George is next on my list.'

Having initially made me very nervous, the phone call then seemed to confirm that I'd got away with it. The box of old paperwork had contained so much rubbish that Stella obviously hadn't sorted through it all yet and I felt sure now that the script would never be missed. Over the next couple of days I performed the routine in the shower, I recited it walking along the beach, I declaimed it from the clifftops, and I whispered it to myself in bed last thing at night. Betty tilted her head to one side as she listened carefully to every line. I could sense she wanted a rewrite. She felt it lacked the words 'walkies' or 'din-dins'.

On Saturday morning I awoke and immediately leapt out of bed. In the newspaper's TV guide the show was listed as 'Pick of the Day' and there was an impressive roll-call of some of the stars who were going to appear, although it seemed that my name hadn't quite made the roll-call. I didn't mind. Most of the people listed there were more famous than me. Except two of them. Not that you can really measure such things. Actually three of them, now I re-read it, but it was no big deal, honestly. And then I wondered if I'd been mentioned in any of the other TV listings. Because the gala night was for charity, all sorts of top stars had been persuaded to take part, and illustrating the feature was a photo of Dame Judi Dench. Wow! I thought. I wonder if I'll get to meet Dame Judi Dench. That really would be something!

One moment I had far too long to think about the evening ahead, and then it seemed I had hardly enough time to rehearse my piece once more before heading up to London. I'd decided to drive there myself and leave my car at my parents' place. I didn't want to be chauffeur-driven all that way in some shiny black Mercedes with an obsequious driver; too much of that kind of treatment can start to affect a man. Although I was a little surprised to realize that I'd absently-mindedly climbed into the back seat of my Nissan Sunny as if someone else was going to drive it away. I had my best suit in a special protective bag beside me, and I kept feeling my script inside my pocket. At traffic lights I would get it out and stare at the words meaninglessly until a car horn sounding behind me set me on my way again.

I arrived at the Palladium a couple of hours before the show began but already there were throngs of fans gathering obediently behind the crash barriers. Above the doors in huge letters were the words 'A Tribute to Billy Scrivens'. It seemed typical of Billy to get top billing even after he'd died. Inside, the security was already far tighter than anything I had experienced. Some areas were even off-limits to the performers. This was the riskiest sort of television show: a live outside broadcast with no dress run, dependent on all the acts keeping to the time they had promised while the channel controller sat behind the director's box praying that nobody said the 'F' word or something even worse, like suggesting viewers switched off their tellies and read a book.

I'd wanted to say hello to Stella and to check that she was OK but I was told that would not be possible. 'Tell her it's me, Jimmy Conway,' I said and they disappeared for a moment but then told me again I couldn't speak to her right now. I tried to tell myself they hadn't even asked her. The security men were polite but very firm – I had walked into a military-style operation where everyone had a clearly defined job and no one was going to bend any rules or make exceptions for people who happened to think that regulations didn't apply to them. I was granted a quick sound-check in which I quickly recounted what I had for breakfast while trying not to look too dumbstruck by the size of the empty auditorium in front of me. For some reason the set on stage was of a huge church, as if we were attending a memorial service to the late St Billy. There were an altar and a pulpit and some lilies, which two set designers were busy spraying because they didn't look quite right. Once the stage manager had terrified me with the enormity of the venue, I was taken to Make-up before being dumped in my dressing room in order that I should have plenty of time in which to panic.

I got changed and lay trembling gently on the sofa in the dressing room. I tried not to listen to a wasp that was buzzing madly by the skylight. It must have been my heightened sense of tension that made me exaggerate the symbolism of this trapped insect. That's what my life had been like, I thought: banging my head endlessly against a pane of glass trying to get out. That's what most people's lives are like: repeatedly coming up against the same barriers whatever they do. They can see there's so much more to the world out there, but it always remains incomprehensibly out of reach.

I was not due onstage for an hour or so into this TV marathon, but although I could hear the stage manager calling the various artists to the wings like some remote minicab controller, there was no way of knowing how the show itself was progressing. I had asked the runner if it was possible to hear what was happening on the stage via the speaker on my wall and she said she would check for me, but she never came back. We were under very strict instructions not to come down until we were called and so I waited and waited and tried to entertain myself as best I could until there was not a single blackhead left on the side of my nose. Because the security was so over the top, I must admit that I momentarily wondered if it was all for my sake; that it wasn't really a variety tribute show, but at long last that surprise edition of *This Is Your Life* for Jimmy Conway. Then I remembered the gala being Pick of the Day in the television listings and I thought that would probably have been taking the cover-up to unnecessary lengths.

Eventually I received my five-minute call and gathered my thoughts together in the calmest, most professional way possible by splashing water all over my trousers and getting caught in Judi Dench's dressing room with a hairdryer pressed against my pants; a focusing exercise that was curiously left out of *An Actor Prepares* by Konstantin Stanislavsky.

In the wings I could feel the heat coming off the

auditorium. The venue was completely full and even though the audience was out of my view I felt I could almost physically touch the expectant excitement. The stage manager attempted to engage me in a little bit of light-hearted banter to put me at my ease, although my jumpiness was exposed when my mobile phone went off.

'Sorry! Sorry!' I whispered and he gave me an exaggerated 'naughty, naughty!' look and then said, 'OK, you're on!' adding, 'I think you might be in for a nice surprise,' which struck me as a curious thing to say. I heard the compère excitedly announcing my name and then suddenly I was out there. To the sound of applause and whistling I strode mock-confidently out onto the stage in the practised way I had seen celebrities jog onto TV chat shows. The first thing that struck me was the brightness. There was a wall of light that almost defied you not to shield your eyes but I knew I had to pretend I was comfortable. I had to make-believe I wanted to be there. The compère patted me on the back like an old friend and then it was just me and a distant microphone stand that looked far too thin for me to hide behind.

I had decided that instead of launching straight into my material, I would take a second or two to look around the space, to stare up into the upper circle and glance at the boxes on either side. I had seen Steve Martin do this on a video I had rented from Fish and Flicks and I thought it had given him the confident air of someone who was entirely comfortable out there. The trouble was that by looking around the audience it was horrifyingly apparent how huge this crowd was, and what a ridiculously tiny figure I must seem to the people at the back of the upper circle. It was like being a tightrope walker and having a good look at how high up you were. 'Goodness me. That would be a very painful way to die if I fell off now!'

But many more thoughts were fighting for space in my spinning head. I was acutely aware that This Was It; that I was finally on stage, no going back, right here, right now, every breath and gesture magnified a hundred times and being scrutinized by thousands and millions of people watching at home. This realization led to another inevitable thought: What the fuck am I doing up here? It wasn't one I felt I should share with all the families watching together at home.

With the applause having died down, I slowly took the microphone from the stand and began. 'Good evening, ladies and gentlemen, my name is Jimmy Conway . . .' and then I delivered the first joke absolutely perfectly, bowled right down the centre to send the middle stump flying, and I paused for the first warm wave of laughter to wash right over me.

Nothing happened. No reaction at all. Not even a small titter from the odd individual in the stalls. It was like the ground disappearing beneath my feet. I was so completely thrown, so surprised that not one person in the audience seemed to understand basic English, that I rushed on to the next joke, wondering if perhaps I'd inadvertently ruined the opening gag by leaving out a key word or something. But as I delivered my second punchline, all circuits were still dead. Quick, flick the buttons, try all the switches, press the alarm, something's happened, there's no pulse, we're losing him! Emergency! Emergency! As I came to the next joke I realized that it was not quite as strong as the previous two but I had always been confident that I would have built up sufficient goodwill by now to get a really big laugh. Still the sea of faces was lifeless: no response, just embarrassed, buttock-clenching silence. In my own personal tribute to a dead comic, I was dying up here live on television.

I ploughed on with the meaningless list of words that was

my monologue, starting to sweat in places that I didn't know had sweat glands and feeling my legs shaking so much it must have been visible. This wasn't fair. I was being cheated. I had learnt this script off by heart, and I clearly remembered there were supposed to be sound effects of people laughing uproariously at regular intervals. Actors in a bad drama can pretend to themselves that the audience is silently but deeply moved, but the success or failure of a comedian is obvious to all. You could try telling yourself that they were laughing *inside*, I suppose, but you'd have to be desperate to believe it. I was really rushing now, gabbling the lines with no consideration or punctuation. I didn't have the wit or experience to find a way to cut to the end of the routine and get off so I just kept going on and on and on. I momentarily wondered if there was a trapdoor somewhere on this stage; maybe I could stand over it in the hope that someone might pull the lever and mercifully send me plummeting into the vaults below.

Despite the glare of the lights I could make out many of the faces in the audience; surprisingly, many of them were smiling at me. I could only presume it was the sort of brave empathetic smile you give an old dog who's off to the vets to be put to sleep. I suppose they were well behaved because this was a live TV recording for charity. No one was heckling or booing. I wasn't interesting enough to provoke that much reaction. They just sat there waiting for me to finish, like brave-faced families in the departure lounge whose flight has been delayed but they aren't going to let it spoil their holiday. Looking directly at them became too painful and after a while most of the monologue was perfunctorily recited to a section of floor a few feet in front of me. There was a bit of blue sticking tape coming off the floor. That's a bit tatty, I thought.

You'd think they'd make sure everything was properly prepared for a big event like this.

Then, just as I had managed to skip a bit of the monologue, the first creative thinking I had done since I had got up there, something inexplicable happened. I got a laugh. It was at the end of what I thought had been a brilliantly observed section about computers, and although the final joke was not the best in the routine, it got a big laugh. I glanced up, surprised, almost put out at being so rudely interrupted in the middle of this private recitation. It had been a big laugh as well. I could feel the atmosphere lifting. Then I got another laugh, a really huge one, with a second ripple, a sort of aftershock chuckle as I suppose they must have thought about what I'd just said, and I could feel my posture changing as I straightened up and puffed out my chest, transforming from defeated prisoner of war to goalscoring hero. This beast in front of me was so dangerously impossible to predict. It had suddenly stirred from hibernation and it appeared that I might have charmed it for the moment. But now I'd woken it up I feared it might choose to turn against me at any second.

My third big laugh was the most perplexing of all. It came halfway through a set-up line. There was no reason for them to laugh and yet as one they spontaneously erupted into joyous, delighted laughter and then applause. The comedian's stock-in-trade response to such a surprise occurrence is to glance down at his trousers and say, 'Unexpected laugh? Check your flies!' Obviously this off-the-peg witty aside did not come into my head in this moment of blind confusion and internal panic. It then struck me that they were not laughing at me at all; that something else had hijacked their attention and it was this that was now engaging them. They laughed once more, in a big powerful wave that washed from the stalls right up to the upper circle, but again it was completely unprovoked by anything I could have possibly said. I stopped spouting my lines and stood there for a second, looking out at them, utterly desolate. 'Behind you!' shouted a delighted voice from the stalls. I was now a mere bit-part player in some wider joke of which I was unaware. I turned round slowly to see if there was indeed anyone behind me and I was struck immediately by an impossible vision, a supernatural apparition, the most surprising, incomprehensible, astonishing thing I had ever seen in my whole life.

Standing on the stage to my rear, grinning at me in his trademark spangly jacket and bow tie, was Billy Scrivens.

* * *

A few weeks after St Peter had witnessed the crucifixion of Jesus Christ, after he had witnessed the death of his Lord and mentor, Peter bumped into Jesus walking on the road to Jerusalem. It must have been a bit of a shock for him, I suppose, although being pretty rock-like Peter probably coped better than I would have done. Especially as he already had Jesus marked down as the Son of God, so if you thought about it you'd be able to rationalize that one pretty quickly. No, the apparition that confronted me was far more surprising. I mean, Billy Scrivens was a big star and a very versatile entertainer, but coming back from the dead? I'd have said that trick was beyond even his great talent.

To suggest that my world turned upside down in that moment would be cautious understatement: my whole existence had been totally invalidated in a split second. A deceased superstar I'd claimed as an old friend, whose dead body I had looted for its celebrity status, whose comic riches I had plundered before criminally pissing away his brilliant material while he stood listening in the wings – well, it was

266

one of those situations in which it's difficult to come up with a perfectly simple explanation.

Billy stood there for a second smiling at me like Banquo's ghost. I was frozen in awestruck dread. I looked to the thousands in the audience now behind me, expecting them to be sharing my incomprehension and astonishment, hoping for some sort of solidarity in this moment of revelation, but they were all laughing at me, revelling in my numb bewilderment.

My instant response was provoked by some primeval survivalist instinct telling me to run away. Of course, I couldn't do that. I was standing up on stage in front of two thousand people; I was live on national television. But I ran for it anyway – bolting for the huge wooden arched door on this church set, only to find it firmly locked against me. I rattled the big metal handle, hearing the delighted laughter of the audience of tricoteuses, cheering at and applauding my terrified reaction to being confronted by this grinning zombie who was now walking towards me with his arms outstretched. To hug me or to strangle me? It was hard to know. The door would not budge. I'd been deliberately trapped onstage, abandoned in this ring with no escape to provide easy prey for this man-eater of light entertainment.

I turned back to face Billy Scrivens, an expression of total horror and fear across my face.

'Jimmy!' he said with a warm smile. 'Long time no see!' And he gave me a huge hug as the crowd burst into joyous applause to see old showbiz friends reunited like this. Although I was too panic-stricken to register this at the time, the audience did not share my stupefaction. On the contrary, they were enjoying witnessing my own incredulity precisely because they'd had this very same surprise played on them at the start of the show. I was later to discover that a procession of major stars were having Billy Scrivens's greatest ever hoax sprung on them live on national television in a two-hour *Gotcha!* special, in which celebrities who had openly wept at his funeral were now paraded onstage in a gala tribute to their late friend, where they would perform in his memory only to find him coming up behind them and tapping him on their shoulder. Billy's death, his funeral and the whole charity gala tribute night were all part of an enormous extended prank contrived by Britain's greatest TV star to top all the scams and tricks ever played out before a television audience. But it was OK because it was all for charity.

And because of my year of wild fabrication, I knew that this was also the moment that I'd be exposed as a charlatan and a liar.

Billy released his bear hug and led me down to centrestage as my mind tried to conjure up any sort of case for the defence.

'So, Jimmy, how do you feel right now?' said Billy finally, his arm around me as we stood facing the jury of two thousand people. In the gap where I was supposed to reply I emitted a pathetic half-giggle, but the euphoric tension in the theatre was so great that this was greeted with a tremendous burst of laughter.

The audience had clearly been aware that Billy was alive by the time I came out to perform. But what else had they been told? While I'd been sitting patiently in my dressing room, prevented from hearing what was happening on stage or coming down to watch from the wings, had Billy revealed the lie of my claims to be an old friend of his? Had the audience been shown photos of me gatecrashing his funeral? Had the pictures of my 'home' from *OK!* magazine been projected up on the monitors, followed by embarrassing secretly taken photos of my real house and an interview with the shocked Korean couple whose luxury flat it really was? Had Billy fore-warned them that I was about to come out and do a comedy routine that I'd burgled from a box of personal documents in his house, stolen from a collection of Billy's papers that I believed was being sorted out by his bereaved wife? I briefly considered making a dash for the huge plywood church door on the other side of the stage, but my guess was that that one would be firmly bolted as well.

'Well, what can I say?' I stammered. 'I feel a bit, you know, embarrassed.'

The mob laughed again. Billy put his hand up to silence them and they obeyed.

'Embarrassed? Why would you feel embarrassed, Jimmy?'

The vicious bastard, he was going to make me go over it all; no detail spared in front of thousands of people.

'Well, all this,' I said, gesturing to the set and the audience. 'You know, and you suddenly being here,' and then I attempted an ironic philosophical laugh which came out as a wheezy semi-snort.

'Bit of a shock, eh?' said Billy.

'Er, yeah, you could say that. But can I just say, that what-ever people think about it all, at the end of the day it's not like anyone got hurt, is it? I mean, there's no actual harm done.'

Still with his arm firmly around my shoulder, Billy nodded sagely and there was a slightly awkward round of applause, which was strangely encouraging. They were clearly prepared to give me a fair hearing.

'Thank you, Jimmy. It's very kind of you to say so. No doubt there'll be the usual killjoys who'll say the whole faked death and funeral thing was somehow in bad taste or not politically correct or something, but I think they'd do well to remember that this event is raising a great deal of money for charity, for *British* kids.' This prompted a knee-jerk round of applause, with a lone 'Yeah!' being shouted out from the stalls. And then Billy punctured the tension by saying, 'And anyway, how else was I supposed to put off paying that tax bill!' and there was a huge laugh and more applause. Billy hadn't realized I'd been talking about myself; he thought I was talking about what he had done. Typical, these celebrities; they're so self-centred.

I could almost touch the love glowing up from the faces below us now. I realized that Billy wasn't going to sour the mood by having it all out with me now on stage. Mr Family Viewing Light Entertainment wasn't going to provoke some bitter row on live television in which he'd be seen throwing accusations and bitterly raking over past events. That would come later in private. No, I discovered that first the bastard was going to make me really suffer. He was going drum home the difference between his total mastery of an audience and my desperate failure even to illicit one titter with his brilliant material. He was going to make me finish my set.

'Anyway, Jimmy – I believe you were in the process of entertaining these good people before you were so rudely interrupted. So why don't I get off stage and let you finish your act?' Then he turned to the audience saying, 'And I'll see you later to see who will be next to get the shock of their lives!' I attempted a half-protest at his suggestion but he was already skipping off and left me totally isolated in the middle of the stage once again. I saw his smile drop the moment he passed through the doorway to the wings, where he was handed a towel with which he wiped his brow.

Now I faced Billy's fans as a condemned man. All right, so they may not know my secret yet, but soon it would be out and

I'd be a national joke: the fantasist who had forged his fame.

'Do you remember when Billy Scrivens came back from the dead?' they'd say to each other. 'There was that supposed comic who'd got famous claiming they'd been old mates, and he managed to get on telly and everything but he was really crap and it turned out he was just some tragic wannabe . . .'

'Oh yeah, I'd forgotten about him. Jimmy something – was it? God, what a sad act he was!'

This was the identity that awaited me as my fourteen and a half minutes of fame now drew to a close. Left onstage to perform the last rites on my fading life as a celebrity; compelled by its crown prince to finish digging my own grave in public. Having failed completely to communicate with this audience first time round, I was now forced to stay out there and face them alone once more. Only now they'd all been reminded what a real comic sounded like.

'Er, right, where was I?' I shrugged, and surprisingly there was a ripple of laughter, I suppose more out of embarrassed empathy with my bizarre situation than anything else. I remembered that I'd been talking about computers when they had mysteriously started laughing at me – because, it now turned out, the late Billy Scrivens had been mugging right behind me in what must surely go down as the greatest bit of upstaging in the history of Western theatre. Gone was the beginning of my glittering career; this was now my swansong. I took the microphone from its stand, a shell-shocked and defeated figure. My fantasy was over, I was done for. I was no longer desperate for the love of the people in front of me. In fact, I felt a vague contempt for them. I had wanted this so much when I first walked out onto this stage what seemed like several hours ago. And now, I thought, I really couldn't give a flying fuck.

I grunted the first joke with a disinterested sneer, not even attempting to hide the fact that I didn't want to be there. And they laughed. They really laughed at the comic conceit that had been served up before them. On paper I had not considered the joke to be any funnier than anything I'd said before, but it seemed that the way I'd delivered it had somehow amused Mistress Audience. I glanced round, half expecting to see Billy Scrivens tiptoeing out behind me – or even Princess Diana and Elvis Presley dancing the tango across the back of the stage. But there was only me. Still exuding the same miserable antipathy I reluctantly wheeled out the next joke and they laughed again. Now they seemed comfortable with me; surprised and amused that I dared to be this rude to them.

It occurred to me that first time out they must have been barely able to concentrate on a single word I was saying, knowing that Billy was going to creep up on me at any second. That might explain my earlier failure. Either that or I'd been a crap comic. But whatever the reason, now that the tension had been released, they were laughing at every joke, exploding every time I pressed the detonator. Some gags got more than I expected, others less than they deserved, but I was finding my balance. I was off and cycling away. I was being a successful stand-up comic.

I focused on maintaining this sneering, disinterested posture that seemed to have them hanging on my every word. Now when I knew that I had a good punchline coming I had the confidence to slow right down, to make them wait a second or two before I deigned to share it with them, holding back till exactly the right moment for maximum comic effect. Then 'Bang!' and their delight was all the greater. I felt so in control; I could make the sea of eager faces still and silent on my command or summon the waves of laughter to break upon the shore. I finished the set to enormous applause and as I took a small and humble bow I could hear increasing numbers of people shouting 'More! More!' Not wanting to push my luck, I decided against performing Billy's planned encore. I wanted to freeze this moment for ever. I was safe out here on stage, I thought; they wouldn't dare hurt me in front of all these witnesses. It would only be when I walked back to the wings that the recriminations would start. Where once I'd been terrified by the prospect of going out onto the stage, now I was frightened at having to leave it. I gave the audience a final farewell wave before I stepped out of the lights and into the darkness. I had no defence I could muster, no mitigating circumstances I could possibly plead. I braced myself for whatever it was that Billy Scrivens was about to say to me.

'Jimmy, me old mate!' he chuckled, ironically I presumed. 'Sorry to do that to you, y'old bastard, but great TV, eh! You have to admit, bloody tip-top TV!' and he gave me a playful punch on the arm, clearly delighted with the way the evening was going. 'When you ran to the door like that, Jimmy, brilliant, brought the bloody house down! You never dreamed, did you, not for a moment, you never imagined what was going to happen?'

'Er, no. No, I didn't,' I stammered, regarding him suspiciously. He muttered contentedly to himself at being reassured of this.

'Well, it's great to see you again, Jimmy, it really is. It's bloody boring being in hiding for twelve months I can tell you. You start to miss all your mates a bit. Know what I mean?'

I still was unsure what I should say. Was this another test? Was he providing another opportunity for me to incriminate myself further? On stage a band I half recognized were playing their hit single and the lead singer shouted, 'Sing along if you know the words . . .'

'Um, yeah, well it's great to have you back, Billy,' I ventured. 'And well done, you know, on pulling this off.'

He liked that. I could almost hear him purr with satisfaction.

'You know, Jimmy, we never saw enough of each other before my little sabbatical. We should make sure we get together more often.'

'Er, yeah. That would be, um, lovely.'

And I just stared at him and he smiled back at me and then looked out at the group on stage, happily tapping a foot in time to the music.

It was at this point that I realized that Billy Scrivens was completely mad. He was so totally self-obsessed that he couldn't remember who he knew and who he didn't. He literally didn't know who his friends were. All the anxiety I had expended about my deception was based on the presumption that Billy Scrivens was a sane person who would have noticed that we'd never properly met before. But the media said that I was an old friend of his, so he presumed it must be true. Were all his friendships so superficial that he couldn't remember who he'd spoken to and who he hadn't?

There had been no mention of all the material I had just done and I wondered if he'd even been listening.

'Oh, and Jimmy – I definitely recognized half of those gags you just did.'

Shit! I thought. He had been listening. Here it comes.

'Typical bloody writers, eh? Billy Scrivens drops dead and the first thing they think is: That means he won't be using that stuff we wrote for him. Let's see if we can flog it a second time; get Jimmy Conway on the phone!' and he slapped me on the back and gave a huge laugh.

'Yeah, writers, coh!' I concurred. 'Who needs 'em?'

'We do, worst luck. Ha ha ha!'

It appeared that I had got away with it scot-free. My mind raced through all the possibilities, all the exits that needed to be covered, and from every angle it suddenly seemed I was in the clear. I had claimed to be a friend of a dead comic and even he had believed me. I had gone on stage as a proper comedian and after a fashion and for whatever reason got a fantastic response. OK, those weren't my jokes, but it transpired they weren't Billy's either. The writers had already been paid for them, so they weren't going to kick up a fuss if Britain's top comic had chosen to pass them on to a friend. I had got away with it, and what's more I'd been good. I had found my voice and been a proper entertainer, and just because I couldn't write the stuff, it didn't mean that I couldn't hire some writers to do it for me like Billy obviously did.

I had achieved everything I had ever wanted. I crept into the hospitality room where a collection of stunned celebrities were exchanging accounts of how it had felt to have a dead superstar come up and tap them on the shoulder while they were onstage. Each one was patiently waiting for the current speaker to stop talking before immediately launching into their own identical account of the same experience. I needed to go back to my dressing room to get my head together so I went to take a bottle of beer from a six pack of fancy Czech lager and then just picked up the whole pack.

It had been less than thirty minutes since I had left this little cocoon, but now I was completely transformed. I lay back on the sofa and drank the first beer straight back and then started on the second one. I was a proper comic. I had done it. I felt euphoric and dizzy and ten foot tall.

And then I remembered that just before I had gone on stage

my mobile phone had rung. Who on earth could have been ringing at such a time? I wondered as I took another swig of beer. I'd ring them back and ask them if they'd seen the show. I turned on the phone and saw that whoever it was had left a message. The voice on the recording was distant and distorted but still unmistakable, even if we hadn't spoken for weeks. It had been Nancy calling me from Seaford. She relayed her message in tears. Tamsin was pregnant.

— | | —

19 Station Road,
Seaford,
Sussex

Dear Jimmy,

When you were thirteen years old you wrote a series of letters
to your future self, sort of time-capsule telegrams to remind
your adult incarnation of all the plans you had for your fame
and fortune. You may remember that when you were reunited
with these letters as a grown-up it seemed that life hadn't
turned out quite as you had hoped. You felt a failure, and went
to some fairly unconventional lengths to try to put that
right. Well, I'm writing this letter to you after all that has
happened. I think I'm now a lot older and wiser than I was two
decades ago, or indeed twelve months ago. At last I know what
it means to be a success.

It seems to me that the process of maturing is learning not
to worry too much about what other people might think of you.
As a teenager you are crippled by this overwhelming anxiety;

countless precious opportunities are not taken out of fear of embarrassment. It is not until you reach your thirties that you finally realize with a huge sigh of relief that you don't much care if a few people don't like you. What a liberating day that is, when someone asks you an unreasonable favour and you have the confidence to say no.

The problem is that evolution hasn't yet found a way of making this curve level out when a person has developed exactly the correct degree of concern for what others might think. Halfway through your life you get it about right, but the trajectory continues inexorably on the same path until you're a pensioner who simply couldn't give a toss. What else could explain Doreen Cutbush's once green, now grubby-grey gilet with its permanent doggy sheen, or the grumpy old man in the bread shop who, when asked if he'd like his loaf sliced for him, replies 'Piss off!' One can be too unconcerned about what people think.

So the only advice I send to my elderly self, Jimmy, is that you try to cling to a fragment of vanity, both physical and social, and make the effort to stand in the post office queue without muttering obscenities. Oh, and if the area of your facial hair has spread upwards, and huge grey tufts are now sprouting above your cheekbones, then it might be an idea to shave those off as well.

But more importantly, when you accidentally come across this final letter in your old age, filed between your money-off catfood coupons and the set of teeth you'd been looking for, I don't want you to start trying to impress the other residents at the Eventide Home for the Elderly by cheating at carpet bowls or forging little scribbled drawings from invented grandchildren. You have been a success; you don't need to lie to anyone. 'To thine own self be true, and it must follow, as the night the day, thou canst not then be false to any man' as you will remember from when you read <u>Hamlet</u>. Oh, all right, I admit, I never read <u>Hamlet</u>. I saw the quote on the back of a matchbox.

Mine sincerely,
Jimmy

Watching the events of that evening back on video was a compelling and cathartic experience. First and foremost I have to acknowledge that it was one of the most memorable nights of television I have ever witnessed. The viewing figures soared during the course of the night as people watching at home telephoned friends and relations to say what was going on over on BBC1. I realized that my own part in it would be forgotten in the wake of the astonishing return of Billy Scrivens, whose status as Britain's foremost entertainer was now established beyond any doubt. The BBC agreed a five-year deal far in excess of anything they had been offering before his apparent demise, and his Christmas special coincided with the publication of his autobiography, which Billy had been busy writing during his year in hiding.

The enormous church set in which I had performed made perfect sense when you saw how Billy revealed himself to the audience. With an angelic choir singing movingly in the background, the audience was shown edited highlights of Billy's career, climaxing with the news reports of his untimely death. As they were reminded of the day he died, a coffin came up out of the ground, at first barely visible in the swirling dry ice and flashing lights. With the audience moved close to tears by music and the sadness of the montage the coffin was hydraulically raised to the vertical position.

The choir were singing a specially arranged version of Billy's old theme tune, suddenly there was an explosion of fireworks and Billy burst out of the coffin and sang, 'Hello, Hello, Good to be Back'. The cameras cut to the reaction of the stunned audience, where individuals were covering their mouths in disbelief while Billy ran up and down the aisles so that people could see it really was him. One elderly woman was kneeling in the aisle, kissing her crucifix and giving thanks to God.

Billy then gradually brought the audience down by explaining how this idea had come to him. Every joke was greeted with a fantastic response in the hysteria of the moment. He said that for this year's Star Appeal Night he had wanted to do something more memorable than ever before, and he joked that coming back from the dead hadn't been done for a couple of thousand years. He thanked the handful of people in authority, the Sussex police and Brighton doctors and the coroner, who had been party to his faked demise knowing that their cooperation would help raise a great deal of money for charity. And then in a conspiratorial mock whisper, he revealed that inside this theatre were dozens of celebrities who were still in the dark about this little secret, and that while these stars were performing tonight they might get a little surprise while they were up on stage.

Different stars had reacted in different ways to the shock. Dame Judi Dench had been in the middle of reading a moving speech from a Shakespeare play unaware that viewers had already phoned in and pledged £203,500 to have Billy come up from behind and goose her in the middle of it. 'Where be your gibes now, your gambols, your songs, your flashes of merriment . . .' she said as a familiar-looking entertainer came up and pinched her on the bum. Dame Judi put her hand to her chest and said, 'Oh my goodness,' which I sensed was marginally more dignified than my panic-stricken attempt at running away. Mick Jagger looked so completely unsurprised to see Billy that I wondered if he'd ever been aware he'd been dead in the first place. Elton John looked like he'd really had the rug pulled from over his head. Gwyneth Paltrow burst into tears, while one of the Spice Girls fainted. It really was great TV.

Seeing myself die on stage during the first part of my

performance did not seem so bad in context. You knew the audience was waiting for something else more exciting to happen, and as a viewer you were concentrating on the door at the back of the stage. My attempts to run for it were generally taken as a brilliant piece of comic improvisation and after that the audience was so completely hyped up that I think if I'd performed my entire act in Norwegian they still would have laughed and cheered at every word. I draw the line at the stuff about Vulcan fish or dodos deserving to be extinct – that would have died whatever.

There was a little feature on what Billy had been doing for the past twelve months including some footage filmed at the cottage outside Seaford, which to my relief did not feature me creeping around downstairs and going through all his papers while he was upstairs in the bath. However, Billy had not spent a year as a total recluse but had gone out and about in disguise. We were treated to some footage of him in a rather ludicrous false beard sitting reading the newspaper outside a café and walking across Trafalgar Square. It must have been a bit of a shock for him to have to queue for the cinema, to be told there were no tables available in the restaurant, to have to start *paying for everything*.

Having had twelve months to plan his comeback show, Billy didn't overlook a single detail and the jokes and set-pieces kept coming all night. Then at the end of the evening all the celebrities and myself were summoned back to the wings ready for the grand finale. I had been sitting alone in my dressing room, surrounded by empty lager bottles, repeatedly calling Nancy's home phone number and her mobile but getting no reply from either.

A Beatles tribute band played onstage while Billy circulated in the wings, chatting and laughing with various other stars. I caught Stella Scrivens's eye across the crowd and she half smiled and raised her eyebrows knowingly at me before continuing a whispered conversation with a TV chef. She was running her hand up and down his lapel as she talked and he panted like a puppy dog and giggled. Honestly, some men are so gullible. Thank goodness I saw through her all those minutes ago, I thought.

The wings were filling up, and the stage manager was miming 'Hush' to the less scary of the celebrities. Near by, Billy was holding court to a circle of old showbiz friends when a young runner came up and brought him a bottle of mineral water on a tray. Without even noticing her he took a swig and his eyes seemed to bulge as he swallowed.

'Is this still?' he snapped at her.

The runner looked terrified. 'Is this still what?' she stammered.

'Don't fucking joke with me,' he said, even though I don't think she had meant to. 'I asked for still; this is fucking sparkling. How fucking difficult is that, you useless piece of shit?'

The stage manager heard a raised voice and said 'Shhh!' and Billy spun round and caught his eye and the SM realized his mistake and said, 'Sorry, sorry, do carry on.'

Billy shook his head in disbelief and then casually resumed his conversation where he had left off. The runner took this as her cue to leave, bursting into tears as she passed me. I tried to offer her a consoling smile but she was too embarrassed to make eye contact with anyone. Actually, I wouldn't have minded drinking the water because I realized I was feeling quite drunk.

The tribute band finished their penultimate number and then we were prodded back out under the spotlights. The church interior was gone – we were now standing in a replica of the set for Billy's TV show. I found myself holding hands with David Beckham and George Michael and singing along to 'All You Need Is Love' as everyone swayed from side to side. When I watched the tape I noticed I was the only one swaying the wrong way. When the singing of the international anthem was over, Billy walked down to the front of the stage to thank the audience for making it such a memorable evening and I listened and nodded, and about two minutes into his speech I realized I was still holding George Michael's hand so I let go. Having heaped praise on all the people in front of him, Billy turned to thank the people with him on stage. Touching piano music was playing and on the giant screens on the back of the stage there was a succession of black and white still shots from Billy's funeral. 'I'm just so grateful still to be alive and to be able to do so much to help all those British kids,' said Billy. And then the sad music was turned up as pictures of Billy holding hands with disabled children were flashed up on the screen. 'Charity' is the backstage pass that says 'Access All Areas', I thought. No grounds of taste are out of bounds if you are going there on behalf of charity. And then I remembered how I had justified the deception involved in doing my advert by deciding to help out Nancy. I'd wanted to do something I shouldn't, so I did it for charity. There were plenty of ways I could have helped Nancy more directly than that. Refraining from telling her daughter to go and get herself pregnant was possibly one of them. The recording of Nancy crying on my mobile phone still ran round in my head as I watched slow-motion footage of Billy pushing a wheelchair. The passenger was not in shot.

I had already come to the conclusion that Billy Scrivens was the most dreadful man I'd ever met, but out there on that stage I decided that I was taking part in the most vulgar, distasteful event I had ever witnessed. I wondered if it may even have been the lowest point in the history of Western civilization, or perhaps the second lowest after Elton John singing a hastily reworded version of *Candle in the Wind* at a funeral in Westminster Abbey in front of the entire British royal family. Holding back the tears because he had in fact survived his own faked death, Billy returned to paying tribute to us suckers who were gathered on stage to pay homage to him. 'For these people are not just the most wonderful and talented group of people you are likely to find gathered together anywhere on the entire planet,' he said, 'they also all happen to be my very dearest and closest friends.' He paused for dramatic effect. 'Every. Single. One of them.'

There was a slightly weak sycophantic round of applause and I winced at his sickening insincerity when I thought of how one of my real friends must be feeling right now. At this point you might say that something inside me snapped, except that I don't think it did snap: it reconnected, it healed, it mended.

'I'm not!' I said, emboldened by too much strong lager. 'I'm not a friend of yours! You said it was great to see me again, but you have never had so much as a single conversation with me before tonight.'

Billy looked momentarily surprised to be interrupted but there was a glint in his eye. He seemed to relish the prospect of a verbal duel here live on stage.

'Celebrities don't have conversations, Jimmy. They just meet up and say, "Enough about me. What did *you* think of my show?"'

The audience laughed heartily at this. Some might even have imagined my intervention was scripted. But even if I was inadvertently making him look even better, I wasn't going to stop now.

'Ah yes, but I'm not a celebrity, you see. I was lying when I claimed I had known you before you died, and then I lied about being a stand-up comic. I forged my reviews, I invented a career, I falsified an entire celebrity lifestyle because I wanted to be famous.'

There was a nervous half-laugh from one or two people in the audience but nothing more. Even Billy could not come up with a brilliantly apposite punchline to that and for the first time ever I saw him momentarily lost for words. Now in his eyes there was almost an expression of pleading. 'Why are you doing this, Jimmy?' his eyes seemed to say. The lines on the autocue machine were maniacally scrolling up and down looking for this section of the script. The theatre was incredibly quiet, though from the headphones of a cameraman I could hear the distorted, frantic screams of some remote director. I didn't dare pause for another second. 'In fact, I never performed a single joke in public before tonight. So I am not your friend, Billy. If anyone's interested, my friends are Nancy, Dave, Chris, Norman and Panda and everyone else back in Seaford,' I said, thinking I had better stop soon because this was starting to sound like a dedication on the Radio 2 Breakfast Show. 'And if you're watching, Nancy, don't worry, it's going to be OK.' And proud that I had made such a speech without slurring my words I made a dignified exit from stage, which was only slightly spoiled when I failed to remember the two steps down from where we were standing at the back of the stage, which caused me to fall flat on my face. And that was the last laugh I ever got as a celebrity stand-up comic.

Having already seen Billy come back from the dead that evening, the audience was suspicious that this whole speech might be part of another elaborate scam. They refused to be impressed or surprised, choosing instead to wait for Billy to explain what on earth was going on. When I watched the tape later I couldn't help but be impressed by what he said after I had walked off the stage.

'Knock, knock!' he shouted to the audience.

'Who's there?' they dutifully replied.

'Jimmy!'

'Jimmy who?' they shouted back.

'Hey, that's show business!' he said, gesturing to where I had disappeared, and then got on with the show. And that old gag kind of said it all.

I was shaking as I got to the wings, but attempting my very best proud and defiant look, I walked straight past the stage manager and out of the door. On the other side was a dimly lit corridor at the end of which I discovered a pair of locked double doors. So I turned round and walked back again. I passed the puzzled stage manager a second time before forcing the handle of the fire exit. I had gone from being under the warm glare of the spotlights, live on stage and simultaneously broadcast into millions of homes, into a dank, urine-soaked alleyway where a couple of people were sleeping under strips of cardboard.

My speech may have been cut from the instant repeat granted to Billy's comeback show but in the acres of newsprint that were given over to his return, a small section was devoted to the novelty story of the hoaxer who'd had everyone believing he was a real celebrity. But the moment that I ceased to be a star was completely overshadowed by the story about someone who still was. My downfall was only really covered to pad out the Billy Scrivens episode yet further. The American reviews I had written were checked and proved never to have been printed; genuine stand-up comics confirmed they'd never seen me on stage. It was strange when the media recounted how I'd pulled the wool over their eyes. Every newspaper and magazine gave the impression that they themselves had remained above all the eager gullibility they mockingly described; this 'media' they referred to was a group of foolish people somewhere over there.

However, my display on live television and the subsequent coverage was sufficiently embarrassing to prompt the agency to halt transmission of the bank adverts. It turns out that banks are quite touchy about being associated with fraud. The agency were furious; they even threatened legal action until the advertisers realized this was one thing they did not want advertised any further. A similar campaign was soon launched featuring a premiership goalkeeper, but not before the agency had been along to a game to check that he really did play in goal and that he could actually catch. I had so far been paid just over two thousand pounds for the advert and after the night of the gala I didn't receive another penny. I never really wanted a stupid jet ski, anyway. But now I wanted to find a way to help Nancy more than ever.

Her tearful message was still on my mobile and I couldn't help listening to it over and over again. There was something in Nancy's tone when she relayed the news about Tamsin that seemed to say, I don't know if you're still interested in any of this but I thought I'd tell you anyway . . . Nancy sounded abandoned, like I'd let her down. So how was she going to feel when she found out I'd been lying to them all for the past year as well?

Unable to track her down that night, I had finally rung Chris the following morning and had a long talk with him about everything that had happened. He'd watched my declamation from the stage of the Palladium and had been amazed. He'd heard my public confession and listened as I explained why I'd rejected the world of celebrity and everything it stood for. I told him how I had been an idiot to be seduced by the fool's gold of fame and hoped he would accept my apology for having deceived them all. I was wasting my time. He kept repeating the same thing. 'Yeah, but it was amazing! You mentioned us on telly! We're famous now!'

'That wasn't really the point of what I was trying to say to you . . .'

'Yeah, but *my* name on telly – in front of all those people! What a result!'

Unfortunately for me, Nancy was far more understanding about why I felt so guilty; in fact, she seemed to totally agree that I should feel that way. Although I was still staying with my parents, I finally managed to speak to her on the phone. My embarrassed apology didn't follow the script at all. When you offer up a repentant statement like, 'I just feel like I've let everyone down', your comforting friend is supposed to say, 'No you haven't, don't be silly, no one feels that way . . .' Nancy said, 'Yes, you have.' Then I said, 'I suppose we all do stupid things sometimes,' to which she replied, 'Not like that we don't.'

There was a defeated depression in her voice that I'd never heard before.

'I'm sorry, Nancy, I really am. Are you totally pissed off with me?'

'Jimmy, what do you expect?' she blurted out. 'You lied to us all. You tried to impress us with all this celebrity bullshit and then you're surprised when your best friends feel hurt. If you'd included us in the secret, that would have been different. But why did you have to deceive all of us as well? We're not *OK!* magazine, we're not daytime TV hosts. Why were you trying to impress us?'

'I just wanted to be a success. I wanted to be noticed.'

'We noticed you more when you were still around, you fuckwit. We always noticed you. I always noticed you. When I saw the piece in the *Sunday Times* I noticed you become artificially over-serious like you always do when you're lying. I noticed you avoid eye contact every time you lied about going to the Comedy Store or having played comedy clubs in the States. I noticed every time you went vague or changed the subject. I always noticed you.'

'You mean you knew all along?'

'I just knew I didn't believe a word of it, that's all. I knew you were lying to me. But I didn't think you were lying as much as that.' And with that she hung up the phone. It turns out she wasn't so easily taken in when it really counted.

After hearing Nancy's angry and disappointed voice I felt I had burnt my boats in Seaford and now I had no life in London either. Once the mirage of my fame had evaporated before me I was left with nothing. Not only had my identity and imagined raison d'être been whisked away in an instant, but worse than that the blind optimism that I'd one day amount to something had also now vanished. The undying faith in my own future success that had sustained me all these years had finally expired.

In the waiting room at the chiropodist's they have *Feet Today* magazine on the table, because while you're getting your verrucas done you're bound to want to catch up on the latest news from the world of feet. On the table at the hairdresser's they have *Hair* magazine, because you're obviously interested in hair otherwise you wouldn't be in there getting a trim. But what magazine would you put in Jimmy Conway's waiting room? *Don't Know Yet* news? *Can't Decide* monthly? *No Point Whatsoever* magazine? It wasn't just that I didn't have a career; I didn't feel like I had any purpose. I was the only person I could think of who'd managed to become famous for *not* being famous.

It is at times like these that a man can make some stupid and destructive decisions. Despairing prisoners serving life sentences will lacerate their arms with broken light bulbs. My self-destruction took another, more subtle form. I decided that taking that a job teaching English in Kuwait would be an excellent career move at this stage. Phrases such as 'turning over a new leaf' and 'wiping the slate clean' came into my head; such hideous clichés that frankly I should never be allowed to teach English again. But I thought, hey, Kuwait, it's a great opportunity; one of the great cultural centres of the world. Paris has the Louvre, New York has Broadway and Kuwait has its famous, erm, sand. I looked the place up in the encyclopaedia. It said that 92 per cent of the terrain was stony desert. But that still left 8 per cent, and I'm sure they could really use an English teacher in Umm Qasr to explain that you're supposed to put a 'u' after the letter 'Q'. I just wanted to get far away from everyone and everything, and suddenly 92 per cent stony desert sounded perfect. I called Doreen Cutbush at the language school and for some strange reason the job hadn't already been snapped up.

'Oh I am pleased, Jimmy,' she said. 'Although it'll be a sad day as well of course.'

'Oh, thanks Doreen.'

'My dogs will miss your Betty.'

I did a short email to my various friends as a way of letting them know without providing them with an opportunity to talk me out of it. Or even worse, not trying to talk me out of it.

Dear All,

I feel I owe you all something of an apology. When I said that I was a successful stand-up comic, what I meant was that I was a tragic fantasist with an ego problem. What can I say? I feel embarrassed and foolish and the only thing I can say in my defence is that I tried to do the right thing in the end, albeit far too late in the day.

I hope you can accept this apology and I hope that none of you have switched to text message banking because frankly it is a stupid bloody idea that will never catch on.

I've decided to make a clean break of things and I've got myself a job teaching English in Kuwait starting in a few weeks. It's a two-year contract. Betty is going to live with my mum and dad till I come back.

I'll miss you all.

Jimmy

P.S. My birthday seems to have come round once again. If anyone would like to let me buy them a farewell drink I'll be down the Red Lion next Sunday from about 8 p.m.

I didn't want to make a big deal about the invitation. I needed a reason why nobody was going to turn up. Part of me was tempted to stay in that night, to have a quiet birthday dinner for two with the one pal I could rely on to be there. That's the thing about Border collies, they never say no to a dinner party. I could have laid on a real feast for Betty, sat her up at the table as she quizzed me about each item on the menu: 'Yes, the *viande pour chien en boîte* – what is that exactly?'

'Ah, that is one of chef's specialities, madam. It is dog meat. From a tin. Scraped into a bowl.'

'Mmmm. Sounds delicious!' she would say, licking her lips. 'And what about this one: traditional meat chunks in their own jelly?'

'That's a tin of dog meat, as well, really, er, served in the traditional manner, chopped up into a big bowl that says "DOG" on the side.'

'Ooh, that sounds lovely too, but then they all do.'

But much as I loved Betty there was something extremely oppressive about having a dog staring at you for every single second that you are in her company. Whatever you did, she wanted to do it with you. 'It's all right, Betty, you don't have to leap up quite so excitedly, I'm only turning the page of my book.' There was no waking hour of the day when you were not being watched, no movement you could make without her being engrossed and excited. I suppose that must be what it's like to be a real celebrity, with a hundred thousand Bettys all watching you wherever you went, with the added risk of them suddenly transforming into a pack of rabid Rottweilers at any given moment. Who'd want to live like that for evermore? I asked myself.

As it happened, the chances of my adoring fans numbering more than one three-year-old Border collie had rapidly faded and as I headed off for my birthday drinks I took her with me so that it would look a little bit less tragic when I was sitting in the pub on my own. We walked down along the seafront and she chased the waves fizzing up and down the shingle and I sat looking out at the horizon for a while until eventually she came and sat next to me. How could it be right for me to abandon the one companion who would always stick by me no matter what? How do you tell your dog that you are going away for two years? She had found a stick and she dropped it beside me. 'Betty. I'm taking a long-term job in Kuwait and you're going to have to live with my mum and dad in London while I'm away.' She nudged the stick closer to me in the hope that I would throw it for her. She always focused too much on the short term. 'I wish I could take you with me, but it's just not practical. I know it's very hard for you to understand and I'm sorry.' She picked up the stick, dropped it in my lap and gave an excited bark. 'Yeah, yeah, two years, whatever, just throw the bloody stick.' I pulled her close to me and buried my face in the back of her thick mane. She liked this attention so much that the tail wagged the dog. Her whole bottom was doing the twist as the creature she loved most in all the world was giving her his undivided love and attention. And then I kept my face pressed hard against her shiny fur because I didn't want her to see that I was trying not to cry.

I have always maintained that there is nothing more ridiculous than the extraordinary amount of emotion people seem to expend on their pets; there is something unhealthy and excessive about a dumb animal being loved and fussed over like a newborn baby. There's only one exception I would make to this and that is if your pet happened to be Betty, my own particular Border collie. In this instance, any amount of emotional attachment would be entirely justified. It's just all those other foolish people who have far less special dogs than my own who get things out of all proportion.

I hugged her tight and wished I could give her everything she wanted in the whole world, and since this merely involved throwing a stick a few yards along the beach, it was quite easy to arrange. As I sat and watched her biting and spitting out bits of wood, I wondered if this was the only meaningful goodbye I'd have to make. It was hard for me to know how many of my old friends I had completely alienated at the end of a whole year of lying. As Betty pulled me reluctantly towards the Red Lion I could feel confident only about one or two people making the effort on my behalf. It was a pub I had been to hundreds of times before, I was going to meet up with friends I had known for years, and yet strangely I felt as nervous approaching those pub doors as I had done when I walked out onstage in front of millions of television viewers. I didn't have butterflies in my stomach. I had flocks of seagulls flapping about in there.

I heaved open the pub door. It was worse than I had feared. Only Chris was present, sipping a lonely lager and heroically attempting to read the beer mat. I had said eight o'clock to everyone, and it was now twenty past. One real friend left in England, and people asked me how I could possibly go and work in Kuwait. It's still quite early, I said to myself. I expect a few more people will come along in a minute, as Robinson Crusoe said when he was washed up on the shore.

Despite being the only person who had bothered to turn up, Chris seemed to feel compelled to apologize for the poor turnout. 'It is the quarter-final of *University Challenge* tonight,' he pointed out as a compelling mitigating factor. 'St Catherine's, Cambridge versus Brunel.'

'Ah, that would explain it. I thought the roads were very quiet,' I said, pretending to be mollified. 'I just hope the national grid can cope with the sudden power surge when it finishes.'

I bought a couple of drinks and a packet of crisps for the dog (no rotted dead fish flavour so I got her ready salted).

'Right, let me make sure that I've got everyone's drinks right. Whose was the half of lager?'

'Oh, that was mine,' said Chris, unironically.

I sat there for a moment in silence. 'I've been a real idiot, Chris,' I said.

'Why, what have you done?'

I think Chris often missed *University Challenge*. We chatted awkwardly about nothing for a while. I owed it to him to make an effort. He was the one person who had bothered to come out, so the least I could do was think of some interesting question I could ask him.

'Well, it tells you where the beer is from,' he replied, passing me his beer mat to read. This subject didn't sustain us for as long as I'd hoped and now that it was obvious no one else was coming I didn't want him to have to stay any longer for my sake.

'Actually, Chris, it's really nice of you to come and everything but I think I might go home now,' I said scraping back my chair as I stood up.

'What?' he exclaimed, showing more concern than I'd been expecting.

'I'm sorry – I'm just a bit down at the moment. You don't want to sit here all night with me moping on my birthday. Thanks for coming out and everything but I think I might just get an early night.'

'No, don't go!' he said leaping to his feet. 'You can't go.'

Suddenly his face looked much less anxious as he spotted something behind me and I turned and saw Nancy approaching.

'Jimmy Conway?' said Nancy rather formally.

'Oh, hi, Nancy, thanks for coming.' I was momentarily confused as she produced a large red photo album decorated with some gold lettering. And then she made an almost ceremonial announcement, the words of which I'd imagined many times, though I'd never believed I'd really hear them.

'Jimmy, you thought you were going for a quiet birthday drink in the Red Lion, but you're not. Because Jimmy Conway, teacher, friend and bloke down the pub: This Is Your Life!'

At that perplexing moment the famous opening four notes of the *This Is Your Life* theme tune boomed, rather distortedly, out of the cheap pub PA system more accustomed to announcing businessmen's sandwich orders. I was a bit unsure how to react to what I presumed to be a rather bizarre joke, when behind me the double doors to the pub's function room swung open and I saw that just about everyone I knew in the town was gathered inside. Dave, Tamsin, Norman and Panda, friends from Brighton and Newhaven, people I had worked with, students I had taught, they were all in there. The theme tune became louder as I was led through and they burst into applause, smiling mischievously and a little proudly at their surprise. Chris and Nancy led me in to where Dave was grinning at me, Norman was standing and applauding, and even Doreen was there with her two miniature schnauzers panting on her lap.

Above the little stage Tamsin was tying up a home-made banner that read 'Jimmy Conway, This Is Your Life!' and then Nancy led me up onto the rostrum. I kept spotting more old faces: people I hadn't seen for a couple of years who'd moved away from the town but who had been persuaded to come back for this special occasion. The applause continued and I felt a great weight lifting off my shoulders as I recognized the affection in everyone's faces. They weren't going to let me leave the country without a real goodbye. Either that or it was an elaborate trap and they were now going to beat me up for being such a lying scumbag.

The clapping died down and there was a moment's pause. 'You bastards!' I said, and they laughed because they knew I meant it in the nicest possible way. I was smiling so broadly I could almost feel it hurting. My face wasn't used to this, I was going to pull a grinning muscle. They should have warned me so I could do a few gentle warm-up smiles beforehand. Betty was going from table to table, wagging her tail and welcoming them all back, until eventually she sat and watched me on stage like everyone else.

Nancy took the microphone from the stand and read from the prepared script inside the album almost like a professional. 'You were born James Elliot Conway and grew up in 27 Elms Crescent, East Grinstead. Disillusionment set in early as you discovered that your road was not actually a crescent and that all the elms had died and been chopped down before you were born. You were a quiet baby, perhaps because being with your mother made it impossible to get a word in edgeways, but you were always accommodating even then, as your mother recalls:

Norman pressed down the 'play' button on the tape deck and the unmistakable free-form experimental jazz speech of my mother poured out of the speakers: 'Oh yes Jimmy was a very easy baby potty-trained at eighteen months one or two accidents of course there's still a stain on the chaise longue are you sure this will record without a microphone he slept right through well I think he did but it's hard to know because we always wore earplugs in those days so the baby didn't wake us up things were different back then there were no disposable nappies no disposable anything if you had a shoebox you'd jolly well hang on to it and use it for keeping old postcards in I think we've got a microphone from our old tape player somewhere I must get it down for Jimmy and we'd cut up the postcards to make collage Jimmy made a lovely bluebird with cut out bits of the Mediterranean, Aegean mostly some Adriatic it's a shame he never wanted to go to art college the little light's flashing does that means it's recording he could have been a successful artist now like Lucy-Anne Freud, she's very good isn't she though I think it's a shame she has to make them quite so fat don't you agree?'

Apparently Mum's short and pithy anecdote, specially recorded for the occasion, still had a little longer to run but they stopped the tape there because they only had the function room booked till closing time. Nancy then continued the narrative: 'As a young man you dreamed one day that you might be a famous comedian. You even went so far as to foolishly write down your plans in order that you might have the piss taken out of you by your brother and all your friends on your thirty-fifth birthday. Well, as we all know, over the past year you did succeed in becoming quite famous, and even performed live on national television before you suddenly decided to quit while you were still behind.' For a moment I was worried that we were going to hear further extracts from the embarrassing teenage scribblings that had been so excruciating this time last year. 'Now you are off to start a new life in the Middle East. Kuwait might seem a long way away, but frankly it's not as far from us all as you have been in the past few months. So we wanted to say that even though you'll be three thousand miles away, Jimmy, it's great to have you back.'

A blast of the *This Is Your Life* theme tune that they had recorded off the telly was played in while at Nancy's invitation Dave stepped up to the microphone. 'I was asked by Nancy if I could say a few nice words about Jimmy Conway. Well, I racked my brains and I'm afraid I really couldn't think of anything.' A laugh went around the room while Doreen Cutbush looked very concerned that this young man should say such a thing. 'Jimmy is a mean, cowardly backstabber who never bought a drink or sent a single birthday card to any of his countless illegitimate children who are scattered around the country. He is cruel to animals and oftens stops to laugh at Seaford's three-legged dog. He is the sort of man who would go up behind a blind person at a pelican crossing and go beep-beep-beep-beep-beep. I was also asked to list some of his achievements but I drew another blank there, I'm afraid. The only thing I can think of is that he is personally responsible for the plague-like spread of pubic lice among the female students at the Sussex Language Centre.'

By now Nancy had got down off the stage and was explaining to an ashen-faced Doreen Cutbush about Dave's perverse sense of humour. At the back of the crowd one of the language students present had got out her English–Hungarian dictionary to look up a couple of words she'd never heard before.

'But apart from those minor quibbles,' continued Dave, 'you're quite a good bloke, Jimmy. I can understand why you might want to escape to Kuwait right now, but we're going to miss you. For a day or two anyway.'

Having prevented Doreen from setting her little dogs on Dave, Nancy now leapt back on the stage and tried to bring the evening a little closer to the spirit of the original TV show format. She thanked Dave and then returned to her red book to read out a little more of my life history. 'Jimmy, you had a happy childhood, two loving parents and an elder brother you could always depend upon to use your head as a fart cushion. Sadly your brother cannot be here tonight

300

because, well, I didn't invite him, but he sends you this message:'

High on the wall of this back room was a large black television which tonight was haphazardly connected to a VCR player on Norman's improvised mixing desk. As the telly sprang into life there was a smattering of applause in appreciation of the effort that must have been involved in setting all this up. It might not have been as technically slick as the editing suites I'd seen during the previous year but whatever it lacked in professionalism it made up for in chaotic charm. 'Hello, Jimmy!' beamed my brother from a sunlounger in his back garden. 'I'm sorry I can't be there this evening but it sounds like they are going to give you a night to remember.' His kids ran into the screen and waved at the camera and shouted, 'Hello, Uncle Jimmy!' at the screen. This was great. This wasn't far off the real *This Is Your Life* that I had dreamt of. All right, as yet there had not been any references to my tireless work for animal charities, but that might have been because I didn't do any.

'You've been a great uncle to these two, Jimmy. They think the world of you and we're all really going to miss you while you're away.' Then the elder of the two boys shoved his little brother out of the way, who fell to the ground and started to cry and Nicholas said, 'Stop it both of you, you're both as bad as each other.'

Nicholas looked back to camera and apologized for the behaviour of his two boys and said that he had managed to unearth some footage of another couple of horrors that he'd transferred to video for me. A cheer went up around the room as we cut to some silent old footage of two small boys, me and my brother, splashing around naked in a paddling pool. Then an even louder hooray as I turned round to wave at the camera revealing a tiny penis, which was shamelessly waving along with me. For some reason the assembled company seemed to find this terrifically amusing. Obviously, I wasn't at all embarrassed by this. I mean, that was me as a child; it bears no relationship to Jimmy Conway the adult.

'It's not what you've got, Jimmy, it's what you do with it!' shouted a voice from the back, and their timing could not have been better as the five-year-old Jimmy proceeded to show exactly what he could do with it: weeing in a great glistening arc against my big brother as he leapt out of the paddling pool in tears. And I'd always thought it was him who had tormented me.

'Some charming early footage there,' said Nancy as the tape ended, 'and if you ever feel the urge to appear on television again, Jimmy, we'd be more than happy to send that clip into *You've Been Framed*.' By now I felt I'd been up there for quite a few minutes so I was very relieved when Chris passed up a pint which I could sip from time to time as something to do during the more embarrassing moments. Nancy skimmed through my undistinguished academic career and remembered my accidental arrival in Seaford. She reminded me of some of the things I had done for her, covering for her lessons when she had childcare problems, for example. Or the time I'd convinced her that because of global warming Eskimos now had over twenty different words for water.

I must admit I couldn't help being pleased that Nancy had noticed I'd surreptitiously tried to help her when she was giving up smoking. 'Jimmy, when I was trying to pack in the ciggies, you kept suggesting we all went to the cinema or café. It was only months later that I realized you had been deliberately arranging social situations away from smoky pubs where you knew I would have caved in. It was subtle and understated, but you were quietly determined to help me quit such a dangerous and disgusting habit and for that, Jimmy, I want to thank you from the bottom of my heart.' And then Nancy took a final drag of her cigarette and stubbed it out on the makeshift stage.

Now it was time for Doreen. She hauled her short but enormous body out of its chair and up onto the stage to begin her own tribute, while under her arms her moustachioed miniature schnauzers glanced around the crowd checking that everyone was listening. If there was anyone I had helped a great deal down the years, I would have to admit it was Doreen Cutbush. I'd always been on hand to exercise her little dogs or to mend the photocopier at the language school or be rung up in the evening to video her favourite programmes when I was in the middle of a rented movie. She was never afraid to ask, and I was always afraid to say no, so it was particularly poignant that she had come along this evening to acknowledge all the hours of my life that I had devoted to helping out my employer and neighbour.

'I was asked by young Nancy here if I might say a few words in praise of my Jimmy. Well, I can tell you I didn't hesitate. I will always have the utmost respect for Jimmy Conway,' she boomed, taking off her glasses-on-a-string where they rested on the horizontal shelf of her bosom. 'For in an age when standards seemed to have gone by the wayside, Jimmy here continues to set an example to so many. Do you know why? Do you know what is so special about this man?'

Around the room I was flattered to see a few people nodding.

'He always, and I mean always, uses the correct word for irregular plurals.'

I double-took slightly from the stage, as she continued.

'You'd never hear Jimmy uttering such hideous modern abominations like curriculums, stadiums or stimuluses – with Jimmy it's curricula, stadia, stimuli every time.'

I did my best to look moved by the warmth of this tribute as I thought about the winter's night when she had got me up at four in the morning because her waterpipe had burst and I had scrambled around in the snow outside her house trying to find the metal flap to turn off the mains supply.

'Radii, alumni, memoranda – what can I say? He's the sort of man who would never say one criteria when he means one criterion. I've always maintained that credit should be given where it is deserved, so there you are.' And with that she stepped down again with the dogs under her arms glancing around as if to say, 'What? What else was there?'

There was a slightly embarrassed pause, punctured by a heckle from Dave.

'Just as long as he never bloody says two cappuccini again.'

'Thank you very much, Doreen,' I said, 'for making the effort to come up onto the rostrums.' Nancy then introduced a slide show of photos from the past. There were pictures of us all from ten years ago where our innocent young faces smiled at the camera oblivious to our appalling sense of fashion. Pictures of a day trip to Dieppe, scenes from parties or picnics or just friends squashing into photo booths. Near the end there was one of Nancy and me in our early twenties sitting on the beach and kissing.

Not everyone stood up and gave a speech. Norman just said that I was 'a good bloke and that' but then added that he wasn't very good at talking in front of people. He said, however, that he would like to pay tribute to me in another language, 'a more, like, universal language, the language of music'. And we all thought, Oh no, he's not, is he? He's not going to finally perform air guitar for us all here and now, is he? However much we had quizzed him about his accomplishments in this unconventional field, none of us had ever been treated to a display.

'This is for you, Jimmy,' he said, and then Panda cued the music and Norman struck a deadly serious pose, fell to his knees and started pretending that he was playing. The moment had come for him to share with us all the joy that was air guitar.

You'd think if you were introducing a group of friends to an unconventional art form that you might try to lead them gently by giving them a brief and accessible taster. If someone had never heard an opera, you wouldn't introduce them to the form by forcing them to sit through the whole of Wagner's Ring Cycle. So what did Norman choose to mime for us? One of the shorter, more popular Beatles tracks maybe? Or a brief snippet of Rodriguez's guitar concerto number 2 perchance? No, for this crowd of air guitar virgins, Norman had selected the Everest of mimed guitar solos: *Freebird* by Lynyrd Skynyrd. All thirteen head-banging minutes of it.

It's quite hard to know what to do when a fully grown man is leaping around in front of you pretending he is playing a rock classic on an imaginary electric string instrument. Some onlookers tried to move their heads from side to side in a jaunty wish-I-could-sing-along-but-don't-know-the-words kind of way. A couple of people attempted to clap in time but this was not picked up by anyone else so they sheepishly stopped again, as if they'd never meant to clap for more than twenty seconds or so anyway. Most of us adopted that benign appreciative fixed smile as worn by Western tourists incomprehensibly watching an intricate dance in the Indian subcontinent. As it happens, he looked as if he was probably pretty good at it. His fingers gave the impression that they were playing the chords that were intended; he strummed and spun and rocked like the real thing. But at the end of the day it was, you know, well, it was air guitar.

The piece took nearly a quarter of an hour to perform but it only felt like twice that. Exhausted and emotionally drained from his athletic and frankly sweaty performance, Norman finally took a bow to an explosion of applause and cheers and whistling. Chris shouted for more, except it came out as 'More–ow!' because someone kicked him under the table to shut him up. As the applause died down, Norman staggered to the bar to get himself another gallon of cider, while Nancy took the stage once more. 'Thank you very much, and Norman will be concluding his tribute to Lynyrd Skynyrd later on this evening by miming a plane crashing into the side of a mountain.'

Nancy had clearly planned out the whole evening but now one or two of the non–speaking onlookers wondered if they might add a spontaneous word or two.

'I was once in a car with Jimmy and we were stuck in a traffic jam and he let two cars out instead of just one.'

'He always follows the country code and closes gates to prevent livestock escaping.'

I wondered if we might be starting to scrape the barrel a bit now. Next I'd be credited with always putting the lid back on the toothpaste, I thought, until I remembered that actually I didn't. Nancy realized the show was coming to an end and stepped in to round things off.

'Jimmy, you explained to me that you made up all that rubbish about being famous because you so wanted to be a success. Well, before you finally leave us all for sunnier climes, your friends and colleagues wanted to reassure you that you always were a great success. I know it was always your dream to appear on *This Is Your Life*, and, OK, maybe now you'll never get to be on the real thing. But you're the biggest star around, Jimmy. So it gives me great pleasure to say to you at last, Jimmy Conway, *This Is* Your *Life*!'

And her emphasis made me realize where I belonged. Standing on that little stage in the back room of an ordinary pub in a nowhere town I felt at ease with myself, so much surer of who I was and where I fitted in than I had done on the huge stage with pretend friends like Billy Scrivens. My real friends were more sincere because they were cynical, more flattering because they could be rude, richer because they were poorer. Nancy passed me the big red book as Norman cued in the signature tune once more and everyone gathered around to laugh at the photos and point out the little mementoes they had done for me. Norman rolled a joint and Panda tried not to wince as he failed to pass it to the left.

We carried on drinking into the evening and then food was served for everyone. And this was a proper meal, not stupid fancy nibbles that leave you starving. Betty went from table to table, doing her very hardest stare at whoever happened to be eating, failing to use her psychic powers to convey the inspired idea that they should give all their food to her immediately. Everyone commented on how sweet she was as she mournfully rested her head on the laps of various diners. Then their legs started to feel damp and they realized she was drooling all over them.

I went round the room talking to people I hadn't seen for ages, and laughed and joked among friends with whom I had so much to catch up. And now that we were all relaxed, they asked me what it had been like to meet all those famous people and be on telly and perform on stage and be in an advert. I gave them the honest answer that there had been moments when it had been thrilling and terrifying, but throughout it all there had been an anxious empty feeling inside me that had never gone away. Until now, I thought: I never felt so much like a celebrity as I did that evening. Everyone was on a high because we knew we'd had a really special night and what was more we'd done it ourselves. Even Tamsin couldn't help but smile. I made sure I had a chat with her on her own in the corner and this time I was going to report every word of it to her mother.

When the evening was over we walked slightly drunkenly along the seafront, laughing about the night that had just been.

'You can't say we didn't give you a good send-off, Jimmy,' said Dave.

'Er, yeah, about that,' I said awkwardly. 'Do you know, walking along the seafront with you here now, I'm not so sure that I want to go.'

'What!'

'Well, after how sad everyone said they'd be to see me leave, it sort of makes me feel like staying now.'

'Really?' said Nancy, seeming pleased.

'What – after Nancy went to all that bloody effort?' objected Dave.

'That's fantastic, Jimmy,' interjected Nancy. 'Would you just come back to working at the language school then?'

'Well, for the time being, I suppose. Tamsin once said she wished I was her teacher. It made me wonder what it would be like to teach kids who actually understood what I was saying to them.'

'You'd be brilliant, Jimmy, I know you would.'

Chris seemed confused by this and said, 'I reckon you

ought to make a go of this stand-up comedy lark, Jimmy. That seemed to be going pretty well for you.' And then he added 'What? Why's everyone stopped walking? Why are you all staring at me like that?'

Eventually each of them peeled off the group and weaved their way up their various streets until it was just Nancy and me walking along the seafront. We left the promenade and crunched our way across the shingle and sat down. I let Betty off the lead so she could run off down to the shore and bite the sea. Twelve years I had lived on the coast and I was still surprised every time I discovered that the waves carried on dutifully crashing on the shore at night-time as well as during the day.

'Nancy, I don't know how to thank you. All that trouble to say goodbye, and now I'm saying hello again.'

'Yeah, well, it worked then, didn't it?' she said with a smile.

'Suddenly it feels like everything in the world is perfect,' I said tactlessly and her face fell. 'Sorry, that was stupid of me.'

We sat in silence for a minute.

'Nancy, I spoke to Tamsin before she went off with Kelvin tonight.'

'The father of my grandchild, God help us . . .'

'Yeah, well, I chatted about that with her this evening.'

'I know, I saw you; why, what did she say?'

'Well, she talked about herself and how awful it was but how she had no moral choice except to go through with it. But there was something about the way she was relishing the drama of it all that made me suddenly wonder if . . . well, you know . . .'

'No, I don't know, tell me!'

'Well, I wondered if she was making the whole thing up.'

Nancy looked completely astonished at this suggestion and

309

yet I saw that it prompted a glimmer of hope in her face.

'What, pretending to be pregnant? Why on earth should she do that?'

'To exercise some sort of power over her mother. To make people talk about her.'

'That's a pretty massive lie to tell just to get a bit of attention.'

'Not the biggest though – remember you're talking to the expert here. And that's what I'm trying to say. I recognized the syndrome. I think it's just desperate attention-seeking; it's not that different to what I did or even what Billy Scrivens did.'

'You didn't ask her outright, did you?'

'Of course I didn't. I was just a sympathetic ear. I asked her about the morning sickness and she said it was awful. I asked her if she'd felt more tired than usual and she said she did. I asked her if her tongue felt larger than normal at the end of the day because of course that's always the first sign, and she said, oh yeah, that's definitely the worst thing about being pregnant, the terrible tongue-swelling . . .'

'Hmmm,' said Nancy. She lay back on the shingle and stared at the stars. 'Do you know, now I think about it, she wouldn't let me see the test. She wouldn't let me take her to the doctor and then last week for the first time ever she did her own laundry. My God, I think you're right. I think you're probably right. How could she do that to me? She's a bloody headcase!'

'But that's better than a pregnant headcase!'

Nancy laughed and burst into tears at the same time. 'Oh Jimmy!' And then in her delirious state she kissed me full on the lips and hugged me tight.

And then we kissed again, more gently this time and now

without any pretend excuse. With the moon reflecting on the water and the waves lapping on the beach it could not have been more romantic and perfect. Perhaps the only tiny detail I would have changed was not to have Betty bringing us a dead half-rotted seagull she found on the beach . . . but maybe I'm being picky.

'Thanks for organizing this evening,' I said. 'It was the best birthday I've ever had.'

'The things a girl has to do to make a man see she's interested in him!'

I realized that I'd got it into my head that nobody would be interested in me until I became somebody special, but I didn't want to go over all that again.

We kissed some more and Nancy said, 'I thought we were supposed to be just friends.'

'We are. I'm a *boy*, who is your *friend*. A sort of "boy-friend", if you will.'

'And I'm a *friend* who is a *girl* . . . there must be a word we can find for that. Look, are you really sure you want a woman with a screwed up teenage daughter in tow?'

'Oh Tamsin's all right. She's pretty balanced compared to some of the kids I've taught at the language school. I really think that together we could help her find herself. She'll pass through this phase soon enough, you watch. And then think of the money we'll make with all that scrap metal.'

We kissed again and then just sat there watching Betty running excitedly in and out of the breaking waves.

A couple of weeks later Tamsin came back from walking the dog and actually brought us both a cup of tea in bed.

'How disgusting!' she said.

'I'm sorry, Tamsin. Would you rather I slept in the spare room?' I said.

'Not you – Mum. When did you get your navel pierced?'

'I thought you'd like it.'

'Urgh, no. It's awful.'

Nancy pulled her T-shirt down to cover her midriff and we sat up in bed sipping the tea, and flicking through the Sunday papers.

'Yuk! What is Kylie wearing!' said Nancy.

'Yeah, but look at Mel Gibson. He's put on weight, hasn't he?'

Eventually I chucked the papers to the side and stared at the ceiling. I think I had disappeared into this mystery tour hoping that I would earn the love and respect of the people I knew by becoming somebody special for all the people that I didn't. At last I no longer craved the love of millions of strangers, now that I was confident I had the real love of just one person right beside me. Because although you can get a certain type of instant synthetic love from an audience, it's not the dependable, forgiving, deep-rooted love that we all really need.

You can't leave your pants on the floor in front of an audience. You can't sit on the toilet and casually chat about what sort of day they had as your fans brush their teeth before bed. You can't be grumpy and monosyllabic with an audience and expect them to work out why you're sulking. You can't row and make up with the general public. You can't take them a cup of tea on Sunday morning and say sorry and lie in bed and chat about nothing for a bit. You can't have a sexual relationship with all your fans, even if a few rock stars might have attempted it. In any case, the public don't really love *you*, they love an invented image of you and a lifestyle they fantasize about having for themselves. *Hello!* magazine doesn't feature photographs of celebrities' homes with all last night's washing-up piled high around the sink, with an unshaven Julio Iglesias yawning and staggering into the kitchen with his willy swinging about under the crumpled T-shirt he wears in bed. You cannot be yourself to the public, and so even if you were adored by millions, you would still feel empty and hollow. There can't be anything lonelier than getting that much phoney love.

Nancy had shown me that there were greater riches in this life than the overvalued currency of celebrity. Every human being is a hero in one way or another, whether it is bringing up a kid on your own or helping Edna Moore understand the prices in the Mr One Pound shop. That is what she had shown us all when she organized that haphazard night of nostalgic tributes in the back room of a pub. It was such an inspired idea. It made me think that everyone deserved a night like that just once in their life. In fact, that would make a really good television programme: a *This Is Your Life* for the common man. I'm sure she wouldn't mind me offering that idea into the BBC: a weekly entertainment show that made heroes out of ordinary people and proved you don't need to be famous to be special.

I decided I should send it in because it was a message that needed to be heard; a programme like that might become the antidote to the celebrity-obsessed culture that was distorting what really mattered in this world. I was going to send it in because it was time some of the real heroes of our society got some credit. I was going to send it in because people had to see that celebrities aren't important; *people* are important.

And anyway, you never know, I thought. They might even let me present it . . .

Acknowledgements

Thanks are due to Bill Scott-Kerr, Georgia Garrett, Mark Burton, Pete Sinclair, John McNally and, most of all, Jackie O'Farrell. With apologies to the real Betty, a slightly less mad Border collie.

JO'F 2002